Spanish

PHRASEBOOK & DICTIONARY

Acknowledgments

Associate Publisher Tali Budlender

Managing Editors Annelies Mertens, Angela Tinson

Editors Laura Crawford, Samantha Forge, Robyn Loughnane, Jodie Martire, Martine Power, Branislava Vladisavljevic

Series Designer Mark Adams

Managing Layout Designer Chris Girdler

Layout Designers Frank Deim, Carol Jackson, Mazzy Prinsep, Jacqui Saunders, Kerrianne Southway

Production Support Yvonne Kirk, Glenn van der Knijff

CD Production Labsonics

Language Writers Marta López, Cristina Hernández Montero

Thanks

Jane Atkin, Sasha Baskett, Yvonne Bischofberger, Helen Christinis, Brendan Dempsey, Indra Kilfoyle, Nic Lehman, Naomi Parker, Trent Paton, Piers Pickard, Averil Robertson, Joseph Spanti, John Taufa, Juan Winata

Published by Lonely Planet Publications Pty Ltd
ABN 36 005 607 983

2nd Edition – October 2012
ISBN 978 1 74220 967 8
Text © Lonely Planet 2012
Cover Image Bruce Bi – Lonely Planet Images

Printed in China 10 9 8 7 6 5 4 3 2 1

Contact lonelyplanet.com/contact

MIX
Paper from
responsible sources
FSC™ C021741
www.fsc.org

Look out for the following icons throughout the book:

 'Shortcut' Phrase
Easy-to-remember alternative to the full phrase

 Q&A Pair
Question-and-answer pair – we suggest a
response to the question asked

 Look For
Phrases you may see on signs, menus etc

 Listen For
Phrases you may hear from officials, locals etc

LANGUAGE TIP **Language Tip**
An insight into the foreign language

CULTURE TIP **Culture Tip**
An insight into the local culture

How to read the phrases:
- Coloured words and phrases throughout the book are
  phonetic guides to help you pronounce the foreign language.
- Lists of phrases with tinted background are options you
  can choose to complete the phrase above them.

These abbreviations will help you choose the right words and phrases in this book:

a	adjective	**m**	masculine	**sg**	singular
f	feminine	**n**	noun	**v**	verb
inf	informal	**pl**	plural		
lit	literal	**pol**	polite		

Contents

PAGE 6

About Spanish
Learn about Spanish, build your own sentences and pronounce words correctly.

PAGE 31

Travel Phrases
Ready-made phrases for every situation – buy a ticket, book a hotel and much more.

Basics 31

Practical 41

PAGE 190

Menu Decoder
Dishes and ingredients explained – order with confidence and try new foods.

PAGE 205

Two-Way Dictionary
Quick reference vocabulary guide – 3500 words to help you communicate.

Spanish

INTRO

español es·pa·*nyol*

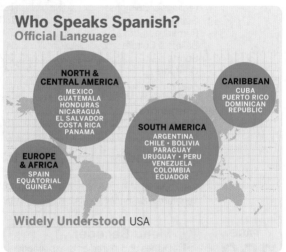

Who Speaks Spanish?
Official Language

NORTH & CENTRAL AMERICA
MEXICO
GUATEMALA
HONDURAS
NICARAGUA
EL SALVADOR
COSTA RICA
PANAMA

CARIBBEAN
CUBA
PUERTO RICO
DOMINICAN REPUBLIC

SOUTH AMERICA
ARGENTINA
CHILE · BOLIVIA
PARAGUAY
URUGUAY · PERU
VENEZUELA
COLOMBIA
ECUADOR

EUROPE & AFRICA
SPAIN
EQUATORIAL GUINEA

Widely Understood USA

Why Bother

You'll be seduced by this melodic language and have fun trying to roll your *rr*'s like the locals – not to mention ordering scrumptious tapas or engaging in all the shouting at the *fútbol*.

Distinctive Sounds

The strong and rolled r, harsh and guttural kh and, in European Spanish, 'lisping' th.

Spanish in the World

Over the last 500 years, Spanish in Latin America has evolved differently to the

300 MILLION
speak Spanish as their
first language

100 MILLION
speak Spanish as their
second language

Spanish of Europe. Among other differences, you'll easily recognise Latin Americans by the lack of lisp in their speech – ie *cerveza* (beer) is ther·*ve*·tha in Europe but ser·*ve*·sa across the Atlantic.

Spanish in Spain

Spanish, or Castilian (*castellano* ka·ste·*lya*·no) is primarily the language of Castille (covering the largest territory in Spain). However, Catalan, Galician and Basque are also official languages, and locals in these regions are very proud of their own language.

False Friends

Warning: many Spanish words look like English words but have a different meaning altogether, eg *suburbio* soo·*boor*·byo is a slum district, not a suburb (which is *barrio ba·ryo* in Spanish).

Language Family

Romance (developed from Vulgar Latin spoken by Roman soldiers and merchants during the conquest from the 3rd to the 1st century BC). Close relatives include Portuguese, Italian, French and Romanian.

Must-Know Grammar

Spanish has a formal and informal word for 'you' (*Usted* oo·*ste* and *tú* too respectively). The verbs also have a different ending for each person, like the English 'I do' vs 'he/she do**es**'.

Donations to English

Thanks to Columbus' discovery of the New World in 1492, a large corpus of words from indigenous American languages has entered English via Spanish. You may recognise *canyon*, *guerrilla*, *ranch*, *tornado*...

5 Phrases to Learn Before You Go

1 **What time does it open/close?**
¿A qué hora abren/cierran? a ke o·ra ab·ren/thye·ran

The Spanish tend to observe the siesta (midday break), so opening times may surprise you.

2 **Are these complimentary?**
¿Son gratis? son gra·tees

Tapas (bar snacks) are available pretty much around the clock at Spanish bars. You'll find they're free in some places.

3 **When is admission free?**
¿Cuándo es la entrada gratuita?
kwan·do es la en·tra·da gra·twee·ta

Many museums and galleries in Spain have admission-free times, so check before buying tickets.

4 **Where can we go (salsa) dancing?**
¿Dónde podemos ir a bailar (salsa)?
don·de po·de·mos eer a bai·lar (sal·sa)

Flamenco may be the authentic viewing experience in Spain, but to actively enjoy the music you'll want to do some dancing.

5 **How do you say this in (Catalan/Galician/Basque)?**
¿Cómo se dice ésto en (catalán/gallego/euskera)?
ko·mo se dee·the es·to en (ka·ta·lan/ga·lye·go/e·oos·ke·ra)

Spain has four official languages, and people in these regions will appreciate it if you try to use their local language.

10 Phrases to Sound Like a Local

What's up?	**¿Qué pasa?**	ke *pa*·sa
Great!	**¡Genial!**	khe·*nyal*
How cool!	**¡Qué guay!**	ke gwai
That's fantastic!	**¡Estupendo!**	es·too·*pen*·do
Really?	**¿En serio?**	en *se*·ryo
You don't say!	**¡No me digas!**	no me *dee*·gas
Sure.	**Seguro.**	se·*goo*·ro
OK.	**Vale.**	*va*·le
Of course!	**¡Por supuesto!**	por soo·*pwes*·to
Whatever.	**Lo que sea.**	lo ke *se*·a

ABOUT Spanish

Pronunciation

Spanish pronunciation isn't difficult, as most sounds are similar
to the sounds found in English. The relationship between Spanish sounds and their spelling is straightforward and consistent.
There are some easy rules to follow and once you learn them
you shouldn't have problems being understood. As in most languages, Spanish pronunciation can vary according to region –
this book focuses on Castilian Spanish.

Vowel Sounds

SYMBOL	ENGLISH EQUIVALENT	SPANISH EXAMPLE	TRANSLITERATION
a	alms	agua	a·gwa
ai	aisle	bailar	bai·lar
e	red	número	noo·me·ro
ee	bee	día	dee·a
ey	hey	seís	seys
o	go	ojo	o·kho
oo	book	gusto	goo·sto
ow	cow	autobús	ow·to·boos
oy	boy	hoy	oy

Consonant Sounds

SYMBOL	ENGLISH EQUIVALENT	SPANISH EXAMPLE	TRANSLITERATION
b	big	barco	*bar*·ko
ch	chilli	chica	*chee*·ka
d	din	dinero	dee·*ne*·ro
f	fun	fiesta	*fye*·sta
g	go	gato	*ga*·to
k	kick	cabeza, queso	ka·*be*·tha, *ke*·so
kh	as in the Scottish *loch*	jardín, gente	khar·*deen*, *khen*·te
l	loud	lago	*la*·go
ly	million	llamada	lya·*ma*·da
m	man	mañana	ma·*nya*·na
n	no	nuevo	*nwe*·vo
ny	canyon	señora	se·*nyo*·ra
p	pig	padre	*pa*·dre
r	run (but stronger and rolled)	ritmo, burro, mariposa	*reet*·mo, *boo*·ro, ma·ree·*po*·sa
s	so	semana	se·*ma*·na
t	tin	tienda	*tyen*·da
th	thin	Barcelona, manzana	bar·the·*lo*·na, man·*tha*·na
v	soft 'b', between 'v' and 'b'	vaca	*va*·ka
w	win	guardia	*gwar*·dya
y	yes	viaje, ya	*vya*·khe, ya

Reading & Writing

There are some key things to remember about consonants in written Spanish:

» The letter *c* is pronounced with a lisp, eg *cerveza* ther·*ve*·tha, except when it comes before *a*, *o* and *u* or a consonant. Then, it's pronounced hard like the *k* in 'king'.

» When ending a word, the letter *d* is also pronounced soft, like a th, or is so slight that it hardly gets pronounced at all.

» The letter *j* stands for a harsh and guttural sound, and we use the kh symbol in our pronunciation guides.

» Try to roll your double r's.

» The letter *q* is pronounced hard, like a k.

» The letter *v* sounds more like a b, said with the lips pressed together.

» There are a few letters which don't appear in the English alphabet: *ch*, *ll* and *ñ*. You'll see that these letters have their own entries in the Spanish–English dictionary.

~ SPANISH ALPHABET ~

A	a	a	B	b	be	C	c	the
CH	ch	che	D	d	de	E	e	e
F	f	e·fe	G	g	khe	H	h	a·che
I	i	ee	J	j	*kho*·ta	K	k	ka
L	l	e·le	LL	ll	e·lye	M	m	e·me
N	n	e·ne	Ñ	ñ	e·nye	O	o	o
P	p	pe	Q	q	koo	R	r	e·re
S	s	e·se	T	t	te	U	u	oo
V	v	oo·ve	W	w	oo·ve do·ble	X	x	e·kees
Y	y	ee·*grye*·ga	Z	z	*the*·ta			

Word Stress

There is word stress in Spanish, which means you emphasise one syllable in a word over another. Rule of thumb: when a written word ends in *n*, *s* or a vowel, the stress falls on the second-last syllable, eg *lejos* le·khos (far), *casa* ka·sa (house). Otherwise, the final syllable is stressed, eg *hablar* a·blar (talk). If you see an accent mark over a syllable, it cancels out these rules and you just stress that syllable instead, eg *número* noo·me·ro (number).

LANGUAGE TIP **False Friends**

Beware of false friends – those words that sound like familiar English, but could land you in a bit of trouble if you use them unwittingly in Spanish. Here are some mistakes that it's a little too easy to make:

el suburbio	el soo·boor·byo slum district, not 'suburb' which is *el barrio*, el ba·ryo
Estoy constipado/a. m/f	es·toy kons·tee·pa·do/a I have a cold, not 'I'm constipated', which is *estoy estreñido/a* **m/f** es·toy es·tre·nyee·do/a
Estoy embarazada.	es·toy em·ba·ra·tha·da I'm pregnant, not 'I'm embarrassed', which is *estoy avergonzado/a* **m/f** es·toy a·ver·gon·tha·do/a
la injuria	la een·khoo·ree·a insult, not 'injury', which is *la herida*, la e·ree·da
los parientes	los pa·ree·yen·tes relatives, not 'parents', which is *los padres*, los pa·dres
sensible	sen·see·ble sensitive, not 'sensible', which is *prudente*, proo·den·te

ABOUT SPANISH PRONUNCIATION

ABOUT Spanish

Grammar

This chapter is designed to explain the main grammatical structures you need in order to make your own sentences. Look under each heading for information on functions which these grammatical categories express in a sentence. For example, demonstratives are used for giving instructions, so you'll need them to tell the taxi driver where your hotel is, etc. A glossary of grammatical terms is included at the end of this chapter to help you.

Adjectives & Adverbs

Describing People/Things • Doing Things

When using an adjective to describe a noun, you need to use a different ending depending on whether the noun is masculine or feminine, and singular or plural (see **gender** and **plurals**). Most adjectives use the following four endings:

~ ADJECTIVES ~

	singular		plural	
m	fantástico	fan·*tas*·tee·ko	fantásticos	fan·*tas*·tee·kos
f	fantástica	fan·*tas*·tee·ka	fantásticas	fan·*tas*·tee·kas

a fantastic hotel un hotel fantástico (lit: a-**m-sg** hotel
fantastic-**m-sg**)
oon o·*tel* fan·*tas*·tee·ko

a fantastic meal	una comida fantástica (lit: a-**f-sg** meal fantastic-**f-sg**) *oo*·na ko·*mee*·da fan·*tas*·tee·ka
some fantastic books	unos libros fantásticos (lit: some-**m-pl** books fantastic-**m-pl**) *oo*·nos *lee*·bros fan·*tas*·tee·kos
some fantastic tapas	unas tapas fantásticas (lit: some-**f-pl** tapas fantastic-**f-pl**) *oo*·nas *ta*·pas fan·*tas*·tee·kas

Adjectives generally come after the noun in Spanish. However, adjectives expressing quantity (such as 'much', 'a lot', 'little', 'few', 'many') always precede the noun. See also **demonstratives** and **possessives**.

a comfortable hotel	un hotel cómodo (lit: a-**m-sg** hotel comfortable-**m-sg**) oon o·*tel* ko·mo·do
many tourists	muchos turistas (lit: many-**m-pl** tourists) *moo*·chos too·*rees*·tas

Most adverbs in Spanish are derived from adjectives by adding the ending -*mente* ·*men*·te to the singular feminine form of the adjective (ie the form ending in -*a*), just like you add the ending '-ly' to the adjective in English. In Spanish, adverbs are generally placed after the verb they refer to.

a slow train	un tren lento (lit: a-**m-sg** train slow-**m-sg**) oon tren *len*·to
to speak slowly	hablar lentamente (lit: to-speak slowly) ab·*lar* len·ta·*men*·te

Articles

Naming People/Things

There are four words for the definite article (ie equivalents of 'the' in English) in Spanish, used depending on the gender and the number of the noun (see **gender** and **plurals**). The masculine singular form of the definite article is joined to some prepositions when it's placed after them, so *a el* (to the-m-sg) becomes *al* al and *de el* (of the-m-sg) becomes *del* del. See also **prepositions**.

~ DEFINITE ARTICLES ~

m sg	**the car**	el coche	el *ko*·che
m pl	**the cars**	los coches	los *ko*·ches
f sg	**the shop**	la tienda	la *tyen*·da
f pl	**the shops**	las tiendas	las *tyen*·das

Similarly, Spanish has four words for the indefinite article (ie 'a/an' in English), depending on the gender and number of the noun.

~ INDEFINITE ARTICLES ~

m sg	**an egg**	un huevo	oon *we*·vo
m pl	**some eggs**	unos huevos	oo·nos *we*·vos
f sg	**a house**	una casa	oo·na *ka*·sa
f pl	**some houses**	unas casas	oo·nas *ka*·sas

Be

Describing People/Things • Making Statements

Spanish has two words for the English verb 'be': *ser* ser and *estar* es·*tar*, which are used depending on the context.

~ USE OF *SER* (TO BE) ~

permanent characteristics of persons/things	Liz es muy guapa. *leez es mooy gwa·pa*	Liz is very pretty.
occupations or nationality	Ana es de España. *a·na es de e·spa·nya*	Ana is from Spain.
time or location of events	Son las tres. *son las tres*	It's 3 o'clock.
possession	¿De quién es este bolso? *de kyen es es·te bol·so*	Whose bag is this?

~ USE OF *ESTAR* (TO BE) ~

temporary characteristics of persons/things	La sopa está fría. *la so·pa es·ta free·a*	The soup is cold.
time or location of persons/things	Estamos en Madrid. *es·ta·mos en ma·dreeth*	We're in Madrid.
mood of a person	Estoy contento/a. m/f *es·toy kon·ten·to/a*	I'm happy.

~ *SER* (TO BE) – PRESENT TENSE ~

I	am	yo	soy	yo	soy
you sg inf	are	tú	eres	too	e·res
you sg pol	are	Usted	es	oo·ste	es
he	is	él	es	el	es
she	is	ella	es	e·lya	es
we	are	nosotros m nosotras f	somos	no·so·tros no·so·tras	so·mos
you pl inf	are	vosotros m vosotras f	sois	vo·so·tros vo·so·tras	soys
you pl pol	are	Ustedes	son	oo·ste·des	son
they	are	ellos m ellas f	son	e·lyos e·lyas	son

~ *ESTAR* (TO BE) – PRESENT TENSE ~				
I	**am**	yo	estoy	yo	es·*toy*
you sg inf	**are**	tú	estás	too	es·*tas*
you sg pol	**are**	Usted	está	oo·*ste*	es·*ta*
he	**is**	él	está	el	es·*ta*
she	**is**	ella	está	e·lya	es·*ta*
we	**are**	nosotros m nosotras f	estamos	no·so·tros no·so·tras	es·*ta*·mos
you pl inf	**are**	vosotros m vosotras f	estáis	vo·so·tros vo·so·tras	es·*tais*
you pl pol	**are**	Ustedes	están	oo·ste·des	es·*tan*
they	**are**	ellos m ellas f	están	e·lyos e·lyas	es·*tan*

Demonstratives

Giving Instructions • Indicating Location • Pointing
Things Out

To point something out, the easiest phrases to use are *es* es (it
is), *esto es* es·to es (this is) or *eso es* e·so es (that is).

It's a guide to Seville.   Es una guía de Sevilla.
(lit: is a-**f**-**sg** guide of Seville)
es *oo*·na *gee*·a de se·*vee*·lya

The Spanish words for 'this' and 'that' vary, depending on whether
something is close (ie 'this'), away from you (ie 'that'), or even
further away in time or space (ie 'that over there'). Each of these
words changes form depending on the gender and number of the
noun it refers to. See also **gender** and **plurals**.

~ DEMONSTRATIVES ~

	m sg		m pl	
this (close)	éste	e·ste	éstos	e·stos
that (away)	ése	e·se	ésos	e·sos
that (further away)	aquél	a·*kel*	aquéllos	a·ke·lyos
	f sg		f pl	
this (close)	ésta	e·sta	éstas	e·stas
that (away)	ésa	e·sa	ésas	e·sas
that (further away)	aquélla	a·ke·lya	aquéllas	a·ke·lyas

Gender

Naming People/Things

In Spanish, all nouns (words which denote a thing, person or idea) have either masculine or feminine gender. You can recognise the noun's gender by the article, demonstrative, possessive or any other adjective accompanying the noun, as they all change form to agree with the noun's gender (see **adjectives & adverbs**, **articles**, **demonstratives**, **possessives**). The gender of words is also indicated in the dictionary, but here are some general rules:

» a word is masculine/feminine if it refers to a man/woman
» words ending in -o or -or are generally masculine
» words ending in -a, -d, -z or -ión are usually feminine

The masculine and feminine forms of words are indicated with m and f throughout this book where relevant. See also p138.

Have

Possessing

Possession can be indicated in various ways in Spanish (see also **possessives**). One way is by using the verb *tener* te·*ner* (have). For negative forms with 'have', see **negatives**.

~ *TENER* (TO HAVE) ~

I	have	yo	tengo	yo	*ten·go*
you sg inf	have	tú	tienes	too	*tye·nes*
you sg pol	have	Usted	tiene	oo·*ste*	*tye·ne*
he	has	él	tiene	el	*tye·ne*
she	has	ella	tiene	e·*lya*	*tye·ne*
we	have	nosotros m nosotras f	ten·emos	no·*so*·tros no·*so*·tras	te·*ne*·mos
you pl inf	have	vosotros m vosotras f	tenéis	vo·*so*·tros vo·*so*·tras	te·*neys*
you pl pol	have	Ustedes	tienen	oo·*ste*·des	*tye*·nen
they	have	ellos m ellas f	tienen	e·*lyos* e·*lyas*	*tye*·nen

The word *hay* ai – which is the impersonal form of the verb *haber* ha·*ber* (have) – is used to mean 'there is/are' and in questions for 'is/are there ...?':

Is there hot water?   ¿Hay agua caliente?
(lit: is-there water hot-f-sg)
ai *a*·gwa ka·*lyen*·te

Negatives

Negating

To make a negative statement in Spanish, just add the word *no* no (not) before the main verb of the sentence:

I'm not going to try that.
No voy a probarlo.
(lit: not I-go to to-try-it)
no voy a pro·*bar*·lo

Contrary to English, Spanish uses double negatives:

I have nothing to declare.
No tengo nada que declarar.
(lit: not I-have nothing that to-declare)
no *ten*·go *na*·da ke dek·la·*rar*

Personal Pronouns

Making Statements • Naming People/Things

Personal pronouns ('I', 'you' etc) change form in Spanish depending on whether they're the subject or the object of a sentence. It's the same in English, which has 'I' and 'me' as subject and object pronouns (eg 'I see her' and 'She sees me'). Note, however, that the subject pronoun is usually omitted in Spanish as the subject is understood from the corresponding verb form (see **verbs**).

I'm a student.
Soy estudiante.
(lit: I-am student-**m&f-sg**)
soy es·too·*dyan*·te

ABOUT SPANISH GRAMMAR

~ SUBJECT PRONOUNS ~

I	yo	yo	**we**	nosotros m nosotras f	no·so·tros no·so·tras
you sg inf	tú	too	**you** pl inf	vosotros m vosotras f	vo·so·tros vo·so·tras
you sg pol	Usted	oo·*ste*	**you** pl pol	Ustedes	oo·*ste*·des
he **she**	él ella	el e·lya	**they**	ellos m ellas f	e·lyos e·lyas

As the tables show, Spanish has two 'you' forms. With people familiar to you or younger than you, it's usual to use the informal form of 'you', *tú* too, rather than the polite form, *Usted* oo·*ste*. Phrases in this book use the form that is appropriate to the situation. Where both forms are used, they are indicated by pol and inf. See also the box **addressing people**, p95.

~ OBJECT PRONOUNS ~

me	me	me	**us**	nos	nos
you sg inf	te	te	**you** pl inf	vos	vos
you sg pol	lo/le m la/le f	lo/le la/le	**you** pl pol	los/les m las/les f	los/les las/les
him **it**	lo/le	lo/le	**them**	los/les m las/les f	los/les las/les
her **it**	la/le	la/le			

In this table, the forms separated by a slash are direct/indirect object pronouns.

The direct and indirect object pronouns differ only for the third person ('he', 'she', 'it', 'they') and the polite 'you' forms.

I don't know her.	No la conozco. (lit: not her I-know)
	no la ko·*noth*·ko
I'm talking to her.	Le hablo. (lit: to-her I-talk)
	le *a*·blo

The object pronouns generally come before the verb. The indirect object pronoun comes before the direct object pronoun.

I'll show it to you.	Te lo mostraré. (lit: to-you-**sg-inf**
	it-**m-sg** I-will-show)
	te lo mos·tra·*re*

Plurals

Naming People/Things

To form plurals in Spanish, add -*s* if the noun ends in a vowel and -*es* if it ends in a consonant. In this book singular and plural forms are shown with **sg** and **pl** respectively where needed.

~ SINGULAR ~			~ PLURAL ~		
bed	cama	*ka*·ma	**beds**	camas	*ka*·mas
woman	mujer	moo·*kher*	**women**	mujeres	moo·*khe*·res

Possessives

Possessing

A common way of indicating possession is by using possessive adjectives before the noun they refer to. Like other adjectives, they agree with the noun in number, and in case of 'our' and 'your' they also agree in gender (see also **gender** and **plurals**).

| our daughter | nuestra hija (lit: our-**f-sg** daughter) |
| | *nwes*·tra *ee*·kha |

~ POSSESSIVE ADJECTIVES ~

my	mi/mis	mee/ mees	**our**	nuestro/ nuestros m nuestra/ nuestras f	nwes·tro/ nwes·tros nwes·tra/ nwes·tras
your sg inf	tu/tus	too/ toos	**your** pl inf	vuestro/ vuestros m vuestra/ vuestras f	vwes·tro/ vwes·tros vwes·tra/ vwes·tras
your sg pol	su/sus	soo/ soos	**your** pl pol	su/sus	soo/soos
his her its	su/sus	soo/ soos	**their**	su/sus	soo/soos

Note that in the table above, the Spanish possessive adjective forms separated by a slash are used with a singular and plural noun respectively.

my child	mi hijo (lit: my-**m-sg** child) mee *ee*·kho
my children	mis hijos (lit: my-**m-pl** children) mees *ee*·khos

Another way to indicate possession is by using possessive pronouns (see the table opposite), which also agree in gender and number with the noun.

The book is mine.	El libro es mío. (lit: the-**m-sg** book is mine-**m-sg**) el *lee*·bro es *mee*·o

~ POSSESSIVE PRONOUNS ~

mine	mío/ míos m mía/ mías f	mee·o/ mee·os mee·a/ mee·as	**ours**	nuestro/ nuestros m nuestra/ nuestras f	nwes·tro/ nwes·tros nwes·tra/ nwes·tras
yours sg inf	tuyo/ tuyos m tuya/ tuyas f	too·yo/ too·yos too·ya/ too·yas	**yours** pl inf	vuestro/ vuestros m vuestra/ vuestras f	vwes·tro/ vwes·tros vwes·tra/ vwes·tras
yours sg pol	suyo/ suyos m suya/ suyas f	soo·yo/ soo·yos soo·ya/ soo·yas	**yours** pl pol	suyo/ suyos m suya/ suyas f	soo·yo/ soo·yos soo·ya/ soo·yas
his **hers** **its**			**theirs**		

The four alternatives in this table are used with **m sg**, **m pl**, **f sg** and **f pl** nouns.

Ownership can also be expressed in Spanish using the construction '*de* de (of) + noun', just like in English. See also **have**.

my friend's bag	el bolso de mi amigo (lit: the-**m-sg** bag of my friend-**m-sg**) el *bol*·so de mee a·*mee*·go

Prepositions

Giving Instructions • Indicating Location • Pointing Things Out

Like English, Spanish uses prepositions to explain where things are in time or space. Some common prepositions are listed in the table that follows. For more prepositions, see the **dictionary**.

When certain prepositions are followed by a definite article, they are contracted into a single word (see **articles**).

~ PREPOSITIONS ~

after	después de	des·pwes de	**from**	de	de
at (time)	a	a	**in (place)**	en	en
before	antes de	an·tes de	**to**	a	a

Questions

Asking Questions • Negating

The easiest way of forming 'yes/no' questions in Spanish is to add the phrase *verdad* ver·*da* (literally 'truth') to the end of a statement, similar to 'isn't it?' in English. You can also turn a statement into a question by putting the verb before the subject of the sentence, just like in English.

This is the right stop, isn't it?	¿Ésta es la parada, verdad? (lit: this-**f-sg** is the-**f-sg** stop truth) es·ta es la pa·*ra*·da ver·*da*
Is this the right stop?	¿Es ésta la parada? (lit: is this-**f-sg** the-**f-sg** stop) es es·ta la pa·*ra*·da

As in English, there are also question words for more specific questions. These words go at the start of the sentence.

~ QUESTION WORDS ~

how	cómo	ko·mo	**where**	dónde	don·de
what	qué	ke	**who**	quién **sg**	kyen
				quiénes **pl**	kye·nes
when	cuándo	kwan·do	**why**	por qué	por ke

Verbs

Doing Things

There are three verb categories in Spanish, depending on whether the infinitive ends in *-ar*, *-er* or *-ir*, eg *hablar* ab·*lar* (talk), *comer* ko·*mer* (eat), *vivir* vee·*veer* (live). Tenses are formed by adding various endings for each person to the verb stem (after removing *-ar*, *-er* or *-ir* from the infinitive) or to the infinitive, and for most verbs these endings follow regular patterns. The verb endings for the present, past and future tenses are presented in the tables on the following pages. For negative forms of verbs, see **negatives**.

~ PRESENT TENSE ~

		hablar	**comer**	**vivir**
I	yo	habl**o**	com**o**	viv**o**
you sg inf	tú	habl**as**	com**es**	viv**es**
you sg pol	Usted	habl**a**	com**e**	viv**e**
he/she	él/ella	habl**a**	com**e**	viv**e**
we	nosotros **m** nosotras **f**	habl**amos**	com**emos**	viv**imos**
you pl inf	vosotros **m** vosotras **f**	habl**áis**	com**éis**	viv**ís**
you pl pol	Ustedes	habl**an**	com**en**	viv**en**
they	ellos **m** ellas **f**	habl**an**	com**en**	viv**en**

See also **be** and **have**.

~ PAST TENSE ~

		hablar	comer	vivir
I	yo	hablé	comí	viví
you sg inf	tú	hablaste	comiste	viviste
you sg pol	Usted	habló	comió	vivió
he/she	él/ella	habló	comió	vivió
we	nosotros m nosotras f	hablamos	comimos	vivimos
you pl inf	vosotros m vosotras f	hablasteis	comisteis	vivisteis
you pl pol	Ustedes	hablaron	comieron	vivieron
they	ellos m ellas f	hablaron	comieron	vivieron

In case of the future tense, the endings follow the same pattern for all three verb categories, and they are simply added to the infinitive (dictionary form of the verb), not the verb stem:

~ FUTURE TENSE ~

		hablar	comer	vivir
I	yo	hablaré	comeré	viviré
you sg inf	tú	hablarás	comerás	vivirás
you sg pol	Usted	hablará	comerá	vivirá
he/she	él/ella	hablará	comerá	vivirá
we	nosotros m nosotras f	hablaremos	comeremos	viviremos
you pl inf	vosotros m vosotras f	hablaréis	comeréis	viviréis
you pl pol	Ustedes	hablarán	comerán	vivirán
they	ellos m ellas f	hablarán	comerán	vivirán

Word Order

Making Statements

Spanish has a basic word order of subject–verb–object, just like English. However, the subject pronoun is usually omitted in Spanish because the subject is understood from the corresponding verb form (see **verbs**). Both of the following examples are correct, but the second one is more common:

I study business.   Yo estudio comercio.
(lit: I I-study business)
yo es·*too*·dyo ko·*mer*·thyo

Estudio comercio. (lit: I-study business)
es·*too*·dyo ko·*mer*·thyo

See also **negatives** and **questions**.

CULTURE TIP   **Proverbs in Spain**

Proverbs are big in Spain. The Marqués de Santillana compiled a national collection in the second half of the 15th century, and one of the characters in *Don Quixote*, Sancho Panza, speaks almost entirely in proverbs. The novel's author, Cervantes, described these popular sayings as 'short sentences based on long experience'.

Ser como el perro del hortelano, que ni come las berzas, ni las deja comer al amo.   ser *ko*·mo el *pe*·ro del or·te·*la*·no ke nee *ko*·me las *ber*·thas nee las *de*·kha ko·*mer* al *a*·mo
(lit: to be like the market gardener's dog, who doesn't eat the cabbages and won't let his master eat them either)

ABOUT LANGUAGE

GRAMMAR

~ GRAMMAR GLOSSARY ~

adjective	a word that describes something – 'he was the **greatest** toreador of his time'
adverb	a word that explains how an action is done – 'he turned around **quickly**'
article	the words 'a', 'an' and 'the'
demonstrative	a word that means 'this' or 'that'
direct object	the thing or person in the sentence that has the action directed to it – 'and the bull missed **him**'
gender	classification of *nouns* into classes (like masculine and feminine), requiring other words (eg *adjectives*) to belong to the same class
indirect object	the person or thing in the sentence that is the recipient of the action – 'the public yelled to **him**'
infinitive	dictionary form of a verb – 'to **be** careful'
noun	a thing, person or idea – 'the **fight** was exciting'
number	whether a word is singular or plural – 'and they sent in new **toreadors**'
personal pronoun	a word that means 'I', 'you' etc
possessive adjective	a word that means 'my', 'your' etc
possessive pronoun	a word that means 'mine', 'yours' etc
preposition	a word like 'for' or 'before' in English
subject	the thing or person in the sentence that does the action – '**his cape** fell on the ground'
tense	form of a *verb* that tells you whether the action is in the present, past or future – eg 'run' (present), 'ran' (past), 'will run' (future)
verb	a word that tells you what action happened – 'when the bull **charged** again'
verb stem	part of a *verb* that doesn't change – eg '**mov**e' in '**mov**ing' and '**mov**ed'

Basics

Understanding

KEY PHRASES

Do you speak English?	¿Habla inglés? pol	*ab*·la een·*gles*
I (don't) understand.	(No) Entiendo.	(no) en·*tyen*·do
What does ... mean?	¿Qué significa ...?	ke seeg·nee·*fee*·ka ...

There are two words for 'Spanish': *español* es·pa·*nyol* and *castellano* kas·te·*lya*·no. *Español* is used in Spain, whereas *castellano* is more likely to be used by Latin Americans.

1a Q **Do you speak English?**	¿Habla inglés? *ab*·la een·*gles*
Q **Does anyone speak (English)?**	¿Hay alguien que hable (inglés)? ai al·*gyen* ke *ab*·le een·*gles*
A **I (don't) speak Spanish.**	(No) Hablo español. (no) *ab*·lo es·pa·*nyol*
A **I speak a little (Spanish).**	Hablo un poco de (español). *ab*·lo oon *po*·ko de (es·pa·*nyol*)
I'd like to practise Spanish.	Me gustaría practicar español. me goos·ta·*ree*·a prak·tee·*kar* es·pa·*nyol*
I need an interpreter who speaks (English).	Necesito un intérprete que hable (inglés). ne·the·*see*·to oon in·*ter*·pre·te ke *ab*·le (een·*gles*)

🔊 LISTEN FOR

¿Cómo?	*ko*·mo	Pardon?
No.	no	No.
Sí.	see	Yes.

Would you like me to teach you some English?	¿Quieres que te enseñe algo de inglés? **inf** *kye*·res ke te en·*se*·nye *al*·go de een·*gles*
1b Q **Do you understand?**	¿Me entiende? me en·*tyen*·de
1c A **I understand.**	Entiendo. en·*tyen*·do
1d A **I don't understand.**	No entiendo. no en·*tyen*·do
How do you pronounce this word?	¿Cómo se pronuncia esta palabra? *ko*·mo se pro·*noon*·thya es·ta pa·*lab*·ra
How do you write 'ciudad'?	¿Cómo se escribe 'ciudad'? *ko*·mo se es·*kree*·be thyu·*da*
What does ... mean?	¿Qué significa ...? ke seeg·nee·*fee*·ka ...
2a **Could you please repeat that?**	¿Puede repetir? *pwe*·de re·pe·*teer*
2b **Could you please write it down?**	¿Puede escribirlo, por favor? *pwe*·de es·kree·*beer*·lo por fa·*vor*
2c **Could you please speak more slowly?**	¿Puede hablar más despacio, por favor? *pwe*·de ab·*lar* mas des·*pa*·thyo por fa·*vor*

| ✂ | **Slowly, please!** | Más despacio, por favor. | mas des·*pa*·thyo por fa·*vor* |

Numbers & Amounts

KEY PHRASES

How much?	¿Cuánto?	*kwan*·to
a little	un poquito	oon po·*kee*·to
some	algunos/as m/f	al·*goo*·nos/as

Cardinal Numbers

3a	0	cero	*the*·ro
3b	1	uno	*oo*·no
3c	2	dos	dos
3d	3	tres	tres
3e	4	cuatro	*kwa*·tro
3f	5	cinco	*theen*·ko
3g	6	seis	seys
3h	7	siete	*sye*·te
3i	8	ocho	o·cho
3j	9	nueve	*nwe*·ve
3k	10	diez	dyeth
	11	once	*on*·the
	12	doce	*do*·the
	13	trece	*tre*·the
	14	catorce	ka·*tor*·the
	15	quince	*keen*·the
	16	dieciséis	dye·thee·*seys*
	17	diecisiete	dye·thee·*sye*·te
4a	20	veinte	*veyn*·te

21	veintiuno	veyn·tee·oo·no
22	veintidós	veyn·tee·dos
4b 30	treinta	*treyn*·ta
4c 40	cuarenta	kwa·*ren*·ta
4d 50	cincuenta	theen·*kwen*·ta
4e 60	sesenta	se·*sen*·ta
4f 70	setenta	se·*ten*·ta
4g 80	ochenta	o·*chen*·ta
4h 90	noventa	no·*ven*·ta
4i 100	cien	thyen
101	ciento uno	*thyen*·to oo·no
500	quinientos	kee·*nyen*·tos
4j 1000	mil	mil
4k 1,000,000	un millón	oon mee·*lyon*

Ordinal Numbers

1st	primero/a m/f	pree·*me*·ro/a
2nd	segundo/a m/f	se·*goon*·do/a
3rd	tercero/a m/f	ter·*the*·ro/a

Amounts

How much?	¿Cuánto?	*kwan*·to
a little	un poquito	oon po·*kee*·to
many	muchos/as m/f	*moo*·chos/as
some	algunos/as m/f	al·*goo*·nos/as
more/less	más/menos	mas/*me*·nos
a quarter/half	un cuarto/medio	oon *kwar*·to/*me*·dyo
a third	un tercio	oon *ter*·thyo
all/none	todo/nada	*to*·do/*na*·da

For other amounts, see **self-catering** (p184).

Times & Dates

KEY PHRASES

What time is it?	¿Qué hora es?	ke o·ra es
At what time ...?	¿A qué hora ...?	a ke o·ra ...
What date?	¿Qué día?	ke dee·a

Telling the Time

5a Q What time is it?	¿Qué hora es?	ke o·ra es
5b A It's (one) o'clock.	Es la (una).	es la oo·na
A It's (10) o'clock.	Son las (diez).	son las (dyeth)
Quarter past one.	Es la una y cuarto.	es la oo·na ee kwar·to
Twenty past one.	Es la una y veinte.	es la oo·na ee veyn·te
Half past one.	Es la una y media.	es la oo·na ee me·dya
Twenty to one.	Es la una menos veinte.	es la oo·na me·nos veyn·te
Quarter to one.	Es la una menos cuarto.	es la oo·na me·nos kwar·to
It's early.	Es temprano.	es tem·pra·no
It's late.	Es tarde.	es tar·de

Q	At what time?	¿A qué hora?
		a ke o·ra

A	At ...	A las ...
		a las ...

am	de la mañana
	de la ma·nya·na

pm	de la tarde
	de la tar·de

The Calendar

6a	Monday	lunes m	loo·nes
6b	Tuesday	martes m	mar·tes
6c	Wednesday	miércoles m	myer·ko·les
6d	Thursday	jueves m	khwe·ves
6e	Friday	viernes m	vyer·nes
6f	Saturday	sábado m	sa·ba·do
6g	Sunday	domingo m	do·meen·go
7a	January	enero m	e·ne·ro
7b	February	febrero m	fe·bre·ro
7c	March	marzo m	mar·tho
7d	April	abril m	a·breel
7e	May	mayo m	ma·yo
7f	June	junio m	khoo·nyo
7g	July	julio m	khoo·lyo
7h	August	agosto m	a·gos·to
7i	September	septiembre m	sep·tyem·bre
7j	October	octubre m	ok·too·bre
7k	November	noviembre m	no·vyem·bre
7l	December	diciembre m	dee·thyem·bre

8a	summer	verano m	ve·ra·no
8b	autumn	otoño m	o·to·nyo
8c	winter	invierno m	een·vyer·no
8d	spring	primavera f	pree·ma·ve·ra

What date?		¿Qué día? ke dee·a
9a Q	**What date is it today?**	¿Qué día es hoy? ke dee·a es oy
🅐	**It's (18 October).**	Es (el dieciocho de octubre). es (el dye·thee·o·cho de ok·too·bre)

Present

now	ahora	a·o·ra
right now	ahora mismo	a·o·ra mees·mo
this afternoon	esta tarde	es·ta tar·de
this month	este mes	es·te mes
this morning	esta manana	es·ta ma·nya·na
this week	esta semana	es·ta se·ma·na
this year	este año	es·te a·nyo
9b today	hoy	oy
tonight	esta noche	es·ta no·che

Past

(three) days ago	hace (tres) días	a·the (tres) dee·as
half an hour ago	hace media hora	a·the me·dya o·ra
a while ago	hace un rato	a·the un ra·to
(five) years ago	hace (cinco) años	a·the (theen·ko) a·nyos

day before yesterday	anteayer	an·te·a·yer
9c last month	el mes pasado	el mes pa·sa·do
last night	anoche	a·no·che
9d last week	la semana pasada	la se·ma·na pa·sa·da
9e last year	el año pasado	el a·nyo pa·sa·do
since (May)	desde (mayo)	des·de (ma·yo)
9f yesterday	ayer	a·yer
yesterday afternoon	ayer por la tarde	a·yer por la tar·de
yesterday evening	ayer por la noche	a·yer por la no·che
yesterday morning	ayer por la mañana	a·yer por la ma·nya·na

Future

in (six) days	dentro de (seis) días	den·tro de (seys) dee·as
in an hour	dentro de una hora	den·tro de oo·na o·ra
in (five) minutes	dentro de (cinco) minutos	den·tro de (theen·ko) mee·noo·tos
in a month	dentro de un mes	den·tro de oon mes
10a tomorrow	mañana	ma·nya·na
10b next month	el mes que viene	el mes ke vye·ne
10c next week	la semana que viene	la se·ma·na ke vye·ne
10d next year	el año que viene	el a·nyo ke vye·ne
tomorrow morning	mañana por la mañana	ma·nya·na por la ma·nya·na

BASICS

TIMES & DATES

tomorrow afternoon	mañana por la tarde	ma·*nya*·na por la *tar*·de
tomorrow evening	mañana por la noche	ma·*nya*·na por la *no*·che
day after tomorrow	pasado manana	pa·*sa*·do ma·*nya*·na
until (June)	hasta (junio)	*as*·ta (*khoo*·nyo)

During the Day

11a afternoon	la tarde f	la *tar*·de
day	día m	*dee*·a
11b evening	la noche f	la *no*·che
midday	mediodía m	me·dyo·*dee*·a
midnight	medianoche f	me·dya·*no*·che
early morning (midnight to 5am)	madrugada f	ma·droo·*ga*·da
11c morning	la mañana f	la ma·*nya*·na
night	noche f	*no*·che
sunrise	amanecer m	a·ma·ne·*ther*
sunset	puesta f del sol	*pwes*·ta del sol

Practical

Transport

KEY PHRASES

What time's the next bus?	¿A qué hora es el próximo autobús?	a ke o·ra es el *prok*·see·mo ow·to·*boos*
Two ... tickets, please.	Dos ... billetes, por favor.	dos ... bee·*lye*·tes, por fa·*vor*
Please tell me when we get to ...?	¿Puede avisarme cuando lleguemos a ...?	*pwe*·de a·vee·*sar*·me *kwan*·do lye·*ge*·mos a ...
Please take me to this address.	Por favor, lléveme a esta dirección.	por fa·*vor*, *lye*·ve·me a es·ta dee·rek·*thyon*
I'd like to hire a car.	Quisiera alquilar un coche.	kee·*sye*·ra al·kee·*lar* oon *ko*·che

Getting Around

At what time does the ... leave/arrive?	¿A qué hora sale/llega el ...?	a ke o·ra *sa*·le/*lye*·ga el ...

boat	barco	*bar*·ko
bus (city)	autobús	ow·to·*boos*
bus (intercity)	autocar	ow·to·*kar*
plane	avión	a·*vyon*
train	tren	tren
tram	tranvía	tran·*vee*·a

12a What time's the first bus?	¿A qué hora es el primer autobús?	a ke *o*·ra es el pree·*mer* ow·to·*boos*
12b What time's the last bus?	¿A qué hora es el último autobús?	a ke *o*·ra es el *ool*·tee·mo ow·to·*boos*
What time's the next bus?	¿A qué hora es el próximo autobús?	a ke *o*·ra es el *prok*·see·mo ow·to·*boos*
12c How long will it be delayed?	¿Cuánto tiempo se retrasará?	*kwan*·to *tyem*·po se re·tra·sa·*ra*
12b Is this seat available?	¿Está libre este asiento?	es·*ta lee*·bre es·te a·*syen*·to
✄ **Is it free?**	¿Está libre?	es·*ta lee*·bre
12e That's my seat.	Ése es mi asiento.	*e*·se es mee a·*syen*·to
I'd like to get off at (Aranjuez).	Me gustaría bajarme en (Aranjuez).	me goos·ta·*ree*·a ba·*khar*·me en (a·ran·*khweth*)
I want to get off here!	¡Quiero bajarme aquí!	*kye*·ro ba·*khar*·me a·*kee*
I'd prefer to walk there.	Prefiero ir a pie.	pre·*fye*·ro eer a pye
Can we get there by public transport?	¿Se puede ir en transporte público?	se *pwe*·de eer en trans·*por*·te *poo*·blee·ko

Buying Tickets

13a Do I need to book a seat?	¿Tengo que reservar?	*ten·go ke re·ser·var*
13b How much is it?	¿Cuánto cuesta?	*kwan·to kwes·ta*
13c Where can I buy a ticket?	¿Dónde puedo comprar un billete?	*don·de pwe·do kom·prar oon bee·lye·te*
13d Is it a direct route?	¿Es un viaje directo?	*es oon vya·khe dee·rek·to*
Is there a toilet?	¿Hay servicios?	*ai ser·vee·thyos*
13e How long does the trip take?	¿Cuánto se tarda?	*kwan·to se tar·da*
Can I get a stand-by ticket?	¿Puede ponerme en la lista de espera?	*pwe·de po·ner·me en la lees·ta de es·pe·ra*
I'd like an aisle seat.	Quisiera un asiento de pasillo.	*kee·sye·ra oon a·syen·to de pa·see·lyo*
I'd like a window seat.	Quisiera un asiento junto a la ventana.	*kee·sye·ra oon a·syen·to khoon·to a la ven·ta·na*
I'd like a (non)smoking seat.	Quisiera un asiento de (no) fumadores.	*kee·sye·ra oon a·syen·to de (no) foo·ma·do·res*

Buying a Ticket

What time is the next ...?

¿A qué hora sale el próximo ...?
a ke *o·ra* sa·le el *prok·see·mo* ...

 boat
barco
bar·ko

 bus
autobús
ow·to·*boos*

 train
tren
tren

One ... ticket, please.

Un billete ..., por favor.
oon bee·*lye·*te ... por fa·*vor*

 one-way
sencillo
sen·*thee·*lyo

 return
de ida y vuelta
de *ee·*da ee *vwel·*ta

I'd like a/an ... seat.

Quisiera un asiento ...
kee·*sye·*ra oon a·*syen·*to ...

aisle
de pasillo
de pa·*see·*lyo

window
junto a la
ventana
*khoon·*to a la
ven·*ta·*na

Which platform does it depart from?

¿De cuál andén sale?
de kwal an·*den* sa·le

14a I'd like to cancel my ticket, please.	Me gustaría cancelar mi billete, por favor. me goos·ta·*ree*·a kan·the·*lar* mee bee·*lye*·te por fa·*vor*
14b I'd like to change my ticket, please.	Me gustaría cambiar mi billete, por favor. me goos·ta·*ree*·a kam·*byar* mee bee·*lye*·te por fa·*vor*
(Two) ... tickets, please.	(Dos) billetes ..., por favor. (dos) bee·*lye*·tes ... por fa·*vor*

1st-class	de primera clase	de pree·*me*·ra *kla*·se
2nd-class	de segunda clase	de se·*goon*·da *kla*·se
child's	infantil	een·fan·*teel*
return	de ida y vuelta	de *ee*·da ee *vwel*·ta
student's	de estudiante	de es·too·*dyan*·te

A one-way ticket to (Barcelona).	Un billete sencillo a (Barcelona). oon bee·*lye*·te sen·*thee*·lyo a (bar·the·*lo*·na)

Luggage

15a My luggage has been damaged.	Mis maletas han sido dañadas. mees ma·*le*·tas an *see*·do da·*nya*·das
15b My luggage has been lost.	Mis maletas han sido perdidas. mees ma·*le*·tas an *see*·do per·*dee*·das

PRACTICAL TRANSPORT

🔊 LISTEN FOR

Esta parada es ...	es·ta pa·ra·da es ... This stop is ...
La próxima parada es ...	la prok·see·ma pa·ra·da es ... The next stop is ...
Está completo.	es·ta kom·ple·to It's full.
El ... está retrasado/ cancelado.	el ... es·ta re·tra·sa·do/ kan·the·la·do The ... is delayed/ cancelled.

15c My luggage has been stolen.	Mis maletas han sido robadas. mees ma·le·tas an see·do ro·ba·das
I'd like a luggage locker.	Quisiera un casillero de consigna. kee·sye·ra oon ka·see·lye·ro de kon·seeg·na

Bus

Which bus goes to (Madrid)?	¿Qué autobús va a (Madrid)? ke ow·to·boos va a (ma·dreeth)
Where's the bus stop?	¿Dónde está la parada del autobús? don·de es·ta la pa·ra·da del ow·to·boos
What's the next stop?	¿Cuál es la próxima parada? kwal es la prok·see·ma pa·ra·da

16a Please tell me when we get to ...	¿Puede avisarme cuando lleguemos a ...?
	pwe·de a·vee·sar·me kwan·do lye·ge·mos a ...
Bus number ...	El autobús número ...
	el ow·to·boos noo·me·ro ...

For bus numbers, see **numbers & amounts**, p34.

Train

16b What station is this?	¿Cuál es esta estación?
	kwal es es·ta es·ta·thyon
16c What's the next station?	¿Cuál es la próxima estación?
	kwal es la prok·see·ma es·ta·thyon
Does this train stop at (Valencia)?	¿Para el tren en (Valencia)?
	pa·ra el tren en (va·len·thya)
Do I need to change trains?	¿Tengo que cambiar de tren?
	ten·go ke kam·byar de tren
Which carriage is for (Bilbao)?	¿Cuál es el coche para (Bilbao)?
	kwal es el ko·che pa·ra (beel·bow)

Boat

Are there life jackets?	¿Hay chalecos salvavidas?
	ai cha·le·kos sal·va·vee·das
What's the sea like today?	¿Cómo está el mar hoy?
	ko·mo es·ta el mar oy
I feel seasick.	Estoy mareado/a. **m/f**
	es·toy ma·re·a·do/a

Taxi

17a I'd like a taxi.	Quisiera un taxi. kee·*sye*·ra oon *tak*·see	
17b I'd like a taxi at (9am).	Quisiera un taxi a (las nueve de la mañana). kee·*sye*·ra oon *tak*·see a (las *nwe*·ve de la ma·*nya*·na)	
Where's the taxi stand?	¿Dónde está la parada de taxis? *don*·de es·*ta* la pa·*ra*·da de *tak*·sees	

PRACTICAL TRANSPORT

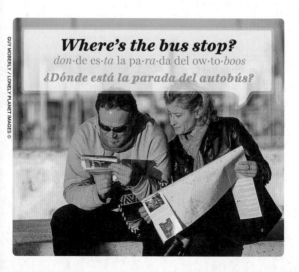

Where's the bus stop?
don·de es·*ta* la pa·*ra*·da del ow·to·*boos*
¿Dónde está la parada del autobús?

PRACTICAL TRANSPORT

17c Is this taxi available?	¿Está libre este taxi? es·*ta* lee·bre es·te tak·see
✂ **Is it free?** ¿Está libre?	es·*ta* lee·bre
How much is the flag fall/hiring charge?	¿Cuánto es la tasa de alquiler? *kwan*·to es la *ta*·sa de al·kee·*ler*
17d Please put the meter on.	Por favor, ponga el taxímetro. por fa·*vor* pon·ga el tak·*see*·me·tro
17e How much is it to ...?	¿Cuánto cuesta ir a ...? *kwan*·to *kwes*·ta eer a ...
17f Please take me to (this address).	Por favor, lléveme a (esta dirección). por fa·*vor* *lye*·ve·me a (es·ta dee·rek·*thyon*)
✂ **To ...** A ...	a ...
How much is the final fare?	¿Cuánto es en total? *kwan*·to es en to·*tal*
18a Please slow down.	Por favor vaya más despacio. por fa·*vor* va·ya mas des·*pa*·thyo
18b Please wait here.	Por favor espere aquí. por fa·*vor* es·*pe*·re a·*kee*
18c Please stop here.	Por favor pare aquí. por fa·*vor* *pa*·re a·*kee*

For other useful phrases, see **directions**, p57.

Car & Motorbike

Where can I hire a ...?	¿Dónde se puede alquilar ...? *don·de se pwe·de al·kee·lar ...*
Does that include insurance/mileage?	¿Incluye el seguro/kilometraje? *een·kloo·ye el se·goo·ro/ kee·lo·me·tra·khe*
19a I'd like to hire a car.	Quisiera alquilar un coche. *kee·sye·ra al·kee·lar oon ko·che*
19b I'd like to hire a motorbike.	Quisiera alquilar una moto. *kee·sye·ra al·kee·lar oo·na mo·to*
How much for hourly hire?	¿Cuánto cuesta el alquiler por hora? *kwan·to kwes·ta el al·kee·ler por o·ra*
19c How much for daily hire?	¿Cuánto cuesta el alquiler por día? *kwan·to kwes·ta el al·kee·ler por dee·a*
19d How much for weekly hire?	¿Cuánto cuesta el alquiler por semana? *kwan·to kwes·ta el al·kee·ler por se·ma·na*
19e Is this the road to ...?	¿Es el camino a ...? *es el ka·mee·no a ...*
Where's a petrol station?	¿Dónde hay una gasolinera? *don·de ai oo·na ga·so·lee·ne·ra*

PRACTICAL TRANSPORT

PRACTICAL TRANSPORT

LOOK FOR

Acceso	ak·*the*·so	Entrance
Aparcamiento	a·par·ka·*myen*·to	Parking
Ceda el Paso	*the*·da el *pa*·so	Give Way
Desvío	des·*vee*·o	Detour
Dirección Única	dee·rek·*thyon* oo·nee·ka	One Way
Frene	*fre*·ne	Slow Down
Peaje	pe·*a*·khe	Toll
Peligro	pe·*lee*·gro	Danger
Prohibido Aparcar	pro·ee·*bee*·do a·par·*kar*	No Parking
Prohibido el Paso	pro·ee·*bee*·do el *pa*·so	No Entry
Stop	es·*top*	Stop
Vía de Acceso	*vee*·a de ak·*the*·so	Exit Freeway

What's the (city) speed limit?	¿Cuál es el límite de velocidad (en la ciudad)? kwal es el *lee*·mee·te de ve·lo·thee·*da* (en la thyu·*da*)
Please fill it up.	Por favor, lléneme el depósito. por fa·*vor* *lye*·ne·me el de·*po*·see·to
I'd like (20) litres of ...	Quiero (veinte) litros de ... *kye*·ro (*veyn*·te) *lee*·tros de ...
Please check the oil/water.	Por favor, revise el nivel del aceite/agua. por fa·*vor* re·*vee*·se el nee·*vel* del a·*they*·te/*a*·gwa

windscreen
parabrisas m
pa·ra·*bree*·sas

petrol
gasolina f
ga·so·*lee*·na

battery
batería f
ba·ta·*ree*·a

engine
motor m
mo·*tor*

headlight
faro m
fa·ro

tyre
rueda f
rwe·da

Please check the tyre pressure.	Por favor, revise la presión de los neumáticos. por fa·*vor* re·*vee*·se la pre·*syon* de los ne·oo·*ma*·tee·kos
(How long) Can I park here?	¿(Por cuánto tiempo) Puedo aparcar aquí? (por *kwan*·to *tyem*·po) *pwe*·do a·par·*kar* a·*kee*
19f I need a mechanic.	Necesito un mecánico. ne·the·*see*·to oon me·*ka*·nee·ko
The car has broken down (at Salamanca).	El coche se ha averiado (en Salamanca). el *ko*·che se a a·ve·*rya*·do (en sa·la·*man*·ka)
I had an accident.	He tenido un accidente. e te·*nee*·do oon ak·thee·*den*·te

Bicycle

Can we get there by bike?	¿Se puede ir en bici? se *pwe*·de eer en *bee*·thee
20a I'd like to hire a bicycle.	Quisiera alquilar una bicicleta. kee·*sye*·ra al·kee·*lar oo*·na bee·thee·*kle*·ta
Where can I buy a (secondhand) bike?	¿Dónde se puede comprar una bicicleta (de segunda mano)? *don*·de se *pwe*·de kom·*prar oo*·na bee·thee·*kle*·ta (de se·*goon*·da *ma*·no)
How much is it per day?	¿Cuánto cuesta por un día? *kwan*·to *kwes*·ta por oon *dee*·a
How much is it per hour?	¿Cuánto cuesta por una hora? *kwan*·to *kwes*·ta por *oo*·na *o*·ra
I have a puncture.	Se me ha pinchado una rueda. se me a peen·*cha*·do *oo*·na *rwe*·da
I'd like to have my bicycle repaired.	Me gustaría arreglar mi bicicleta. me goo·sta·*ree*·a a·reg·*lar* mee bee·thee·*kle*·ta
Are there cycling paths?	¿Hay carril bicicleta? ai ka·*reel* bee·thee·*kle*·ta
Is there bicycle parking?	¿Hay aparcamiento de bicicletas? ai a·par·ka·*myen*·to de bee·thee·*kle*·tas
Can I take my bike on the train?	¿Puedo llevar mi bicicleta en el tren? *pwe*·do lye·*var* mee bee·thee·*kle*·ta en el tren

Border Crossing

KEY PHRASES

I'm here for ... days.	Estoy aquí por ... días.	es·*toy* a·*kee* por ... *dee*·as
I'm staying at ...	Me estoy alojando en ...	me es·*toy* a·lo·*khan*·do en ...
I have nothing to declare.	No tengo nada que declarar.	no *ten*·go *na*·da ke de·kla·*rar*

Passport Control

21a I'm here on business.	Estoy aquí por negocios. es·*toy* a·*kee* por ne·*go*·thyos
21b I'm here on holiday.	Estoy aquí de vacaciones. es·*toy* a·*kee* de va·ka·*thyo*·nes
I'm here in transit.	Estoy aquí en tránsito. es·*toy* a·*kee* en *tran*·see·to
I'm here for ... days.	Estoy aquí por ... días. es·*toy* a·*kee* por ... *dee*·as
I'm here for ... weeks.	Estoy aquí por ... semanas. es·*toy* a·*kee* por ... se·*ma*·nas
I'm here for ... months.	Estoy aquí por ... meses. es·*toy* a·*kee* por ... *me*·ses
I'm going to (Salamanca).	Voy a (Salamanca). voy a (sa·la·*man*·ka)
I'm staying at ...	Me estoy alojando en ... me es·*toy* a·lo·*khan*·do en ...

🔊 LISTEN FOR

Su pasaporte, por favor.	soo pa·sa·*por*·te por fa·*vor*
	Your passport, please.
Su visado, por favor.	soo vee·*sa*·do por fa·*vor*
	Your visa, please.
¿Está viajando en un grupo?	es·*ta* vya·*khan*·do en oon *groo*·po
	Are you travelling in a group?
¿Está viajando con familia?	es·*ta* vya·*khan*·do kon fa·*mee*·lya
	Are you travelling with family?
¿Está viajando solo/a? m/f	es·*ta* vya·*khan*·do *so*·lo/a
	Are you travelling on your own?

Customs

21c I have nothing to declare.	No tengo nada que declarar. no *ten*·go *na*·da ke de·kla·*rar*
21d I have something to declare.	Quisiera declarar algo. kee·*sye*·ra de·kla·*rar al*·go
That's (not) mine.	Eso (no) es mío. e·so (no) es *mee*·o
I didn't know I had to declare it.	No sabía que tenía que declararlo. no sa·*bee*·a ke te·*nee*·a ke de·kla·*rar*·lo

For phrases on payments and receipts, see **money & banking**, p91.

Directions

KEY PHRASES

Where's the ...?	¿Dónde está ...?	*don*·de es·*ta* ...
What's the address?	¿Cuál es la dirección?	kwal es la dee·rek·*thyon*
How far is it?	¿A cuánta distancia está?	a *kwan*·ta dees·*tan*·thya es·*ta*

Excuse me.	Perdón. per·*don*
Could you help me, please?	¿Perdón, puede ayudarme, por favor? per·*don* pwe·de a·yoo·*dar*·me por fa·*vor*
22a Where's the ...?	¿Dónde está ...? *don*·de es·*ta* ...
I'm looking for ...	Busco ... *boos*·ko ...
Which way is ...?	¿Por dónde se va a ...? por *don*·de se va a ...
22b How do I get there?	¿Cómo se puede ir? *ko*·mo se *pwe*·de eer
22c How far away is it?	¿A qué distancia está? a ke dees·*tan*·thya es·*ta*
22d What's the address?	¿Cuál es la dirección? kwal es la dee·rek·*thyon*

22e Can you show me on the map?	¿Me lo puede indicar en el mapa? me lo *pwe*·de een·dee·*kar* (en el *ma*·pa)
23a It's far.	Está lejos. es·*ta le*·khos
23b It's near.	Está cerca. es·*ta ther*·ka
23c It's next to ...	Está al lado de ... es·*ta* al *la*·do de ...
23d here	aquí a·*kee*
23e there	allí a·*yee*
23f opposite ...	frente a ... *fren*·te a ...
23g straight ahead	todo recto *to*·do *rek*·to
24a Turn at the corner.	Doble en la esquina. *do*·ble en la es·*kee*·na
24b Turn at the traffic lights.	Doble en el semáforo. *do*·ble en el se·*ma*·fo·ro
24c Turn left.	Doble a la izquierda. *do*·ble a la eeth·*kyer*·da
24d Turn right.	Doble a la derecha. *do*·ble a la de·*re*·cha
(two) kilometres	(dos) kilómetros (dos) kee·*lo*·me·tros
(three) metres	(tres) metros (tres) *me*·tros
(six) minutes	(seis) minutos (seys) mee·*noo*·tos

traffic lights
semáforo m
se·*ma*·fo·ro

shop
tienda f
tyen·da

pedestrian crossing
paso de cebra m
pa·so de *the*·bra

bus
autobús m
ow·to·*boos*

intersection
cruce m
kroo·the

corner
esquina f
es·*kee*·na

taxi
taxi m
tak·see

25a **by bus**	en autobús	en ow·to·*boos*
25b **by taxi**	en taxi	en *tak*·see
25c **by train**	en tren	en tren
25d **on foot**	a pie	a pye
avenue	avenida f	a·ve·*nee*·da
lane	callejón m	ka·lye·*khon*
street	calle f	*ka*·lye

For locations and compass directions, see the **dictionary**.

Accommodation

KEY PHRASES

Where's a hotel?	¿Dónde hay un hotel?	*don*·de ai on *o*·tel
Do you have a double room?	¿Tiene una habitación doble?	*tye*·ne *oo*·na a·bee·ta·*thyon do*·ble
How much is it per night?	¿Cuánto cuesta por noche?	*kwan*·to *kwes*·ta por *no*·che
Is breakfast included?	¿El desyauno está incluído?	el de·sa·*yoo*·no es·*ta* een·kloo·ee·do
What time is checkout?	¿A qué hora hay que dejar libre la habitación?	a ke *o*·ra ai ke de·*khar lee*·bre la a·bee·ta·*thyon*

Finding Accommodation

26a Where's a guesthouse?	¿Dónde hay una pensión? *don*·de ai *oo*·na pen·*syon*	
26b Where's a hotel?	¿Dónde hay un hotel? *don*·de ai oon o·*tel*	
26c Where's a youth hostel?	¿Dónde hay un albergue juvenil? *don*·de ai oon al·*ber*·ge khoo·ve·*neel*	
26d Where's a camping ground?	¿Dónde hay una zona de acampada? *don*·de ai *oo*·na *tho*·na de a·kam·*pa*·da	

27a **Can you recommend somewhere cheap?**	¿Puede recomendar un sitio barato?	*pwe·*de re·ko·men·*dar* oon *see·*tyo ba·*ra·*to
27b **Can you recommend somewhere nearby?**	¿Puede recomendar un sitio cercano?	*pwe·*de re·ko·men·*dar* oon *see·*tyo ther·*ka·*no
27c **Can you recommend somewhere luxurious?**	¿Puede recomendar un sitio de lujo?	*pwe·*de re·ko·men·*dar* oon *see·*tyo de *loo·*kho
What's the address?	¿Cuál es la dirección?	kwal es la dee·rek·*thyon*

For more on how to get there, see **directions** (p57).

Booking Ahead & Checking In

27d **I'd like to book a room, please.**	Quisiera reservar una habitación.	kee·*sye·*ra re·ser·*var* oo·na a·bee·ta·*thyon*

✂	**Are there rooms?**	¿Hay habitaciones?	ai a·bee·ta·*thyo·*nes

27e **I have a reservation.**	Tengo una reserva.	*ten·*go oo·na re·*ser·*va
My name's ...	Me llamo ...	me *lya·*mo ...
For (three) nights/weeks.	Por (tres) noches/semanas.	por (tres) *no·*ches/se·*ma·*nas
From (July 2) to (July 6).	Desde (el dos de julio) hasta (el seis de julio).	*des·*de (el dos de *khoo·*lyo) *as·*ta (el seys de *khoo·*lyo)

🔊 LISTEN FOR

Lo siento, está completo.	lo *syen*·to es·*ta* kom·*ple*·to I'm sorry, we're full.
¿Por cuántas noches?	por *kwan*·tas *no*·ches For how many nights?
Su pasaporte, por favor.	soo pa·sa·*por*·te por fa·*vor* Your passport, please.

Do I need to pay upfront?	¿Necesito pagar por adelantado? ne·the·*see*·to pa·gar por a·de·lan·*ta*·do
Do you offer (long-stay) discounts?	¿Ofrecen descuentos (por larga estancia)? of·*re*·then des·*kwen*·tos (por *lar*·ga es·*tan*·thya)
Is breakfast included?	¿El desyauno está incluído? el de·sa·*yoo*·no es·*ta* een·kloo·*ee*·do
Is there parking?	¿Hay aparcamiento? ai a·par·ka·*myen*·to
28a How much is it per night?	¿Cuánto cuesta por noche? *kwan*·to *kwes*·ta por *no*·che
How much is it per week?	¿Cuánto cuesta por semana? *kwan*·to *kwes*·ta por se·*ma*·na
28b How much is it per person?	¿Cuánto cuesta por persona? *kwan*·to *kwes*·ta por per·*so*·na
Can I pay by credit card?	¿Puedo pagar con tarjeta de crédito? *pwe*·do pa·*gar* con tar·*khe*·ta de *kre*·dee·to

Finding a Room

Do you have a ... room?

¿Tiene una habitación ...?
tye·ne oo·na a·bee·ta·*thyon* ...

 double
doble
do·ble

 single
individual
een·dee·vee·*dwal*

How much is it per ...?

¿Cuánto cuesta por ...?
kwan·to *kwes*·ta por ...

 night
noche
no·che

 person
persona
per·*so*·na

Is breakfast included?

¿El desayuno está incluído?
el de·sa·*yoo*·no es·*ta* een·kloo·*ee*·do

Can I see the room?

¿Puedo verla?
pwe·do·*ver*·la

I'll take it. / **I won't take it.**

La alquilo.
la al·*kee*·lo

No la alquilo.
no la al·*kee*·lo

Can I pay by travellers cheque?	¿Puedo pagar con cheques de viajero? *pwe·do pa·gar con che·kes de vya·khe·ro*

For other methods of payment, see **money & banking**, p91.

28c Do you have a double room?	¿Tiene una habitación doble? *tye·ne oo·na a·bee·ta·thyon do·ble*
28d Do you have a single room?	¿Tiene una habitación individual? *tye·ne oo·na a·bee·ta·thyon een·dee·vee·dwal*
28e Do you have a twin room?	¿Tiene una habitación con dos camas? *tye·ne oo·na a·bee·ta·thyon con dos ka·mas*
Do you have a room with/ without (a) ...?	¿Tiene una habitación con/sin ...? *tye·ne oo·na a·bee·ta·thyon kon/seen ...*
Can I see it?	¿Puedo verla? *pwe·do ver·la*
It's fine, I'll take it.	Vale, la alquilo. *va·le la al·kee·lo*

Requests & Queries

29a When's breakfast served?	¿Cuándo se sirve el desayuno? *kwan·do se seer·ve el de·sa·yoo·no*
29b Where's breakfast served?	¿Dónde se sirve el desayuno? *don·de se seer·ve el de·sa·yoo·no*

29c Please wake me at (seven).	Por favor, despiérteme a (las siete). *por fa·vor des·pyer·te·me a (las sye·te)*
Can I get another ...?	¿Puede darme otro/a ...? m/f *pwe·de dar·me o·tro/a ...*
Can I use the ...?	¿Puedo usar ...? *pwe·do oo·sar ...*

kitchen	la cocina	la ko·thee·na
laundry	el lavadero	el la·va·de·ro
telephone	el teléfono	el te·le·fo·no

29d I'd like to get internet access.	Quisiera usar el internet. *pwe·do oo·sar el een·ter·net*
30a Is there an elevator?	¿Hay ascensor? *ai as·then·sor*
30b Is there a safe?	¿Hay una caja fuerte? *ai oo·na ka·kha fwer·te*
Do you arrange tours here?	¿Aquí organizan recorridos? *a·kee or·ga·nee·than re·ko·ree·dos*
Do you change money here?	¿Aquí cambian dinero? *a·kee kam·byan dee·ne·ro*
Is there a message for me?	¿Tiene un mensaje para mí? *tye·ne oon men·sa·khe pa·ra mee*
I'm locked out of my room.	Cerré la puerta y se me olvidaron las llaves dentro. *the·re la pwer·ta y se me ol·vee·da·ron las lya·ves den·tro*

| The (bathroom) door is locked. | La puerta (del baño) está cerrada.
la *pwer*·ta (del *ba*·nyo) es·*ta* the·*ra*·da |
| There's no need to change my sheets. | No hace falta cambiar las sábanas.
no *a*·the *fal*·ta kam·*byar* las *sa*·ba·nas |

Complaints

| It's too ... | Es demasiado ...
es de·ma·*sya*·do ... |

cold	fría f	*free*·a
dark	oscura f	os·*koo*·ra
light/bright	clara f	*kla*·ra
noisy	ruidosa f	rwee·*do*·sa
small	pequeña f	pe·*ke*·nya

30c The air-conditioning doesn't work.	No funciona el aire acondicionado. no foon·*thyo*·na el *ai*·re a·kon·dee·thyo·*na*·do
30d The fan doesn't work.	No funciona el ventilador. no foon·*thyo*·na el ven·tee·la·*dor*
30e The toilet doesn't work.	No funciona el retrete. no foon·*thyo*·na el re·*tre*·te
This ... isn't clean.	Éste/Ésta ... no está limpio/a. m/f es·te/es·ta ... no es·ta *leem*·pyo/a
There's no hot water.	No hay agua caliente. no ai *a*·gwa ka·*lyen*·te

TV
televisión f
te·le·vee·*syon*

fan
ventilador m
ven·tee·la·*dor*

air-conditioning
aire acondicionado m
ai·re a·kon·dee·thyo·*na*·do

bed
cama f
ka·ma

key
llave f
lya·ve

toilet
retrete m
re·*tre*·te

bathroom
baño m
ba·nyo

Answering the Door

Who is it?	¿Quién es? kyen es
Just a moment.	Un momento. oon mo·*men*·to
Come in.	Adelante. a·de·*lan*·te
Can you come back later, please?	¿Puede volver más tarde, por favor? *pwe*·de vol·*ver* mas *tar*·de por fa·*vor*

PRACTICAL ACCOMMODATION

Checking Out

31a **What time is checkout?**	¿A qué hora hay que dejar la habitación?	a ke o·ra ai ke de·*khar* la a·bee·ta·*thyon*
How much extra to stay until (6 o'clock)?	¿Cuánto más cuesta quedarse hasta (las seis)?	*kwan*·to mas *kwes*·ta ke·*dar*·se *as*·ta (las seys)
Can I have a late checkout?	¿Puedo dejar la habitación más tarde?	*pwe*·do de·*khar* la a·bee·ta·*thyon* mas *tar*·de
31b **Can I leave my luggage here?**	¿Puedo dejar las maletas aquí?	*pwe*·do de·*khar* las ma·*le*·tas a·*kee*
31c **There's a mistake in the bill.**	Hay un error en la cuenta.	ai oon e·*ror* en la *kwen*·ta
I'm leaving now.	Me voy ahora.	me voy a·o·ra
Can you call a taxi for me (for 11 o'clock)?	¿Me puede pedir un taxi (para las once)?	me *pwe*·de pe·*deer* oon *tak*·see (*pa*·ra las *on*·the)
31d **Could I have my deposit, please?**	¿Me puede dar mi depósito, por favor?	me *pwe*·de dar mee de·*po*·see·to por fa·*vor*

31e Could I have my passport, please?	¿Me puede dar mi pasaporte, por favor? me *pwe*·de dar mee pa·sa·*por*·te por fa·*vor*
31f Could I have my valuables, please?	¿Me puede dar mis objetos de valor, por favor? me *pwe*·de dar mees ob·*khe*·tos de va·*lor* por fa·*vor*
I'll be back on (Tuesday).	Volveré el (martes). vol·ve·*re* el (*mar*·tes)
I'll be back in (three) days.	Volveré en (tres) días. vol·ve·*re* en (tres) *dee*·as

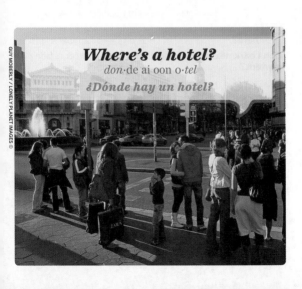

Where's a hotel?
don·de ai oon o·*tel*
¿Dónde hay un hotel?

I had a great stay, thank you.	He tenido una estancia muy agradable, gracias.
	e te·*nee*·do oo·na es·*tan*·thya mooy a·gra·*da*·ble *gra*·thyas
You've been terrific.	Han sido estupendos.
	an *see*·do es·too·*pen*·dos
I'll recommend it to my friends.	Se lo recomendaré a mis amigos.
	se lo re·ko·men·da·*re* a mees a·*mee*·gos

Camping

Where's the nearest camp site?	¿Dónde está el terreno de cámping más cercano?
	don·de es·*ta* el te·*re*·no de *kam*·peeng mas ther·*ka*·no
32a Am I allowed to camp here?	¿Se puede acampar aquí?
	se *pwe*·de a·kam·*par* a·*kee*
Can I park next to my tent?	¿Se puede aparcar al lado de la tienda?
	se *pwe*·de a·par·*kar* al *la*·do de la *tyen*·da
Do you have ...?	¿Tiene ...?
	tye·ne ...

electricity	electricidad	e·lek·tree·thee·*da*
shower facilities	duchas	*doo*·chas
a site	un sitio	oon *see*·tyo
tents for hire	tiendas de campaña para alquilar	*tyen*·das de kam·*pa*·nya *pa*·ra al·kee·*lar*

How much is it per ...?	¿Cuánto vale por ...?
	kwan·to *va*·le por ...

caravan	caravana	ka·ra·*va*·na
person	persona	per·*so*·na
tent	tienda	*tyen*·da
vehicle	vehículo	ve·*ee*·koo·lo

Is the water drinkable?	¿Se puede beber el agua?
	se *pwe*·de be·ber el *a*·gwa

I'm looking for the nearest showers.	Estoy buscando las duchas más cercanas.
	es·*toy* boos·*kan*·do las *doo*·chas mas ther·*ka*·nas

I'm looking for the nearest toilet block.	Estoy buscando los servicios más cercanos.
	es·*toy* boos·*kan*·do los ser·*vee*·thyos mas ther·*ka*·nos

Could I borrow ...?	¿Me puede prestar ...?
	me *pwe*·de pres·*tar* ...

For cooking utensils, see **self-catering** (p186) and the **dictionary**.

PRACTICAL ACCOMMODATION

🔍 LOOK FOR

Caballeros	ka·ba·*lye*·ros	Men
Caliente	ka·*lyen*·te	Hot
Dirección Prohibida	dee·rek·*thyon* pro·hee·*bee*·da	No Entry
Frío	*free*·o	Cold
Señoras	se·*nyo*·ras	Women

Renting

Do you have a/an ... for rent?	¿Tiene ... para alquilar? tye·ne ... pa·ra al·kee·lar

apartment	un piso	oon pee·so
cabin	una cabaña	oo·na ka·ba·nya
house	una casa	oo·na ka·sa
room	una habitación	oo·na a·bee·ta·thyon
villa	un chalet	oon cha·le

furnished	amueblado/a m/f a·mwe·bla·do/a
partly furnished	semi amueblado/a m/f se·mee a·mwe·bla·do/a
unfurnished	sin amueblar seen a·mwe·blar

Staying with Locals

Can I stay at your place?	¿Me puedo quedar en su/tu casa? pol/inf me pwe·do ke·dar en soo/too ka·sa
Thanks for your hospitality.	Gracias por su/tu hospitalidad. pol/inf gra·thyas por soo/too os·pee·ta·lee·da
I have my own mattress.	Tengo mi propio colchón. ten·go mee pro·pyo kol·chon
I have my own sleeping bag.	Tengo mi propio saco de dormir. ten·go mee pro·pyo sa·ko de dor·meer

Can I bring anything for the meal?	¿Puedo traer algo para la comida? *pwe·do tra·er al·go pa·ra la ko·mee·da*
Can I use your telephone?	¿Puedo usar su/tu teléfono? **pol/inf** *pwe·do oo·sar soo/too te·le·fo·no*
Can I help?	¿Puedo ayudar? *pwe·do a·yoo·dar*
Can I set/clear the table?	¿Puedo poner/quitar la mesa? *pwe·do po·ner/kee·tar la me·sa*
Can I do the dishes?	¿Puedo lavar los platos? *pwe·do la·var los pla·tos*
Can I take out the rubbish?	¿Puedo sacar la basura? *pwe·do sa·kar la ba·soo·ra*

For compliments to the chef, see **eating out** (p174).

Shopping

KEY PHRASES

I want to buy ...	Quisiera comprar ...	kee·sye·ra kom·prar ...
Can I look at it?	¿Puedo verlo?	pwe·do ver·lo
Can I try it on?	¿Me lo puedo probar?	me lo pwe·do pro·bar
How much?	¿Cuánto cuesta?	kwan·to kwes·ta
That's too expensive.	Es muy caro.	es mooy ka·ro

Looking For ...

Where's a (super)market?	¿Dónde está un (super)mercado? *don·de es·ta oon (soo·per·)mer·ka·do*
Where's a camping store?	¿Dónde está una tienda de camping? *don·de es·ta oo·na tyen·da de kam·peeng*
Where can I buy locally produced goods/souvenirs?	¿Dónde puedo comprar recuerdos de la zona? *don·de pwe·do kom·prar re·kwer·dos de la tho·na*
33a Where can I buy (a padlock)?	¿Dónde puedo comprar (un candado)? *don·de pwe·do kom·prar (oon kan·da·do)*

For more on shops and how to get there, see **directions** (p57) and the **dictionary**.

Making a Purchase

How much is this?	¿Cuánto cuesta esto?	*kwan·*to *kwes·*ta es·to

✂ **How much?** · ¿Cuánto cuesta? · *kwan·*to *kwes·*ta

33b I want to buy ...	Quisiera comprar ...	kee·*sye·*ra kom·*prar* ...
I'm just looking.	Sólo estoy mirando.	so·lo es·*toy* mee·*ran·*do
33c Can I look at it?	¿Puedo verlo?	*pwe·*do *ver·*lo
33d Do you have any others?	¿Tiene otros?	*tye·*ne o·tros
What is this made from?	¿De qué está hecho?	de ke es·*ta* e·cho
34a Do you accept credit cards?	¿Aceptan tarjetas de crédito?	a·*thep·*tan tar·*khe·*tas de *kre·*dee·to
34b Do you accept debit cards?	¿Aceptan tarjetas de débito?	a·*thep·*tan tar·*khe·*tas de *de·*bee·to
34c I'd like a bag, please.	¿Podría darme una bolsa, por favor?	po·*dree·*a *dar·*me oo·na *bol·*sa por fa·*vor*
34d I'd like a receipt, please.	¿Podría darme un recibo, por favor?	po·*dree·*a *dar·*me oon re·*thee·*bo por fa·*vor*

✂ **Receipt, please.** · El recibo, por favor. · el re·*thee·*bo por fa·*vor*

🔊 LISTEN FOR

¿En qué le puedo servir?	en ke le *pwe*·do ser·*veer*
	Can I help you?
No tengo.	no *ten*·go
	I don't have any.
¿Algo más?	*al*·go mas
	Anything else?

I don't need a bag, thanks.	No necesito bolsa, gracias.
	no ne·the·*see*·to *bol*·sa *gra*·thyas
35a Can you write down the price?	¿Puede escribir el precio?
	pwe·de es·kree·*beer* el *pre*·thyo
Could I have it wrapped?	¿Me lo podría envolver?
	me lo po·*dree*·a en·vol·*ver*
35b Does it have a guarantee?	¿Tiene garantía?
	tye·ne ga·ran·*tee*·a
Can I pick it up later?	¿Puedo recogerlo más tarde?
	pwe·do re·ko·*kher*·lo mas *tar*·de
Can I have it sent overseas?	¿Pueden enviarlo por correo a otro país?
	pwe·den en·vee·*ar*·lo por ko·*re*·o a *o*·tro pa·*ees*
35c It's faulty.	Es defectuoso.
	es de·fek·*two*·so
35d I'd like my change, please.	Quisiera mi cambio, por favor.
	kee·*sye*·ra mee *kam*·byo por fa·*vor*

Making a Purchase

 ### I'd like to buy ...
Quisiera comprar ...
kee·sye·ra kom·prar ...

 ### How much is it?
¿Cuánto cuesta esto?
kwan·to kwes·ta es·to

OR

 ### Can you write down the price?
¿Puede escribir el precio?
pwe·de es·kree·beer el pre·thyo

 ### Do you accept credit cards?
¿Aceptan tarjetas de crédito?
a·thep·tan tar·khe·tas de kre·dee·to

 ### Could I have a ..., please?
¿Podría darme ..., por favor?
po·dree·a dar·me ... por fa·vor

 receipt
un recibo
oon re·thee·bo

 bag
una bolsa
oo·na bol·sa

🔊 LISTEN FOR

cazador m **de ofertas**	ka·tha·*dor* de o·*fer*·tas	bargain hunter
estafa f	es·*ta*·fa	rip-off
ganga f	*gan*·ga	bargain
rebajas f pl	re·*ba*·khas	specials
ventas f pl	*ven*·tas	sale

36a I'd like a refund, please.	Quisiera que me devuelva el dinero, por favor. kee·*sye*·ra ke me de·*vwel*·va el dee·*ne*·ro por fa·*vor*
36b I'd like to return this, please.	Quisiera devolver esto, por favor. kee·*sye*·ra de·vol·*ver* es·to por fa·*vor*

Bargaining

36c That's too expensive.	Es muy caro. es mooy *ka*·ro
Do you have something cheaper?	¿Tiene algo más barato? *tye*·ne *al*·go mas ba·*ra*·to
36d Can you lower the price?	¿Puede bajar el precio? *pwe*·de·a ba·*khar* el *pre*·thyo
I'll give you ...	Le/Te daré ... pol/inf le/te da·*re* ...

Clothes

37a Can I try it on?	¿Me lo puedo probar?
	me lo *pwe*·do pro·*bar*
37b My size is (32).	Uso la talla (treinta y dos).
	oo·so la *ta*·lya (*treyn*·ta ee dos)
37c It doesn't fit.	No me queda bien.
	no me *ke*·da byen
small	pequeño/a m/f
	pe·*ke*·nyo/a
medium	mediano/a m/f
	me·*dya*·no/a
large	grande m&f
	gran·de

For clothing items, see the **dictionary**. For sizes, see **numbers & amounts** (p34).

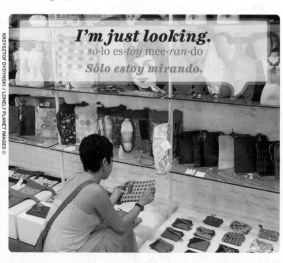

I'm just looking.
so·lo es·*toy* mee·*ran*·do
Sólo estoy mirando.

KRZYSZTOF DYDYNSKI / LONELY PLANET IMAGES ©

Repairs

Can I have my (camera) repaired here?	¿Puede reparar mi (cámara) aquí? *pwe*·de re·pa·*rar* mee (*ka*·ma·ra) a·*kee*
37d When will it be ready?	¿Cuándo estará listo? *kwan*·do es·ta·*ra lees*·to
When will my shoes be ready?	¿Cuándo estarán listos mis zapatos? *kwan*·do es·ta·*ran lees*·tos mees tha·*pa*·tos

Books & Reading

Is there a/an (English-language) bookshop?	¿Hay una librería (en inglés)? ai *oo*·na lee·bre·*ree*·a (en een·*gles*)
Is there a/an (English-language) section?	¿Hay una sección (en inglés)? ai *oo*·na sek·*thyon* (en een·*gles*)
I (don't) like ...	(No) Me gusta/gustan ... sg/pl (no) me *goos*·ta/*goos*·tan ...
I'm looking for something by (Javier Marías).	Estoy buscando algo de (Javier Marías). es·*toy* boos·*kan*·do *al*·go de (kha·*vyer* ma·*ree*·as)

For more on books and reading, see **interests** (p124).

CULTURE TIP

Hispanic Literature

Spanish-language literature has a long history, dating from the 12th century and written across the Spanish-speaking world. Today's thriving industry includes such authors as Ana María Matute, Isabel Allende, Jorge Luis Borges, Miguel de Unamuno, Carmen Martín Gaite, Juan Goytisolo, Miguel Delibes, 1982 Nobel Prize winner Gabriel García Márquez and the 1989 Nobel Prize winner, Camilo José Cela.

Music & DVD

I heard a band called ...	Escuché a un grupo que se llama ... es·koo·*che* a oon *groo*·po ke se *lya*·ma ...
What's their best recording?	¿Cuál es su mejor disco? kwal es soo me·*khor dees*·ko
Can I listen to this?	¿Puedo escuchar esto? *pwe*·do es·koo·*char es*·to
What region is this DVD for?	¿Para qué región es este DVD? *pa*·ra ke re·*khyon* es *es*·te de·oo·ve·de
I'd like a CD/DVD.	Quisiera un compact/DVD. kee·*sye*·ra oon kom·pak/de·oo·ve·de
Is this a pirated copy?	¿Es copia pirata? es *ko*·pya pee·*ra*·ta
I'd like some headphones.	Quisiera unos auriculares. kee·*sye*·ra oo·nos ow·ree·koo·*la*·res

Video & Photography

Can you print digital photos?	¿Podría imprimir fotos digitales? po·*dree*·a eem·pree·*meer* fo·tos dee·khee·*ta*·les
Can you transfer my photos from camera to CD?	¿Podría pasar las fotos de mi cámara a un compact? po·*dree*·a pa·*sar* las *fo*·tos de mee *ka*·ma·ra a oon *kom*·pak
How much is it to develop this film?	¿Cuánto cuesta revelar este carrete? *kwan*·to *kwes*·ta re·ve·*lar* es·te ka·*re*·te
Do you have slide film?	¿Tiene diapositivas? *tye*·ne dee·a·po·see·*tee*·vas
I need a cable to connect my camera to a computer.	Necesito un cable para conectar mi cámara al ordenador. ne·the·*see*·to oon *ka*·ble *pa*·ra ko·nek·*tar* mee *ka*·ma·ra al or·de·na·*dor*
I need a cable to recharge this battery.	Necesito un cable para recargar esta batería. ne·the·*see*·to oon *ka*·ble *pa*·ra re·kar·*gar* es·ta ba·te·*ree*·a
Do you have batteries for this camera?	¿Tiene pilas para esta cámara? *tye*·ne *pee*·las *pa*·ra es·ta *ka*·ma·ra
Do you have memory cards for this camera?	¿Tiene tarjetas de memoria para esta cámara? *tye*·ne tar·*khe*·tas de me·*mo*·rya *pa*·ra es·ta *ka*·ma·ra

CULTURE TIP

The Spanish Lisp

According to a popular legend, one Spanish king – some say Felipe IV, others Ferdinand I – was unable to pronounce the *s* sound properly and his court, and eventually all of Spain, mimicked his lisp. Of course, the tale is a myth. Indeed, only the letters *c* and *z* are pronounced th (when they precede an *i* or an *e*), while the letter *s* remains the same as in English – a selectiveness due to the way Spanish evolved from Latin. So when you hear someone say *gracias* gra·thyas, they are no more lisping than when you say 'thank you' in English.

Do you have (a) ... for this camera?	¿Tiene ... para esta cámara? *tye*·ne ... *pa*·ra es·ta *ka*·ma·ra
38a I need a B&W film for this camera.	Necesito película blanco y negro para esta cámara. ne·the·*see*·to pe·*lee*·koo·la *blan*·ko y *ne*·gro *pa*·ra es·ta *ka*·ma·ra
38b I need a colour film for this camera.	Necesito película color para esta cámara. ne·the·*see*·to pe·*lee*·koo·la ko·*lor pa*·ra es·ta *ka*·ma·ra
I need a (400) speed film for this camera.	Necesito película de sensibilidad (cuatrocientos) para esta cámara. ne·the·*see*·to pe·*lee*·koo·la de sen·see·bee·lee·*da* (kwa·tro·*thyen*·tos) *pa*·ra es·ta *ka*·ma·ra
I need a passport photo taken.	Necesito fotos de pasaporte. ne·the·*see*·to *fo*·tos de pa·sa·*por*·te

PRACTICAL COMMUNICATIONS

Communications

KEY PHRASES

Where's the local internet cafe?	¿Dónde hay un cibercafé cercano?	don·de ai oon thee·ber·ka·fe ther·ka·no
I'd like to check my email.	Quisiera revisar mi correo electrónico.	kee·sye·ra re·vee·sar mee ko·re·o e·lek·tro·nee·ko
I want to send a parcel.	Quisiera enviar un paquete.	kee·sye·ra en·vee·ar oon pa·ke·te
I'd like a SIM card.	Quisiera una tarjeta SIM.	kee·sye·ra oo·na tar·khe·ta seem

Post Office

39a I want to send a parcel.	Quisiera enviar un paquete. kee·sye·ra en·vee·ar oon pa·ke·te	
39b I want to send a postcard.	Quisiera enviar una postal. kee·sye·ra en·vee·ar oo·na pos·tal	
39c I want to buy an envelope.	Quisiera comprar un sobre. kee·sye·ra kom·prar oon so·bre	
39d I want to buy stamps.	Quisiera comprar sellos. kee·sye·ra kom·prar se·lyos	
Please send it by air/ surface mail to ...	Por favor, mándelo por vía aérea/terrestre a ... por fa·vor man·de·lo por vee·a a·e·re·a/te·res·tre a ...	

🔊 LISTEN FOR

buzón m	boo·*thon*	mail box
código m **postal**	*ko*·dee·go pos·*tal*	postcode
correo m **certificado**	ko·*re*·o ther·tee·fee·*ka*·do	registered mail
por vía aérea	por *vee*·a a·e·re·a	airmail
correo m **urgente**	ko·*re*·o oor·*khen*·te	express mail
declaración f **de aduana**	de·kla·ra·*thyon* de a·*dwa*·na	customs declaration
frágil	*fra*·kheel	fragile
internacional	een·ter·na·thyo·*nal*	international
nacional	na·thyo·*nal*	domestic

It contains ...	Contiene ... kon·*tye*·ne ...
Where's the poste restante section?	¿Dónde está la lista de correos? *don*·de es·*ta* la *lees*·ta de ko·*re*·os
Is there any mail for me?	¿Hay alguna carta para mí? ai al·*goo*·na *kar*·ta *pa*·ra mee

Phone

40a **Q** **What's your phone number?**	¿Cuál es su número de teléfono? **pol** kwal es soo *noo*·me·ro de te·*le*·fo·no
Q **What's your phone number?**	¿Cuál es tu número de teléfono? **inf** kwal es too *noo*·me·ro de te·*le*·fo·no
A **The number is ...**	El número es ... el *noo*·me·ro es ...

40b Where's the nearest public phone?	¿Dónde hay una cabina telefónica?	don·de ai oo·na ka·bee·na te·le·fo·nee·ka
Can I look at a phone book?	¿Puedo mirar la guía de teléfonos?	pwe·do mee·rar la gee·a de te·le·fo·nos
What's the area code for ...?	¿Cuál es el prefijo de la zona de ...?	kwal es el pre·fee·kho de la tho·na de ...
What's the country code for ...?	¿Cuál es el prefijo del país de ...?	kwal es el pre·fee·kho del pa·ees de ...

For telephone numbers, see **numbers & amounts**, page 34.

I want to...	Quiero ...	kye·ro ...
make a call to (Singapore)	hacer una llamada a (Singapur)	a·ther oo·na lya·ma·da a (seen·ga·poor)
make a local call	hacer una llamada local	a·ther oo·na lya·ma·da lo·kal
a reverse-charge/ collect call	una llamada a cobro revertido	oo·na lya·ma·da a ko·bro re·ver·tee·do

40c I'd like to buy a phonecard.	Quisiera comprar una tarjeta telefónica. kee·sye·ra kom·prar oo·na tar·khe·ta te·le·fo·nee·ka
It's engaged.	Está comunicando. es·ta ko·moo·nee·kan·do

🔊 **LISTEN FOR**

¿De parte de quién?	de *par*·te de kyen	Who's calling?
¿Con quién quiere hablar?	kon kyen *kye*·re a·*blar*	Who do you want to speak to?
Lo siento, pero ahora no está.	lo *syen*·to *pe*·ro a·o·ra no es·*ta*	I'm sorry, he/she is not here.
Lo siento, tiene el numero equivocado.	lo *syen*·to *tye*·ne el *noo*·me·ro e·kee·vo·*ka*·do	Sorry, you have got the wrong number.

The connection's bad.	Es mala conexión. es *ma*·la ko·nek·*syon*
Hello. (calling)	Hola. o·la
Hello? (answering)	¿Diga? *dee*·ga
Can I speak to ...?	¿Está ...? es·*ta* ...
It's (Julio) ...	Soy (Julio) ... soy (Julio) ...
I've been cut off.	Me han cortado. me an kor·*ta*·do
Can I leave a message?	¿Puedo dejar un mensaje? *pwe*·do de·*khar* oon men·*sa*·khe
Please tell him/her I called.	Sí, por favor, dile que he llamado. see por fa·*vor* *dee*·le ke e lya·*ma*·do
I'll call back later.	Ya llamaré más tarde. ya lya·ma·*re* mas *tar*·de

Mobile/Cell Phone

I'd like a/an ...	Quisiera ...
	kee·sye·ra ...

charger for my phone	un cargador para mi teléfono	oon kar·ga·dor pa·ra mee te·le·fo·no
mobile/cell phone for hire	un móvil para alquilar	oon mo·veel pa·ra al·kee·lar
prepaid phone	una tarjeta prepagada	oo·na tar·khe·ta pre·pa·ga·da

40d I'd like a SIM card (for your network).	Quisiera una tarjeta SIM (para su red). kee·sye·ra oo·na tar·khe·ta seem (pa·ra soo red)
What are the rates?	¿Cuál es la tarifa? kwal es la ta·ree·fa

The Internet

41a Where's the local internet cafe?	¿Dónde hay un cibercafé cercano? don·de ai oon thee·ber·ka·fe ther·ka·no
Do you have public internet access here?	¿Tiene acceso público a internet? tye·ne ak·the·so poo·blee·ko a een·ter·net
Is there wireless internet access here?	¿Hay acceso inalámbrico a internet aquí? ai ak·the·so een·a·lam·bree·ko a een·ter·net a·kee

Can I connect my laptop here?	¿Puedo conectar mi ordenador portátil aquí? *pwe*·do ko·nek·*tar* mee or·de·na·dor por·*ta*·teel a·*kee*
Do you have headphones (with a microphone)?	¿Tiene auriculares (con micrófono)? *tye*·ne ow·ree·koo·*la*·res (kon mee·*kro*·fo·no)
I'd like to buy a card/ USB for prepaid mobile internet.	Quisiera comprar una tarjeta/USB para internet móvil de prepago. kee·*sye*·ra kom·*prar* oo·na tar·*khe*·ta/oo·e·se·be *pa*·ra *een*·ter·net *mo*·veel de pre·*pa*·go
How do I log on?	¿Cómo entro al sistema? *ko*·mo *en*·tro al sees·*te*·ma

⊙ LOOK FOR

Here are some Spanish substitutes for common internet-related terms.

charlar	*char*·lar	chat
ciberespacio m	thee·ber·e·*spa*·thyo	cyberspace
correr tabla por la red	ko·*rer ta*·bla por la re	surf
descargar	des·kar·*gar*	download
en línea	en *lee*·ne·a	online
nombre m **de usuario**	*nom*·bre de oo·*swa*·ryo	username
página f **Web inicial**	*pa*·khee·na web ee·nee·*thyal*	homepage
sistema f **de búsqueda**	sees·*te*·ma de *boos*·ke·da	search engine
sitio m **Web**	*see*·tyo web	website

I'd like to ...		Quisiera ... kee·sye·ra ...
burn a CD	copiar un disco	ko·*pyar* oon *dees*·ko
check my email	revisar mi correo electrónico	re·vee·*sar* mee ko·*re*·o e·lek·*tro*·nee·ko
download my photos	descargar mis fotos	des·kar·*gar* mees *fo*·tos
use a scanner	usar un escáner	oo·*sar* oon es·*ka*·ner
use Skype	usar Skype	oo·*sar* es·*kaip*

41b I'd like to use a printer.	Quisiera usar una impresora. kee·*sye*·ra oo·*sar* oo·na eem·pre·so·ra
How much per page?	¿Cuánto cuesta por página? *kwan*·to *kwes*·ta por *pa*·khee·na
41c How much is it per hour?	¿Cuánto cuesta por hora? *kwan*·to *kwes*·ta por o·ra
It's crashed.	Se ha quedado colgado. se a ke·*da*·do kol·*ga*·do
I've finished.	He terminado. e ter·mee·*na*·do
media player (MP3)	equipo m MP3 e·*kee*·po e·me·pe·*tres*
portable hard drive	disco duro m portátil *dees*·ko *doo*·ro por·*ta*·teel
PSP	PSP m pe·e·se·pe
USB flash drive (memory stick)	memoria f USB me·*mo*·rya oo·e·se·be

Money & Banking

KEY PHRASES

How much is it?	¿Cuánto cuesta esto?	kwan·to kwes·ta es·to
What's the exchange rate?	¿Cuál es el tipo de cambio?	kwal es el tee·po de kam·byo
Where's an ATM?	¿Dónde hay un cajero automático?	don·de ai oon ka·khe·ro ow·to·ma·tee·ko

Paying the Bill

Q How much is it?	¿Cuánto cuesta esto? kwan·to kwes·ta es·to
A It's (12) euros.	Son (doce) euros. son (do·the) e·oo·ros
A It's free.	Es gratis. es gra·tees
There's a mistake in the bill.	Hay un error en la cuenta. ai oon e·ror en la kwen·ta
Do you accept credit/ debit cards?	¿Aceptan tarjetas de crédito/débito? a·thep·tan tar·khe·tas de kre·dee·to/de·bee·to
42a Do you accept travellers cheques?	¿Aceptan cheques de viajero? a·thep·tan che·kes de vya·khe·ro

I'd like my change, please.	Quisiera mi cambio, por favor. kee·sye·ra mee *kam*·byo por fa·*vor*
Could I have a receipt, please?	¿Podría darme un recibo, por favor? po·*dree*·a *dar*·me oon re·*thee*·bo por fa·*vor*

See also **bargaining** (p78).

Banking

Where can I ...?	¿Dónde puedo ...? *don*·de *pwe*·do ...
42b I'd like to change money.	Me gustaría cambiar dinero. me goos·ta·*ree*·a kam·*byar* dee·*ne*·ro
42c I'd like to change travellers cheques.	Me gustaría cobrar un cheque de viajero. me goos·ta·*ree*·a ko·*brar* oon *che*·ke de vya·*khe*·ro
42d I'd like to withdraw money.	Me gustaría sacar dinero. me goos·ta·*ree*·a sa·*kar* dee·*ne*·ro
43a Where's an ATM?	¿Dónde hay un cajero automático? *don*·de ai oon ka·*khe*·ro ow·to·*ma*·tee·ko

🔊 LISTEN FOR

No le quedan fondos.
no le *ke*·dan *fon*·dos
You have no money left.

Hay un problema con su cuenta.
ai oon pro·*ble*·ma kon soo *kwen*·ta
There's a problem with your account.

¿Puedo ver su identificación, por favor?
pwe·do ver soo ee·den·tee·fee·ka·*thyon* por fa·*vor*
Can I see your ID, please?

Por favor firme aquí.
por fa·*vor* *feer*·me a·*kee*
Please sign here.

43b Where's a foreign exchange office?
¿Dónde está la oficina de cambio más cercano?
don·de es·*ta* la o·*fee*·*thee*·na de *kam*·byo mas ther·*ka*·no

---

43c What's the exchange rate?
¿Cuál es el tipo de cambio?
kwal es el *tee*·po de *kam*·byo

What's the charge for that?
¿Cuánto hay que pagar por eso?
kwan·to ai ke pa·*gar* por *e*·so

The ATM took my card.
El cajero automático se ha tragado mi tarjeta.
el ka·*khe*·ro ow·to·*ma*·tee·ko se a tra·*ga*·do mee tar·*khe*·ta

---

I've forgotten my PIN.
Me he olvidado del NPI.
me e ol·vee·*da*·do del e·ne·pe·ee

Has my money arrived yet?
¿Ya ha llegado mi dinero?
ya a lye·*ga*·do mee dee·*ne*·ro

How long will it take to arrive?
¿Cuánto tiempo tardará en llegar?
kwan·to *tyem*·po tar·da·*ra* en lye·*gar*

PRACTICAL BUSINESS

Business

I'm attending a conference.	Asisto a un congreso.	a·sees·to a oon kon·gre·so
I have an appointment with ...	Tengo una cita con ...	ten·go oo·na thee·ta kon ...
Can I have your business card?	¿Puede darme su tarjeta de visita?	pwe·de dar·me soo tar·khe·ta de vee·see·ta

People usually chit-chat for a while before they get down to business. For titles and greetings, see **meeting people** (p106).

I'm attending a ...
Asisto a ...
a·sees·to a ...

conference	un congreso	oon kon·gre·so
course	un curso	oon koor·so
meeting	una reunión	oo·na re·oo·nyon
trade fair	una feria de muestras	oo·na fe·rya de mwes·tras

I'm with my colleagues.	Estoy con mis colegas. m&f es·toy kon mees ko·le·gas
I'm alone.	Estoy solo/a. m/f es·toy so·lo/a
Where's the business district?	¿Dónde está el centro financiero? don·de es·ta el then·tro fee·nan·thye·ro

LANGUAGE TIP

Addressing People

To show formality or respect, you should use the polite form of address *Usted* sg pol oo·*ste* or *Ustedes* pl pol oo·*ste*·des in business and with any service providers (be they kiosk attendants or doctors). It's best to take the lead from how people address you, and respond in the same way. For more on polite forms, see **personal pronouns** in the **grammar** chapter, p21.

Where's the conference?	¿Dónde está el congreso? *don*·de es·*ta* el kon·*gre*·so
Where's the meeting?	¿Dónde es la reunión? *don*·de es la re·oo·*nyon*
I have an appointment with ...	Tengo una cita con ... *ten*·go oo·na *thee*·ta kon ...
Q Can I have your business card?	¿Puede darme su tarjeta de visita? *pwe*·de *dar*·me soo tar·*khe*·ta de vee·*see*·ta
A Here's my business card.	Aquí tiene mi tarjeta de visita. a·*kee tye*·ne mee tar·*khe*·ta de vee·*see*·ta
That went very well.	Eso fue muy bien. *e*·so fwe mooy byen
Thank you for your interest/time.	Gracias por su interés/tiempo. *gra*·thyas por soo een·te·*res*/*tyem*·po
Shall we go for a drink/meal?	¿Vamos a tomar/comer algo? *va*·mos a to·*mar*/ko·*mer* al·go
It's on me.	Invito yo. een·*vee*·to yo

Sightseeing

KEY PHRASES

Can we hire a guide?	¿Podemos alquilar un guía?	po·*de*·mos al·kee·*lar* oon *gee*·a
Can I take a photo?	¿Puedo tomar fotos?	*pwe*·do to·*mar* fo·tos
When's the museum open?	¿A qué hora abren el museo?	a ke o·ra *ab*·ren el moo·*se*·o

Requests & Queries

I'd like a/an ...	Quisiera ... kee·*sye*·ra ...

audio set	un equipo audio	oon e·*kee*·po *ow*·dyo
catalogue	un catálogo	oon ka·*ta*·lo·go
guidebook in English	una guía turística en inglés	*oo*·na *gee*·a too·*rees*·tee·ka en een·*gles*

44a I'd like a local map.	Quisiera un mapa de la zona. kee·*sye*·ra oon *ma*·pa de la *tho*·na
44b I'd like to see ...	Me gustaría ver ... me goos·ta·*ree*·a ver ...

Do you have information on local sights?	¿Tiene información sobre los lugares de interés local? *tye*·ne een·for·ma·*thyon so*·bre los loo·*ga*·res de een·te·*res* lo·*kal*
Do you have information on historical sights?	¿Tiene información sobre los lugares de interés histórico? *tye*·ne een·for·ma·*thyon so*·bre los loo·*ga*·res de een·te·*res* ees·to·ree·ko
Do you have information on religious sights?	¿Tiene información sobre los lugares de interés religioso? *tye*·ne een·for·ma·*thyon so*·bre los loo·*ga*·res de een·te·*res* re·lee·*khyo*·so
Can we hire a guide?	¿Podemos alquilar un guía? po·*de*·mos al·kee·*lar* oon *gee*·a
`44c` **Can I take a photo?**	¿Puedo tomar fotos? *pwe*·do to·*mar fo*·tos
Can I take photographs of you?	¿Le/Te Puedo tomar fotos? pol/inf le/te *pwe*·do to·*mar fo*·tos
I'll send you the photograph.	Le/Te mandaré la foto. pol/inf le/te man·da·*re* la *fo*·to
Could you take a photograph of me?	¿Me puede hacer una foto? me *pwe*·de a·*ther* oo·na *fo*·to
`44d` **What's that?**	¿Qué es eso? ke es *e*·so
How old is it?	¿De qué época es? de ke *e*·po·ka es

Getting In

`45a` **What time does it open?**	¿A qué hora abre? a ke *o*·ra *ab*·re
`45b` **What time does it close?**	¿A qué hora cierra? a ke *o*·ra *thye*·ra

45c What's the admission charge?
¿Cuánto cuesta la entrada?
kwan·to kwes·ta la en·tra·da

45d Is there a discount for children?
¿Hay descuentos para niños?
ai des·kwen·tos pa·ra nee·nyos

45e Is there a discount for students?
¿Hay descuentos para estudiantes?
ai des·kwen·tos pa·ra es·too·dyan·tes

Galleries & Museums

When's the gallery open?
¿A qué hora abren la galería?
a ke o·ra a·bren la ga·le·ree·a

When's the museum open?
¿A qué hora abren el museo?
a ke o·ra ab·ren el moo·se·o

Q What's in the collection?
¿Qué hay en la colección?
ke ai en la ko·lek·thyon

A It's a/an ... exhibition.
Es una exposición de ...
es oo·na eks·po·see·thyon de ...

I like the works of ...
Me gustan las obras de ...
me goos·tan las o·bras de ...

It reminds me of ...
Me recuerda a ...
me re·kwer·da a ...

... art
arte m ...
ar·te ...

graphic	gráfico	*gra·fee·ko*
impressionist	impresionista	*eem·pre·syo·nees·ta*
modernist	modernista	*mo·der·nees·ta*
Renaissance	renacentista	*re·na·then·tees·ta*

Abierto	a·*byer*·to	Open
Cerrado	the·*ra*·do	Closed
Prohibido	pro·ee·*bee*·do	Prohibited

🔍 **LOOK FOR**

Tours

Are there organised walking tours?	¿Organizan recorridos a pie? or·ga·*nee*·than re·ko·*ree*·dos a pye
I'd like to take cooking/ language classes.	Me gustaría ir a clases de cocina/idiomas. me goos·ta·*ree*·a eer a *kla*·ses de ko·*thee*·na/ee·*dyo*·mas

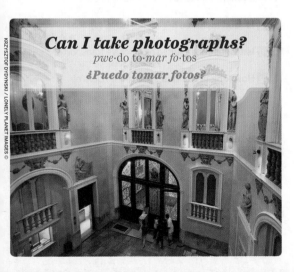

Can I take photographs?
pwe·do to·*mar fo*·tos
¿Puedo tomar fotos?

KRZYSZTOF DYDYNSKI / LONELY PLANET IMAGES ©

Can you recommend a ...?	¿Puede recomendar algún/alguna ...? m/f pwe·de re·ko·men·dar al·goon/al·goo·na ...
46a When's the next day trip?	¿Cuándo es la próxima excursión de un día? kwan·do es la prok·see·ma eks·koor·syon de oon dee·a
46b When's the next tour?	¿Cuándo es la próxima excursión? kwan·do es la prok·see·ma eks·koor·syon
Do I need to take (food) with me?	¿Necesito llevar (comida)? ne·the·see·to lye·var (ko·mee·da)
Is equipment included?	¿Incluye equipo? een·kloo·ye e·kee·po
46c Is food included?	¿Incluye comida? een·kloo·ye ko·mee·da
46d Is transport included?	¿Incluye transporte? een·kloo·ye trans·por·te
46e How long is the tour?	¿Cuánto dura el recorrido? kwan·to doo·ra el re·ko·ree·do
46f What time should we be back?	¿A qué hora debo regresar? a ke o·ra de·bo re·gre·sar
Be back here at ...	Vuelva ... vwel·va ...
I've lost my group.	He perdido a mi grupo. e per·dee·do a mee groo·po

Senior & Disabled Travellers

KEY PHRASES

I need assistance.	Necesito asistencia.	ne·the·*see*·to a·sees·*ten*·thya
Is there wheelchair access?	¿Hay acceso para la silla de ruedas?	ai ak·*the*·so *pa*·ra la *see*·lya de *rwe*·das
Are there toilets for people with a disablity?	¿Hay aseos para minusválidos?	ai a·*se*·os *pa*·ra mee·noos·*va*·lee·dos

I have a disability.	Soy minusválido/a. **m/f** soy mee·noos·*va*·lee·do/a
I need assistance.	Necesito asistencia. ne·the·*see*·to a·sees·*ten*·thya
Are guide dogs permitted?	¿Se permite la entrada a los perros lazarillos? se per·*mee*·te la en·*tra*·da a los *pe*·ros la·tha·*ree*·lyos
Is there wheelchair access?	¿Hay acceso para la silla de ruedas? ai ak·*the*·so *pa*·ra la *see*·lya de *rwe*·das
Are there parking spaces for people with a disability?	¿Tiene aparcamiento para minusválidos? *tye*·ne a·par·ka·*myen*·to *pa*·ra mee·noos·*va*·lee·dos
Are there rails in the bathroom?	¿Hay pasamanos en el baño? ai pa·sa·*ma*·nos en el *ba*·nyo

LOOK FOR

Acceso para Sillas de Ruedas	ak·*the*·so pa·ra *see*·lyas de *rwe*·das	Wheelchair Entrance
Ascensor	a·*then*·sor	Elevator/Lift

Are there toilets for people with a disability?	¿Hay aseos para minusválidos? ai a·*se*·os pa·ra mee·noos·*va*·lee·dos
Is there somewhere I can sit down?	¿Hay algun sitio dónde me pueda sentar? ai al·*goon see*·tyo *don*·de me *pwe*·da sen·*tar*
Could you help me cross this street?	¿Me puede ayudar a cruzar la calle? me *pwe*·de a·yoo·*dar* a kroo·*thar* la *ka*·lye
Could you call me a taxi for the disabled?	¿Podría llamar a un taxi para minusválidos? po·*dree*·a lya·*mar* a oon *tak*·see *pa*·ra mee·noos·*va*·lee·dos
crutches	muletas f pl moo·*le*·tas
guide dog	perro m lazarillo *pe*·ro la·tha·*ree*·lyo
ramp	rampa f *ram*·pa
walking frame	andador m an·da·*dor*
walking stick	bastón m bas·*ton*
wheelchair	silla f de ruedas *see*·lya de *rwe*·das

Travel with Children

KEY PHRASES

Are children allowed?	¿Se admiten niños?	se ad·*mee*·ten *nee*·nyos
Is there a child discount?	¿Hay descuento para niños?	ai des·*kwen*·to *pa*·ra *nee*·nyos
Is there a baby change room?	¿Hay una sala en la que cambiar el pañal al bebé?	ai *oo*·na *sa*·la en la ke kam·*byar*·le el pa·*nyal* al be·*be*

I need a ...   Necesito ...
ne·the·*see*·to ...

baby/child seat	un asiento de seguridad para bebés/niños	oon a·*syen*·to de se·goo·ree·*da pa*·ra be·*bes*/*nee*·nyos
cot	una cuna	*oo*·na *koo*·na
potty	un orinal de niños	oon o·ree·*nal* de *nee*·nyos
stroller	un cochecito	oon ko·che·*thee*·to

Do you sell baby wipes?	¿Vende toallitas para bebés? *ven*·de to·a·*lyee*·tas *pa*·ra be·*bes*
Do you sell disposable nappies/diapers?	¿Vende pañales de usar y tirar? *ven*·de pa·*nya*·les de oo·*sar* ee tee·*rar*

Do you sell milk formula?	¿Vende leche de fórmula? *ven·de le·che de for·moo·la*
Is there a/an ...?	¿Hay ...? *ai ...*

baby change room	una sala en la que cambiarle el pañal al bebé	*oo·na sa·la en la ke kam·byar·le el pa·nyal al be·be*
child discount	descuento para niños	*des·kwen·to pa·ra nee·nyos*
child-minding service	servicio de cuidado de niños	*ser·vee·thyo de kwee·da·do de nee·nyos*
children's menu	menú infantil	*me·noo een·fan·teel*
family discount	descuento familiar	*des·kwen·to fa·mee·lyar*
highchair	trona	*tro·na*

Do you mind if I breastfeed here?	¿Le molesta que dé de pecho aquí? *le mo·les·ta ke de de pe·cho a·kee*
Are children allowed?	¿Se admiten niños? *se ad·mee·ten nee·nyos*
Is this suitable for (three)-year-old children?	¿Es apto para niños de (tres) años? *es ap·to pa·ra nee·nyos de (tres) a·nyos*

If your child is sick, see **health** (p158).

Social

SOCIAL MEETING PEOPLE

Meeting People

KEY PHRASES

My name is ...	Me llamo ...	me *lya*·mo ...
I'm from ...	Soy de ...	soy de ...
I work in (education).	Trabajo en (enseñanza).	tra·*ba*·kho en (en·se·*nyan*·tha)
I'm ... years old.	Tengo ... años.	*ten*·go ... *a*·nyos
And you?	¿Y Usted/tú? pol/inf	ee oos·*te*/too

Basics

47a Yes.	Sí. see
47b No.	No. no
47c Please.	Por favor. por fa·*vor*
47d Thank you.	Gracias. *gra*·thyas
47e You're welcome.	De nada. de *na*·da
47f Excuse me.	Perdón/Discúlpeme. per·*don*/dees·*kool*·pe·me
47g Sorry.	Lo siento. lo *syen*·to

Greetings

In Spain people are often quite casual in their social interactions.
It's fine to use the following expressions in both formal and informal
situations.

48a	Hello.	Hola. *o·*la
	Good morning.	Buenos días. *bwe·*nos *dee·*as
	Good afternoon. (until 8pm)	Buenas tardes. *bwe·*nas *tar·*des
	Good evening/night.	Buenas noches. *bwe·*nas *no·*ches
48b	See you later.	Hasta luego. *as·*ta *lwe·*go
48c	Goodbye.	Adiós. a·*dyos*
48d Q	How are you?	¿Qué tal? ke tal
48e A	Good, thanks.	Bien, gracias. byen *gra·*thyas
	And you?	¿Y Usted/tú? **pol/inf** ee oos·*te*/too
49a Q	What's your name?	¿Cómo se llama Usted? **pol** *ko·*mo se *lya·*ma oos·*te*
49b Q	What's your name?	¿Cómo te llamas? **inf** *ko·*mo te *lya·*mas
49c A	My name is ...	Me llamo ... me *lya·*mo ...
49d	I'm pleased to meet you.	Mucho gusto. *moo·*cho *goos·*to

I'd like to introduce you to ...	Quisiera presentarle a ... **pol**
	kee·*sye*·ra pre·sen·*tar*·le a ...
	Quisiera presentarte a ... **inf**
	kee·*sye*·ra pre·sen·*tar*·te a ...

| ✂ **This is ...** | Ésto es... | *es*·to es ... |

| This is my friend. | Éste/a es mi amigo/a. **m/f** |
| | *es*·te/a es mee a·*mee*·go/a |

Titles & Addressing People

Señor and *Señora* tend to be used in everyday speech. *Doña*, although rare, is used as a mark of respect towards older women, while *Don* is sometimes used to address men. An elderly neighbour, for example, might be called *Doña Lola*. For more on polite forms, see **addressing people** (p95), and **personal pronouns** (p21).

`50a` **Mr**	Señor
	se·*nyor*
Sir	Don
	don
`50b` **Mrs**	Señora
	se·*nyo*·ra
`50c` **Miss**	Señorita
	se·nyo·*ree*·ta
Ms	Señora
	se·*nyo*·ra
Madam	Doña
	do·nya

Making Conversation

Spain is known for its distinct regional personalities. A great conversation starter in Spain is to ask someone where they come from. Other good topics are sport, politics, history and travel.

| Do you live here? | ¿Vives aquí? |
| | vee·ves a·*kee* |

> **LANGUAGE TIP**
>
> **Addressing Friends**
>
> You may hear friends calling each other *tío* m *tee*·o, or *tía* f *tee*·a, but these words are usually used when talking about others. They're a bit crass (a little like using 'sheila' to describe a girl in Australia). Guys use *colega* ko·*le*·ga, and *hombre* *om*·bre, to address their workmates or male friends. In the south, people call their friends *pixas* *pee*·chas or *xoxos* *cho*·chos.

Where are you going?	¿Adónde vas? a·*don*·de vas	
What are you doing?	¿Qué haces? ke a·thes	
Are you here on holidays?	¿Estás aquí de vacaciones? es·*tas* a·*kee* de va·ka·*thyo*·nes	
I'm here for a holiday.	Estoy aquí de vacaciones. es·*toy* a·*kee* de va·ka·*thyo*·nes	
I'm here on business.	Estoy aquí en viaje de negocios. es·*toy* a·*kee* en *vya*·khe de ne·*go*·thyos	
I'm here to study.	Estoy aquí estudiando. es·*toy* a·*kee* es·too·*dyan*·do	
That's (beautiful), isn't it?	¿Es (precioso), no? es (pre·*thyo*·so) no	
How long are you here for?	¿Cuánto tiempo te vas a quedar? *kwan*·to *tyem*·po te vas a ke·*dar*	
I'm here for ... weeks/days.	Estoy aquí por ... semanas/días. es·*toy* a·*kee* por ... se·*ma*·nas/*dee*·as	

Nationalities

You'll find that many country names are similar to English, so even if you don't know the Spanish name, it's more than likely you'll be understood. For more countries, see the **dictionary**.

51a Q Where are you from?	¿De dónde es Usted? pol de *don*·de es oos·*te*
Q Where are you from?	¿De dónde eres? inf de *don*·de e·res
51b A I'm from (Singapore).	Soy de (Singapur). soy de (seen·ga·poor)
A I'm from (Canada).	Soy de (Canadá). soy de (ka·na·*da*)

Age

51c Q How old are you?	¿Cuántos años tiene? *kwan*·tos *a*·nyos *tye*·ne
51d A I'm (25) years old.	Tengo (veinticinco) años. *ten*·go (veyn·tee·*theen*·ko) *a*·nyos
Q How old is your son/daughter?	¿Cuántos años tiene tu hijo/hija? *kwan*·tos *a*·nyos *tye*·ne too *ee*·kho/*ee*·kha
A He's/She's ... years old.	Tiene ... años. *tye*·ne ... *a*·nyos
I'm younger than I look.	Soy más joven de lo que parezco. soy mas *kho*·ven de lo ke pa·*reth*·ko
Too old!	¡Demasiado viejo! de·ma·*sya*·do *vye*·kho

For your age, see **numbers & amounts** (p34).

LISTEN FOR

¡Cojonudo!	ko·kho·*noo*·do	Great!
¿De veras?	de *ve*·ras	Really?
¡Enhorabuena!	e·no·ra·*bwe*·na	Congratulations!
¡Estupendo!	es·too·*pen*·do	That's fantastic!
¡No me digas!	no me *dee*·gas	You don't say!
¡Qué guay!	ke gwai	How cool!
¿Qué hay?	ke ai	What's up?
¡Qué interesante!	ke een·te·re·*san*·te	How interesting!

Occupations & Study

Q What do you do?	¿A qué te dedicas?	a ke te de·*dee*·kas
A I work in (education/ hospitality).	Trabajo en (enseñanza/ hostelería).	tra·*ba*·kho en (en·se·*nyan*·tha/ os·te·le·*ree*·a)
A I'm a/an ...	Soy ...	soy ...

architect	arquitecto/a m/f	ar·kee·*tek*·to/a
mechanic	mecánico/a m/f	me·*ka*·nee·ko/a
student	estudiante m&f	es·too·*dyan*·te
teacher	profesor/ profesora m/f	pro·fe·*sor*/ pro·fe·*so*·ra

A I'm self-employed.	Soy trabajador/ trabajadora autónomo/a. m/f	soy tra·ba·kha·*dor*/ tra·ba·kha·*do*·ra ow·*to*·no·mo/a

🅰 I'm retired.	Estoy jubilado/a. m/f es·*toy* khoo·bee·*la*·do/a
🅰 I'm unemployed.	Estoy en el paro. es·*toy* en el *pa*·ro
❓ What are you studying?	¿Qué estudias? ke es·*too*·dyas
🅰 I'm studying (languages).	Estudio (idiomas). es·*too*·dyo (ee·*dyo*·mas)
I'm studying at ...	Estudio en ... es·*too*·dyo en ...

For more occupations and studies, see the **dictionary**.

Family

| ❓ Do you have (a) ...? | ¿Tiene ...? pol
tye·ne ...
¿Tienes ...? inf
tye·nes ... |
| 🅰 I (don't) have (a) ... | (No) Tengo ...
(no) *ten*·go ... |

brother	un hermano	oon er·*ma*·no
children	hijos	*ee*·khos
family	una familia	oo·na fa·*mee*·lya
partner	una pareja m&f	oo·na pa·*re*·kha
sister	una hermana	oo·na er·*ma*·na

52a ❓ Are you married?	¿Está casado? m es·*tas* ka·*sa*·do
❓ Are you married?	¿Está casada? f es·*tas* ka·*sa*·da
52b 🅰 I'm married.	Estoy casado. m es·*toy* ka·*sa*·do
52c 🅰 I'm married.	Estoy casada. f es·*toy* ka·*sa*·da

| **52d** **A** I'm single. | Soy soltero. m |
| | soy sol·*te*·ro |

| **52e** **A** I'm single. | Soy soltera. f |
| | soy sol·*te*·ra |

| **A** I live with someone. | Vivo con alguien. |
| | *vee*·vo kon al·gyen |

| **A** I'm separated. | Estoy separado/a. m/f |
| | es·*toy* se·pa·*ra*·do/a |

Talking with Children

| Do you go to school or kindergarten? | ¿Vas al colegio o a la guardería? |
| | vas al ko·*le*·khyo o a la gwar·de·*ree*·a |

| What grade are you in? | ¿En qué curso estás? |
| | en ke *koor*·so es·*tas* |

| Do you like school? | ¿Te gusta el colegio? |
| | te *goos*·ta el ko·*le*·khyo |

| Do you like sport? | ¿Te gusta el deporte? |
| | te *goos*·ta el de·*por*·te |

| Do you learn (English)? | ¿Aprendes (inglés)? |
| | a·*pren*·des (een·*gles*) |

| I come from very far away. | Vengo de muy lejos. |
| | *ven*·go de mooy *le*·khos |

Farewells

| It's been great meeting you. | Me ha encantado conocerte. |
| | me a en·kan·*ta*·do ko·no·*ther*·te |

| Keep in touch! | ¡Nos mantendremos en contacto! |
| | nos man·ten·*dre*·mos en kon·*tak*·to |

| Are you on Facebook? | ¿Estás en Facebook? |
| | es·*tas* en *feys*·book |

LANGUAGE TIP

Spanish Idioms

Even idioms translate across languages. Here are a few golden oldies:

It's like casting pearls before swine.
Es como echar margaritas a los cerdos. (lit: it's like feeding daisies to the pigs)
es *ko*·mo e·*char* mar·ga·*ree*·tas a los *ther*·dos

When it rains, it pours.
Éramos pocos y parió la abuela. (lit: there were a few of us then granny gave birth)
e·*ra*·mos *po*·kos y pa·*ree*·o la a·*bwe*·la

This is like watching grass grow.
Es más largo que un día sin pan. (lit: it's longer than a day without bread)
es mas *lar*·go ke oon *dee*·a seen pan

If you ever visit (South Africa), you can stay with me.
Si algún día visitas (Sudáfrica), te puedes quedar conmigo.
see al·*goon dee*·a vee·*see*·tas (soo·*da*·free·ka) te *pwe*·des ke·*dar* kon·*mee*·go

---

53a **Q** **What's your address?**
¿Cuál es tu dirección?
kwal es too dee·rek·*thyon*

A **Here's my ...**
Ésta es mi ... m/f
es·te/*es*·ta es mee ...

53b **A** **Here's my address.**
Ésta es mi dirección.
es·ta es mee dee·rek·*thyon*

53c **A** **Here's my email address.**
Ésta es mi dirección de email.
es·ta es mee dee·rek·*thyon* de *ee*·mayl

For more on addresses, see **directions** (p57).

Basque

Basque (*euskara*, in Basque), is spoken at the western end of the Pyrenees and along the Bay of Biscay – from Bayonne in France to Bilbao in Spain, and inland, almost to Pamplona. Dialects are also spoken, including Bizkaian, Gipuzkoan, High Navarrese, Aezkoan, Salazarese, Lapurdian, Low Navarrese and Suberoan. No one quite knows its origin, but the most likely theory is that Basque is the lone survivor of a language family that once extended across Europe, and was wiped out by the languages of the Celts, Germanic tribes and Romans.

Speaking Spanish in the Basque-speaking towns might be expected from a foreigner, but is not as warmly received as an attempt at one of the most ancient languages of Europe.

Hi!	Kaixo! *kai*·sho
Good morning.	Egun on. e·goon *on*
Good afternoon/evening.	Arratsalde on. a·ra·chyal·de *on*
Goodbye.	Agur. a·*goor*
Take care.	Ondo ibili. on·do ee·*beel*·ee
How are you?	Zer moduz? ser mo·*doos*
Fine, thank you.	Ongi, eskerrik asko. on·gee e·*ske*·reek *as*·ko

🔊 **LISTEN FOR**

Euskal Herrian beti jai!	e·oos·*kal* e·*ree*·an *be*·tee yai The Basque Country's always partying!
Gora gu 'ta gutarrak!	*go*·ra goo ta *goo*·ta·rak Hurray for us!

Excuse me.	Barkatu. bar·*ka*·too
Please.	Mesedez. me·*se*·des
Thank you.	Eskerrik asko. es·*ke*·reek *as*·ko
You're welcome.	Ez horregatik. es o·*re*·ga·teek
Do you speak English?	Ingelesez ba al dakizu? een·*ge*·le·ses ba al da·kee·*soo*
I know a little Basque.	Euskara apur bat badakit. e·*oos*·ka·ra a·*poor* bat ba·da·*keet*
I don't understand.	Ez dut ulertzen. es toot oo·*ler*·tzen
Could you speak in Castillian, please?	Erdaraz egingo al didazu, mesedez? er·da·ras e·*geen*·go al dee·*da*·soo me·*se*·des
How do you say that in Basque?	Nola esaten da hori euskara? *no*·la e·*sa*·ten da o·ree e·oo·ska·*ra*

> **CULTURE TIP**
>
> **Spanish in America**
>
> Columbus' arrival in the New World in 1492 launched the era of Spanish expansion in America, one which is also reflected in the language. *Patata*, *tomate*, *cacao* and *chocolate* are just a few examples of words that entered Spanish (and consequently English) from the indigenous American languages. Bear in mind that Spanish has evolved differently in the Americas, and it's a good idea to take Lonely Planet's *Latin American Spanish* phrasebook if that's your destination.

Catalan

Catalan (*català*, in Catalan) is spoken by up to 10 million people in the northeast of Spain, a territory that comprises Catalonia, coastal Valencia and the Balearic Islands (Majorca, Minorca and Ibiza).

Outside Spain, Catalan is also spoken in Andorra, the south of France and the town of Alguer in Sardinia. Many famous creatives have been Catalan speakers: painters like Dalí, Miró and Picasso, architects like Gaudí, and writers like Mercé Rodoreda.

Despite the fact that almost all Catalan speakers from Spain are bilingual, they appreciate it when visitors attempt to communicate, if even in the simplest way, in Catalan.

Hello!	Hola! o·la
Good morning.	Bon dia. bon *dee*·a
Good afternoon.	Bona tarda. *bo*·na *tar*·da
Good evening.	Bon vespre. bon *bes*·pra
Goodbye.	Adéu. a·*the*·oo
How are you?	Com estàs? kom as·*tas*
(Very) Well.	(Molt) Bé. (mol) be
Excuse me.	Perdoni. par·*tho*·nee
Sorry.	Ho sento. oo *sen*·to
Please.	Sisplau. sees·*pla*·oo
Thank you.	Gràcies. *gra*·see·as

🔊 LISTEN FOR

Això rai!	a·*sho* ra·ee	No problem!
Quin tip de riure!	kin tip da ri·a·*oo*·ra	What a laugh!

Yes./No.	Sí./No.
	see/no
Do you speak English?	Parla anglès?
	par·la an·*gles*
Could you speak in Castilian, please?	Pot parlar castellà sisplau?
	pot par·*la* kas·ta·*lya* sees·*pla*·oo
I (don't) understand.	(No) Ho entenc.
	(no) oo an·*teng*
How do you say ...?	Com es diu ...?
	kom az *dee*·oo ...

Galician

Galician (*galego,* in Galician), is an official language of the Autonomous Community of Galicias and is also widely understood in the neighbouring regions of Asturias and Castilla-Léon. It's very similar to Portuguese, as the two languages have roots in Vulgar Latin.

Galicians are likely to revert to Spanish when addressing a stranger, especially a foreigner, but making a small effort to communicate in Galician will always be welcomed.

Hello!	Ola!
	o·la
Good day.	Bon dia.
	bon *dee*·a
Good afternoon/evening.	Boa tarde.
	bo·a *tar*·de

Goodbye.	Adeus. *a·de·oos* Até logo. *a·te lo·go*
Excuse me.	Perdón. *per·don*
Please.	Por favor. *por fa·vor*
Thank you.	Grácias. *gra·see·as*
Many thanks.	Moitas grácias. *moy·tas gra·see·as*
That's fine.	De nada. *de na·da*
Yes./No.	Si./Non. *see/non*
Do you speak English?	Fala inglés? *fa·la een·gles*
Could you speak in Castilian, please?	Pode falar en español, por favor? *po·de fa·la en e·spa·nyol por fa·bor*
I (don't) understand.	(Non) Entendo. *(non) en·ten·do*
What's this called in Galician?	Como se chama iso en galego? *ko·mo se cha·ma ee·so en ga·le·go*

Interests

KEY PHRASES

What do you do in your spare time?	¿Qué te gusta hacer en tu tiempo libre?	ke te *goos*·ta a·*ther* en too *tyem*·po *lee*·bre
Do you like (travelling)?	¿Te gusta (viajar)?	te *goos*·ta (vya·*khar*)
I (don't) like ...	(No) Me gusta ...	(no) me *goos*·ta ...

Common Interests

What do you do in your spare time?	¿Qué te gusta hacer en tu tiempo libre? ke te *goos*·ta a·*ther* en too *tyem*·po *lee*·bre
54a Q Do you like ...?	¿Te gusta ...? te *goos*·ta ...
54b A I like ...	Me gusta ... me *goos*·ta ...
54c A I don't like ...	No me gusta ... no me *goos*·ta ...
I (don't) like photography.	(No) Me gusta la fotografía. (no) me *goos*·ta la fo·to·gra·*fee*·a
I (don't) like shopping.	(No) Me gusta ir de compras. (no) me *goos*·ta eer de *kom*·pras

For more activities, see **sports** (p142) and the **dictionary**.

Music

Do you like to ...?   ¿Te gusta ...?
te *goos*·ta ...

dance	ir a bailar	eer a bai·*lar*
go to concerts	ir a conciertos	eer a kon·*thyer*·tos
listen to music	escuchar música	es·koo·*char moo*·see·ka
play an instrument	tocar algún instrumento	*to*·kar al·*goon* eens·troo·*men*·to
sing	cantar	*kan*·tar

NEIL SETCHFIELD / LONELY PLANET IMAGES ©

What music do you like?
ke *moo*·see·ka te *goos*·ta
¿Qué música te gusta?

Which bands do you like?	¿Qué grupos te gustan? ke *groo*·pos te *goos*·tan
Which singers do you like?	¿Qué cantantes te gustan? ke kan·*tan*·tes te *goos*·tan
What music do you like?	¿Qué música te gusta? ke *moo*·see·ka te *goos*·ta
classical music	música f clásica *moo*·see·ka *kla*·see·ka
jazz	jazz m khath
pop	música f pop *moo*·see·ka pop
rock	música f rock *moo*·see·ka rok
world music	música f étnica *moo*·see·ka *et*·nee·ka

Cinema & Theatre

I feel like going to (a comedy).	Tengo ganas de ir a (una comedia). *ten*·go *ga*·nas de eer a (*oo*·na ko·*me*·dya)
What's showing at the cinema (tonight)?	¿Qué película dan en el cine (esta noche)? ke pe·*lee*·koo·la dan en el *thee*·ne (*es*·ta *no*·che)
Is it in (English)?	¿Es en (inglés)? es en (een·*gles*)
Is it dubbed?	¿Está doblada? es·*ta* dob·*la*·da
Does it have (English) subtitles?	¿Tiene subtítulos (en inglés)? *tye*·ne soob·*tee*·too·los (en een·*gles*)

Have you seen ...?	¿Has visto ...? as *vees*·to ...
Q Who's in it?	¿Quién actúa? kyen ak·*too*·a
A It stars ...	Actúa ... ak·*too*·a ...
Are those seats taken?	¿Están ocupados estos asientos? es·*tan* o·koo·pa·dos *es*·tos a·*syen*·tos
Q Did you like the film/ play?	¿Te gustó el cine/teatro? te goos·*to* el *thee*·ne/te·a·tro
A I thought it was excellent/OK.	Pienso que fue excelente/regular. *pyen*·so ke fwe eks·the·*len*·te/re·goo·*lar*
A I thought it was long.	Pienso que fue largo. *pyen*·so ke fwe *lar*·go
I (don't) like ...	(No) Me gusta/gustan ... sg/pl (no) me *goos*·ta/*goos*·tan ...

animated films	películas f pl de dibujos animados	pe·*lee*·koo·las de dee·*boo*·khos a·nee·*ma*·dos
comedy	comedia f	ko·*me*·dya
documentary	documentales m pl	do·koo·men·*ta*·les
drama	drama m	*dra*·ma
(Spanish) cinema	cine m (español)	*thee*·ne (es·pa·*nyol*)
horror movies	cine m de terror	*thee*·ne de te·*ror*
sci-fi	cine m de ciencia ficción	*thee*·ne de *thyen*·thya feek·*thyon*

Off to a show? See **buying tickets** (p44) and **going out** (p130).

SOCIAL INTERESTS

Books & Reading

What kind of books do you read?	¿Qué tipo de libros lees? ke *tee*·po de *lee*·bros *le*·es
On this trip I'm reading ...	En este viaje estoy leyendo ... en *es*·te *vya*·khe es·*toy* le·*yen*·do ...
Have you read ...?	¿Has leído ...? as le·*ee*·do ...
Q Which (Spanish) author do you recommend?	¿Qué autor (español) recomiendas? ke ow·*tor* (es·pa·*nyol*) re·ko·*myen*·das
A I'd recommend ...	Recomiendo a ... re·ko·*myen*·do a ...
Where can I exchange books?	¿Dónde puedo cambiar libros? *don*·de *pwe*·do kam·*byar* *lee*·bros

For more on books and reading, see **shopping** (p80).

Volunteering

I'd like to volunteer my skills.	Me gustaría ofrecer mis conocimientos. me goos·ta·*ree*·a o·fre·*ther* mees ko·no·thee·*myen*·tos
Are there any volunteer programs available in the area?	¿Hay programas de voluntariado en la zona? ai pro·*gra*·mas de vo·loon·ta·*rya*·do en la *tho*·na

Feelings & Opinions

KEY PHRASES

Are you ...?	¿Tienes/Estás ...?	tye·nes/es·tas ...
I'm (not) ...	(No) Tengo/ Estoy ...	(no) ten·go/ es·toy ...
What did you think of it?	¿Qué pensaste de eso?	ke pen·sas·te de e·so
I thought it was ...	Pienso que fue ...	pyen·so ke fwe ...
Did you hear about ...?	¿Has oído que ...?	as o·ee·do ke ...

Feelings

Feelings are described with either nouns or adjectives: the nouns use 'have' in Spanish (eg, 'I have hunger') and the adjectives use 'be' (like in English).

55a	**Q** Are you cold?	¿Tienes frío?	tye·nes free·o
55b	**A** I'm cold.	Tengo frío.	ten·go free·o
55c	**A** I'm not cold.	No tengo frío.	no ten·go free·o
55d	**Q** Are you hot?	¿Tienes calor?	tye·nes ka·lor
55e	**A** I'm hot.	Tengo calor.	ten·go ka·lor
55f	**A** I'm not hot.	No tengo calor.	no ten·go ka·lor

56a Q Are you hungry?
¿Tienes hambre?
tye·nes am·bre

56b A I'm hungry.
Tengo hambre.
ten·go am·bre

56c A I'm not hungry.
No tengo hambre.
no ten·go am·bre

56d Q Are you thirsty?
¿Tienes sed?
tye·nes se

56e A I'm thirsty.
Tengo sed.
ten·go se

56f A I'm not thirsty.
No tengo sed.
no ten·go se

57a Q Are you tired? m
¿Estás cansado? m
es·tas kan·sa·do

57b A I'm tired. m
Estoy cansado. m
es·toy kan·sa·do

57c A I'm tired. f
Estoy cansada. f
es·toy kan·sa·da

57d A I'm not tired. m
No estoy cansado. m
no es·toy kan·sa·do

57e A I'm not tired. f
No estoy cansada. f
no es·toy kan·sa·da

I'm a little (sad).
Estoy un poco (triste). m&f
es·toy oon po·ko (trees·te)

I'm quite (disappointed).
Estoy bastante
(decepcionado/a). m/f
es·toy bas·tan·te
(de·thep·thyo na·do/a)

I feel very (lucky).
Me siento muy
(afortunado/a). m/f
me syen·to mooy
(a·for·too·na·do/a)

If you're not feeling well, see **health** (p158).

Opinions

Q Did you like it?	¿Te gustó? te goos·*to*
Q What did you think of it?	¿Qué pensaste de eso? ke pen·*sas*·te de *e*·so
A I thought it was ...	Pienso que fue ... *pyen*·so ke fwe ...
A It's ...	Es ... es ...

beautiful	bonito/a **m/f**	bo·*nee*·to/a
bizarre	raro/a **m/f**	*ra*·ro/a
entertaining	entretenido/a **m/f**	en·tre·te·*nee*·do/a
excellent	fantástico/a **m/f**	fan·*tas*·tee·ko/a
horrible	horrible **m&f**	o·*ree*·ble

I thought it was OK.	Pienso que estaba bien. *pyen*·so ke es·*ta*·ba byen
He's/She's the best.	Es un trozo de pan. (lit: he's/she's a piece of bread) es oon *tro*·tho de pan
I disagree!	No estoy de acuerdo! no es·*toy* de a·*kwer*·do
Yes, but ...	Sí, pero ... see *pe*·ro ...

Politics & Social Issues

Q Who do you vote for?	¿A quién votas? a kyen *vo*·tas
A I support the ... party.	Apoyo al partido ... a·*po*·yo al par·*tee*·do ...

🔊 LISTEN FOR

Claro.	*kla·ro*	Sure.
¡Claro que sí!	*kla·ro ke see*	Of course!
¡De ningún modo!	de neen·*goon mo*·do	No way!
Era broma.	*e*·ra *bro*·ma	Just joking.
Está bien.	es·*ta* byen	It's OK.
57f Estoy bien.	es·*toy* byen	I'm OK.
Quizás.	kee·*thas*	Maybe.
Sin problema.	seen pro·*ble*·ma	No problem.
Un momento.	oon mo·*men*·to	Just a minute.
Vale.	*va*·le	OK.
¡Ya lo creo!	ya lo *kre*·o	You bet!

Did you hear about ...?	¿Has oído que ...? as o·*ee*·do ke ...
Are you in favour of ...?	¿Estás a favor de ...? es·*tas* a fa·*vor* de ...
How do people feel about ...?	¿Cómo se siente la gente de ...? *ko*·mo se *syen*·te la *khen*·te de ...
the economy	economía **f** e·ko·no·*mee*·a
health care	seguro **m** médico se·*goo*·ro *me*·dee·ko
immigration	inmigración **f** een·mee·gra·*thyon*
war in ...	guerra **f** en ... *ge*·ra en ...

The Environment

Is there an environmental problem here?	¿Aquí hay un problema con el medio ambiente? a·*kee* ai oon pro·*ble*·ma kon el *me*·dyo am·*byen*·te
Is this (forest) protected?	¿Está este (bosque) protegido? es·*ta* es·te (*bos*·ke) pro·te·*khee*·do
Where can I recycle this?	¿Dónde se puede reciclar esto? *don*·de se *pwe*·de re·thee·*klar* es·to
climate change	cambio m climático *kam*·byo klee·*ma*·tee·ko
pollution	contaminación f kon·ta·mee·na·*thyon*
recycling	reciclaje m re·thee·*kla*·khe

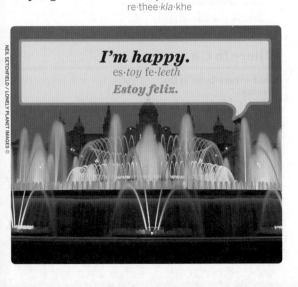

I'm happy.
es·*toy* fe·*leeth*
Estoy feliz.

Going Out

KEY PHRASES

What's on tonight?	¿Qué hay esta noche?	ke ai es·ta no·che
Where are the clubs?	¿Dónde están las discotecas?	don·de es·tan las dees·ko·te·kas
Would you like to go for a coffee?	¿Quieres que vayamos a tomar un café?	kye·res ke va·ya·mos a to·mar oon ka·fe
What time shall we meet?	¿A qué hora quedamos?	a ke o·ra ke·da·mos
Where will we meet?	¿Dónde quedamos?	don·de ke·da·mos

Where to Go

What's there to do in the evenings?	¿Qué se puede hacer por las noches? ke se pwe·de a·ther por las no·ches
What's on ...?	¿Qué hay ...? ke ai ...

locally	en la zona	en la tho·na
this weekend	este fin de semana	es·te feen de se·ma·na
today	hoy	oy
tonight	esta noche	es·ta no·che

58a **Where can I find ...?**	¿Dónde hay ...?	don·de ai ...

58b Where can I find a gay venue?	¿Dónde hay lugares gay?	*don·de ai loo·ga·res gai*
Where are there places to eat?	¿Dónde hay lugares para comer?	*don·de ai loo·ga·res pa·ra ko·mer*
Where are the clubs?	¿Dónde están las discotecas?	*don·de es·tan las dees·ko·te·kas*
58c Where can I find a pub?	¿Dónde hay pubs?	*don·de ai poobs*
Is there a local ... guide?	¿Hay una guía ... de la zona?	*ai oo·na gee·a ... de la tho·na*

entertainment	del ocio	del o·thyo
film	de cine	de thee·ne
gay	de lugares gay	de loo·ga·res gai
music	de música	de moo·see·ka

59a I feel like going to a concert.	Tengo ganas de ir a un concierto.	*ten·go ga·nas de eer a oon kon·thyer·to*
59b I feel like going to the movies.	Tengo ganas de ir al cine.	*ten·go ga·nas de eer al thee·ne*
59c I feel like going to a party.	Tengo ganas de ir a una fiesta.	*ten·go ga·nas de eer a oo·na fyes·ta*
59d I feel like going to the theatre.	Tengo ganas de ir al teatro.	*ten·go ga·nas de eer al te·a·tro*

SOCIAL GOING OUT

Invitations

What are you doing this evening?	¿Qué haces esta noche? ke *a*·thes es·ta *no*·che
What are you up to (right now)?	¿Qué haces (ahora)? ke *a*·thes (a·o·ra)
Would you like to go for a ...?	¿Quieres que vayamos a ...? *kye*·res ke va·*ya*·mos a ...

coffee	tomar un café	to·*mar* oon ka·*fe*
drink	tomar algo	to·*mar* al·go
meal	comer	ko·*mer*
walk	pasear	pa·se·*ar*

I feel like going dancing.	Me apetece ir a bailar. me a·pe·*te*·the eer a bai·*lar*
I feel like going out somewhere.	Me apetece salir. me a·pe·*te*·the sa·*leer*
My round.	Invito yo. een·*vee*·to yo
Do you know a good restaurant?	¿Conoces algún buen restaurante? ko·*no*·thes al·*goon* bwen res·tow·*ran*·te
Do you want to come to the (...) concert with me?	¿Quieres venir conmigo al concierto (de ...)? *kye*·res ve·*neer* kon·*mee*·go al kon·*thyer*·to (de ...)
We're having a party.	Vamos a dar una fiesta. *va*·mos a dar *oo*·na *fyes*·ta
Do you want to come?	¿Por qué no vienes? por ke no *vye*·nes
Are you ready?	¿Estás listo/a? m/f es·*tas* lees·to/a

CULTURE TIP

Movie Subtitles

Foreign movies are usually dubbed into Spanish, but in bigger cities you'll find that some films have Spanish subtitles. Look out for *v.o.* (*version original* ver·*syon* o·ree·khee·*nal*, 'original version') or *v.o.s.* (*version original subtitulada* ver·*syon* o·ree·khee·*nal* soob·tee·too·*la*·da, 'original version with subtitles') in listings.

Responding to Invitations

Sure!	¡Por supuesto! por soo·*pwes*·to
Yes, I'd love to.	Me encantaría. me en·kan·ta·*ree*·a
Where will we go?	¿A dónde vamos? a *don*·de va·*mos*
That's very kind of you.	Es muy amable por tu parte. es mooy a·*ma*·ble por too *par*·te
No, I'm afraid I can't.	Lo siento pero no puedo. lo *syen*·to *pe*·ro no *pwe*·do
Sorry, I can't sing/dance.	Lo siento, no sé cantar/bailar. lo *syen*·to no se kan·*tar*/bai·*lar*
What about tomorrow?	¿Qué tal mañana? ke tal ma·*nya*·na

🔊 LISTEN FOR

¡Eh, tú!	e *too*	Hey!
¡Escucha (esto)!	es·*koo*·cha (es·to)	Listen (to this)!
¡Mira!	*mee*·ra	Look!

Arranging to Meet

Q What time shall we meet?
¿A qué hora quedamos?
a ke *o*·ra ke·*da*·mos

A Let's meet at (eight) o'clock.
Quedamos a las (ocho).
ke·*da*·mos a las (*o*·cho)

Q Where will we meet?
¿Dónde quedamos?
don·de ke·*da*·mos

A Let's meet at the (entrance).
Quedamos en (la entrada).
ke·*da*·mos en (la en·*tra*·da)

I'll pick you up.
Paso a recogerte.
pa·so a re·ko·*kher*·te

I'll be coming later.
Iré más tarde.
ee·*re* mas *tar*·de

Where will you be?
¿Dónde estarás?
don·de es·ta·*ras*

OK!
¡Hecho!
e·cho

I'll see you then.
Nos vemos.
nos *ve*·mos

See you later/tomorrow.
Hasta luego/mañana.
as·ta *lwe*·go/ma·*nya*·na

I'm looking forward to it.
Tengo muchas ganas de ir.
ten·go *moo*·chas *ga*·nas de eer

Sorry I'm late.	Siento llegar tarde. *syen*·to lye·*gar* tar·de
Never mind.	No pasa nada. no *pa*·sa *na*·da

Nightclubs & Bars

Where can we go (salsa) dancing?	¿Dónde podemos ir a bailar (la salsa)? *don*·de po·*de*·mos eer a bai·*lar* (la *sal*·sa)
Q What type of music do you like?	¿Qué tipo de música prefieres? ke *tee*·po de *moo*·see·ka pre·*fye*·res
A I really like (reggae).	Me encanta (el reggae). me en·*kan*·ta (el *re*·gai)
Come on!	¡Vamos! *va*·mos
This place is great!	¡Este lugar me encanta! *es*·te loo·*gar* me en·*kan*·ta

For more on bars and drinks, see **eating out** (p177).

Drugs

I don't take drugs.	No consumo ningún tipo de drogas. no kon·*soo*·mo neen·*goon* *tee*·po de *dro*·gas
I take ... occasionally.	Tomo ... de vez en cuando. *to*·mo ... de veth en *kwan*·do
Do you want to have a smoke?	¿Nos fumamos un porro? nos foo·*ma*·mos oon *po*·ro
Do you have a light?	¿Tienes fuego? *tye*·nes *fwe*·go

See also **police** (p156).

Romance

KEY PHRASES

Would you like to do something?	¿Quieres hacer algo?	kye·res a·ther al·go
I love you.	Te quiero.	te kye·ro
Leave me alone, please	Déjame en paz, por favor.	de·kha·me en path por fa·vor

Asking Someone Out

Don't be surprised if invitations come late in the day. Social life in Spain continues well into the night: sometimes people begin to eat dinner at 10pm and many clubs open at midnight.

Q Would you like to do something (tonight)?	¿Quieres hacer algo (esta noche)? kye·res a·ther al·go (es·ta no·che)
A Yes, I'd love to.	Me encantaría. me en·kan·ta·ree·a
A I'm busy.	Estoy ocupado/a. m/f es·toy o·koo·pa·do/a

Pick-up Lines

Would you like a drink?	¿Te apetece una copa? te a·pe·te·the oo·na ko·pa
Do you have a light?	¿Tienes fuego? tye·nes fwe·go

You're great.	Eres estupendo/a. m/f *e·res es·too·pen·do/a*
You mustn't come here much, because I would have noticed you sooner.	No debes venir mucho por aquí porque me habría fijado en ti antes. *no de·bes ve·neer moo·cho por a·kee por·ke me a·bree·a fee·kha·do en tee an·tes*

Rejections

I'm here with my boyfriend/girlfriend.	Estoy aquí con mi novio/a. m/f *es·toy a·kee kon mee no·vyo/a*
Excuse me, I have to go now.	Lo siento, pero me tengo que ir. *lo syen·to pe·ro me ten·go ke eer*
Leave me alone, please.	Déjame en paz, por favor. *de·kha·me en path por fa·vor*
Go away!	¡Vete! *ve·te*
Hey, I'm not interested in talking to you.	Mira tío/a, es que no me interesa hablar contigo. m/f *mee·ra tee·o/a es ke no me een·te·re·sa ab·lar kon·tee·go*

Getting Closer

Can I kiss you?	¿Te puedo besar? te *pwe·do be·sar*
Do you want to come inside for a drink?	¿Quieres entrar a tomar algo? *kye·res en·trar a to·mar al·go*

> **LANGUAGE TIP** **Masculine & Feminine**
> In this book, masculine forms appear before the feminine forms. If you see a word ending in *-o/a*, it means the masculine form ends in *-o* and the feminine form ends in *-a* (ie you replace the *-o* ending with the *-a* ending to make it feminine), eg hijo/a *ee*·kho/a **m/f** (son/daughter). The same goes for the plural endings *-os/as*, eg *hijos/as* *ee*·khos/as **m/f** (sons/daughters). If you see an *(a)* between brackets at the end of a word, it means you have to add it in order to make that word feminine, eg *español(a)* es·pa·*nyol*/es·pa·*nyo*·la **m/f** (Spanish). In other cases we spell out the whole word, eg *actor/actriz* ak·*tor*/ak·*treeth* **m/f** (actor/actress). See also **gender** (p19).

Do you want a massage?	¿Quieres un masaje? *kye*·res oon ma·*sa*·khe
Let's go to bed!	¡Vámonos a la cama! *va*·mo·nos a la *ka*·ma

Sex

Kiss me!	¡Dame un beso! *da*·me oon *be*·so
I want you.	Te deseo. te de·*se*·o
I want to make love to you.	Quiero hacerte el amor. *kye*·ro a·*ther*·te el a·*mor*
Do you have a condom?	¿Tienes un condón? *tye*·nes oon kon·*don*
🇶 **Do you like this?**	¿Esto te gusta? *es*·to te *goos*·ta
🇦 **I (don't) like that.**	Eso (no) me gusta. *e*·so (no) me *goos*·ta

I think we should stop now.	Pienso que deberíamos parar. *pyen*·so ke de·be·*ree*·a·mos pa·*rar*
Oh yeah!	¡Así! a·*see*
That was amazing.	Eso fue increíble. *e*·so fwe een·kre·*ee*·ble
Can I stay over?	¿Puedo quedarme? *pwe*·do ke·*dar*·me

Love

Q Do you love me?	¿Me quieres? me *kye*·res
A I love you.	Te quiero. te *kye*·ro
I think we're good together.	Creo que estamos muy bien juntos. *kre*·o ke es·*ta*·mos mooy byen *khoon*·tos

SOCIAL ROMANCE

LANGUAGE TIP

Endearments

Here are a few terms of endearment you might use with the one you love.

heart	corazón m&f	ko·ra·*thon*
heaven	cielo m&f	*thye*·lo
little love	amorcito/a m/f	a·mor·*thee*·to/a
my life	mi vida m&f	mee *vee*·da
my love	mi amor m&f	mee a·*mor*
treasure	tesoro m&f	te·*so*·ro

Beliefs & Culture

KEY PHRASES

What's your religion?	¿Cuál es su/tu religión? pol/inf	kwal es soo/too re·lee·*khyon*
I'm ...	Soy ...	soy ...
I'm sorry, it's against my beliefs.	Lo siento, eso va en contra de mis creencias.	lo *syen*·to e·so va en *kon*·tra de mees kre·*en*·thyas

Religion

Q What's your religion?   ¿Cuál es su/tu religión? pol/inf
kwal es soo/too re·lee·*khyon*

A I'm (not) ...   (No) Soy ...
(no) soy ...

agnostic	agnóstico/a m/f	ag·*nos*·tee·ko/a
Buddhist	budista m&f	boo·*dees*·ta
Catholic	católico/a m/f	ka·*to*·lee·ko/a
Christian	cristiano/a m/f	krees·*tya*·no/a
Hindu	hindú m&f	een·*doo*
Jewish	judío/a m/f	khoo·*dee*·o/a
Muslim	musulmán m	moo·sool·*man*
	musulmana f	moo·sool·*ma*·na

I'm (not) religious.   (No) Soy religioso/a. m/f
(no) soy re·lee·*khyo*·so/a

I (don't) believe in God.	(No) Creo en Dios. (no) *kre*·o en *dyos*
I (don't) believe in destiny/fate.	(No) Creo en el destino. (no) *kre*·o en el des·*tee*·no
Can I pray here?	¿Puedo rezar aquí? *pwe*·do re·*thar* a·*kee*

Cultural Differences

Is this a local custom?	¿Esto es una costumbre local? *es*·to es *oo*·na kos·*toom*·bre lo·*kal*
This is fun.	Esto es divertido. *es*·to es dee·ver·*tee*·do
This is (very) interesting.	Esto es (muy) interesante. *es*·to es (mooy) een·te·re·*san*·te
This is (very) different.	Esto es (muy) diferente. *es*·to es (mooy) dee·fe·*ren*·te
I'm not used to this.	No estoy acostumbrado/a a esto. **m/f** no es·*toy* a·kos·*toom*·bra·do/a a *es*·to
I'm sorry, it's against my beliefs.	Lo siento, eso va en contra de mis creencias. lo *syen*·to *e*·so va en *kon*·tra de mees kre·*en*·thyas
I'll try it.	Lo probaré. lo pro·ba·*re*
Sorry, I didn't mean to do/ say anything wrong.	Lo siento, lo hice/dije sin querer. lo *syen*·to lo *ee*·the/*dee*·khe seen ke·*rer*

Sports

KEY PHRASES

What sport do you play?	¿Qué deporte practicas?	ke de·*por*·te prak·*tee*·kas
What's your favourite team?	¿Cuál es tu equipo favorito?	kwal es too e·*kee*·po fa·vo·*ree*·to
What's the score?	¿Cómo van?	*ko*·mo van

Sporting Interests

Q What sport do you play?	¿Qué deporte practicas?	ke de·*por*·te prak·*tee*·kas
Q What sport do you follow?	¿A qué deporte eres aficionado/a? **m/f**	a ke de·*por*·te e·res a·fee·thyo·*na*·do/a
A I play/do ...	Practico ...	prak·*tee*·ko ...
A I follow ...	Soy aficionado/a al ... **m/f**	soy a·fee·thyo·*na*·do/a al ...

basketball	baloncesto m	ba·lon·*thes*·to
cycling	ciclismo m	thee·*klees*·mo
football (soccer)	fútbol m	*foot*·bol
tennis	tenis m	*te*·nis
volleyball	voleibol m	*vo*·ley·bol

For more sports, see the **dictionary**.

Do you like sport?	¿Te gustan los deportes? te *goos*·tan los de·*por*·tes
I like watching it.	Me gusta mirar. me *goos*·ta mee·*rar*
Who's your favourite sportsperson?	¿Quién es tu deportista favorito/a? **m/f** kyen es too de·por·*tees*·ta fa·vo·*ree*·to/a
What's your favourite team?	¿Cuál es tu equipo favorito? kwal es too e·*kee*·po fa·vo·*ree*·to

Going to a Game

Would you like to go to a (basketball) game?	¿Te gustaría ir a un partido de (baloncesto)? te goos·ta·*ree*·a eer a oon par·*tee*·do de (ba·lon·*thes*·to)
Who are you supporting?	¿Con qué equipo vas? kon ke e·*kee*·po vas
Who's playing?	¿Quién juega? kyen *khwe*·ga
Who's winning?	¿Quién gana? kyen *ga*·na
That was a (boring) game.	Ese partido fue (aburrido). *e*·se par·*tee*·do fwe (a·boo·*ree*·do)
That was a (great) game!	¡Ese partido fue (cojonudo)! *e*·se par·*tee*·do fwe (ko·kho·*noo*·do)
What's the score?	¿Cómo van? *ko*·mo van

> **CULTURE TIP** · **Local Sports**
> If you hear the sounds of bat, ball and exertion, it may be *pelotari* (pelota players) enjoying the traditional game of *pelota vasca*, Basque handball. It's also known as *jai-alai* in Basque.
>
> | ball | pelota f | pe·*lo*·ta |
> |---|---|---|
> | striker | delantero/a m/f | de·lan·*te*·ro/a |
> | wall | frontón m | fron·*ton* |

Playing Sport

Q **Do you want to play?**	¿Quieres jugar?	kye·res khoo·gar
A **Yeah, that'd be great.**	Sí, me encantaría.	see me en·kan·ta·ree·a
A **Not at the moment, thanks.**	Ahora mismo no, gracias.	a·o·ra mees·mo no gra·thyas
A **I have an injury.**	Tengo una lesión.	ten·go oo·na le·syon
Can I join in?	¿Puedo jugar?	pwe·do khoo·gar
Where's the best place to run around here?	¿Cuál es el mejor sitio para hacer footing por aquí cerca?	kwal es el me·khor see·tyo pa·ra a·ther foo·teen por a·kee ther·ka
Where's the nearest gym?	¿Dónde está el gimnasio más cercano?	don·de es·ta el kheem·na·syo mas ther·ka·no
Do I have to be a member to attend?	¿Hay que ser socio/a para entrar? m/f	ai ke ser so·thyo/a pa·ra en·trar

Where's the nearest swimming pool?	¿Dónde está la piscina más cercana?	*don·de es·ta la pees·thee·na mas ther·ka·na*
Where's the nearest tennis court?	¿Dónde está la pista de tenis más cercana?	*don·de es·ta la pees·ta de te·nees mas ther·ka·na*
Where are the change rooms?	¿Dónde están los vestuarios?	*don·de es·tan los ves·twa·ryos*
What's the charge per ...?	¿Cúanto cobran por ...?	*kwan·to ko·bran por ...*

day	día	*dee·a*
game	partida	*par·tee·da*
hour	hora	*o·ra*
visit	visita	*vee·see·ta*

Can I hire a ...?	¿Es posible alquilar una ...?	*es po·see·ble al·kee·lar oo·na ...*

ball	pelota	*pe·lo·ta*
bicycle	bicicleta	*bee·thee·kle·ta*
court	cancha	*kan·cha*
racquet	raqueta	*ra·ke·ta*

What a goal/pass!	¡Qué gol/pase!	*ke gol/pa·se*
Your/My point.	Tu/Mi punto.	*too/mee poon·to*
Kick it to me!	¡Pásamelo!	*pa·sa·me·lo*

🔊 LISTEN FOR

fuera de juego	*fwe*·ra de *khwe*·go	offside
penalty m	pe·*nal*·tee	penalty
portero m	por·*te*·ro	goalkeeper
saque m **de esquina**	*sa*·ke de es·*kee*·na	corner
tiro m **libre**	*tee*·ro *lee*·bre	free kick

You're a good player.	Juegas bien. *khwe*·gas byen
Thanks for the game.	Gracias por el partido. *gra*·thyas por el par·*tee*·do

Soccer/Football

Who plays for (Real Madrid)?	¿Quién juega en el (Real Madrid)? kyen *khwe*·ga en el (re·*al* ma·*dreeth*)
What a terrible team!	¡Qué equipo más espantoso! ke e·*kee*·po mas es·pan·*to*·so
He's a great player.	Es un gran jugador. es oon gran khoo·ga·*dor*
He played brilliantly in the match against (Italy).	Jugó de fenomenal en el partido contra (Italia). khoo·*go* de fe·no·me·*nal* en el par·*tee*·do *kon*·tra (ee·*ta*·lya)
Which team is at the top of the league?	¿Qué equipo está en primera posición en la liga? ke e·*kee*·po es·*ta* en pree·*me*·ra po·see·*thyon* en la *lee*·ga

Outdoors

KEY PHRASES

Do we need a guide?	¿Se necesita un guía?	se ne·the·*see*·ta oon *gee*·a
I'm lost.	Estoy perdido/a. m/f	es·*toy* per·*dee*·do/a
What's the weather like?	¿Qué tiempo hace?	ke *tyem*·po a·the

Hiking

There's plenty of walking, hiking and mountaineering to do in Spain. A recognised cross-country walking trail is known as *Gran Recorrido (GR)* gran re·ko·*ree*·do, while the shorter walking paths scattered throughout the country are called *Pequeños Recorridos (PR)* pe·*ke*·nyos re·ko·*ree*·dos.

Where can I find out about hiking trails?	¿Dónde hay información sobre caminos rurales de la zona? *don*·de ai een·for·ma·*thyon* so·bre ka·*mee*·nos roo·*ra*·les de la *tho*·na
Do we need a guide?	¿Se necesita un guía? se ne·the·*see*·ta oon *gee*·a
Are there guided treks?	¿Se organizan excursiones guiadas? se or·ga·*nee*·than eks·koor·*syo*·nes gee·*a*·das

Where can I ...?	¿Dónde puedo ...?	
	don·de pwe·do ...	
buy supplies	comprar	kom·*prar*
	víveres	*vee*·ver·es
find someone who knows this area	encontrar a alguien que conozca el área	en·kon·*trar* a *al*·gyen ke ko·*noth*·ka el *a*·re·a
get a map	obtener un mapa	ob·te·*ner* oon *ma*·pa
hire hiking gear	alquilar un equipo para ir de excursion	al·kee·*lar* oon e·*kee*·po *pa*·ra eer de eks·koor·*syon*

How long is the trail?	¿Cuántos kilómetros tiene el camino? *kwan*·tos kee·*lo*·me·tros *tye*·ne el ka·*mee*·no
How high is the climb?	¿A qué altura se escala? a ke al·*too*·ra se es·*ka*·la
Do we need to take bedding?	¿Se necesita llevar algo en qué dormir? se ne·the·*see*·ta lye·*var al*·go en ke dor·*meer*
Do we need to take food/water?	¿Se necesita llevar comida/agua? se ne·the·*see*·ta lye·*var* ko·*mee*·da/*a*·gwa
Is the track (well-)marked?	¿Es (bien) marcado el sendero? es (byen) mar·*ka*·do el sen·*de*·ro
Is the track open?	¿Es abierto el sendero? es a·*byer*·to el sen·*de*·ro

LOOK FOR

Por Aquí a ...	por a·*kee* a ...	This Way To ...
Prohibido Acampar	pro·ee·*bee*·do a·kam·*par*	No Camping
Terreno de Cámping	te·*re*·no de *kam*·peen	Camping Ground

SOCIAL OUTDOORS

Is the track scenic?	¿Es pintoresco el sendero? es peen·to·*res*·ko el sen·*de*·ro
Which is the easiest/ shortest route?	¿Cuál es el camino más fácil/corto? kwal es el ka·*mee*·no mas *fa*·theel/*kor*·to
Which is the most interesting route?	¿Cuál es el camino más interesante? kwal es el ka·*mee*·no mas een·te·re·*san*·te
Where's a/the ...?	¿Dónde hay ...? *don*·de ai ...

camping site	un cámping	oon *kam*·peen
village	un pueblo	oon *pwe*·blo
showers	duchas	*doo*·chas
toilets	servicios	ser·*vee*·thyos

Where have you come from?	¿De dónde vienes? de *don*·de *vye*·nes
How long did it take?	¿Cuánto ha tardado? *kwan*·to a tar·*da*·do
Does this path go to ...?	¿Este camino va a ...? *es*·te ka·*mee*·no va a ...
Can we go through here?	¿Se puede pasar por aquí? se *pwe*·de pa·*sar* por a·*kee*

SOCIAL OUTDOORS

¡Prohibido Nadar! pro·ee·*bee*·do na·*dar* No Swimming!

Is the water OK to drink?	¿Se puede beber el agua? se *pwe*·de be·*ber* el *a*·gwa
Is it safe?	¿Es seguro? es se·*goo*·ro
Is there a hut there?	¿Hay una cabaña allí? ai *oo*·na ka·*ba*·nya a·*lyee*
When does it get dark?	¿A qué hora oscurece? a ke *o*·ra os·koo·*re*·the
I'm lost.	Estoy perdido/a. **m/f** es·*toy* per·*dee*·do/a

At the Beach

Where's the best beach?	¿Dónde está la playa mejor? *don*·de es·*ta* la *pla*·ya me·*khor*
Where's the nearest beach?	¿Dónde está la playa más cercana? *don*·de es·*ta* la *pla*·ya mas ther·*ka*·na
Is it safe to dive/swim here?	¿Es seguro bucear/nadar aquí? es se·*goo*·ro boo·the·*ar*/na·*dar* a·*kee*
What time is high/low tide?	¿A qué hora es la marea alta/baja? a ke *o*·ra es la ma·*re*·a *al*·ta/*ba*·kha
How much to rent a chair?	¿Cuánto por alquilar una silla? *kwan*·to por al·kee·*lar* *oo*·na *see*·lya

How much to rent an umbrella? (for sun)	¿Cuánto por alquilar un parasol? kwan·to por al·kee·lar oon pa·ra·sol

Weather

60a Q What's the weather like?	¿Qué tiempo hace? ke tyem·po a·the
A Today it's ...	Hoy hace ... oy a·the ...

freezing	un frío que pela	oon free·o ke pe·la
sunny	sol	sol
warm	calor	ka·lor
windy	viento	vyen·to

60b A It's raining.	Está lloviendo. es·ta lyo·vyen·do
60c A It's cold.	Hace frío. a·the free·o
60d A It's hot.	Hace calor. a·the ka·lor
A (Today) It's snowing.	(Hoy) Está nevando. (oy) es·ta ne·van·do
Q What's the weather forecast?	¿Cuál es el pronóstico del tiempo? kwal es el pro·nos·tee·ko del tyem·po
A (Tomorrow) It will be raining.	(Mañana) Lloverá. (ma·nya·na) lyo·ve·ra
Where can I buy a rain jacket?	¿Dónde puedo comprar un impermeable? don·de pwe·do kom·prar oon eem·per·me·a·ble

Where can I buy sunblock?	¿Dónde puedo comprar crema solar? *don·de pwe·do kom·prar kre·ma so·lar*
Where can I buy an umbrella? (for rain)	¿Dónde puedo comprar un paraguas? *don·de pwe·do kom·prar oon pa·ra·gwas*
hail	granizo m *gra·nee·tho*
storm	tormenta f *tor·men·ta*
sun	sol m *sol*

Flora & Fauna

| What ... is that? | ¿Qué ... es ése/ésa? m/f
ke ... es e·se/e·sa |

animal	animal m	*a·nee·mal*
bird	pájaro m	*pa·kha·ro*
flower	flor f	*flor*
plant	planta f	*plan·ta*
tree	árbol m	*ar·bol*

Can you eat the fruit?	¿Se puede comer la fruta? *se pwe·de ko·mer la froo·ta*
Is it endangered?	¿Está en peligro de extinción? *es·ta en pe·lee·gro de eks·teen·thyon*
Is it common?	¿Es común? *es ko·moon*

For geographical and agricultural terms, and names of animals and plants, see the **dictionary**.

Safe Travel

Emergencies

KEY PHRASES

Help!	¡Socorro!	so·*ko*·ro
There's been an accident.	Ha habido un accidente.	a a·*bee*·do oon ak·thee·*den*·te
It's an emergency!	¡Es una emergencia!	es oo·na e·mer·*khen*·thee·ya

61a Help!	¡Socorro! so·*ko*·ro
61b Stop!	¡Pare! *pa*·re
61c Go away!	¡Váyase! *va*·ya·se
Leave me alone!	¡Déjame en paz! *de*·kha·me en path
61d Thief!	¡Ladrón! lad·*ron*
61e Fire!	¡Fuego! *fwe*·go
61f It's an emergency!	¡Es una emergencia! es oo·na e·mer·*khen*·thee·ya
There's been an accident.	Ha habido un accidente. a a·*bee*·do oon ak·thee·*den*·te
Do you have a first-aid kit?	¿Tiene un botiquín de primeros auxilios? *tye*·ne oon bo·tee·*keen* de pree·*me*·ros owk·*see*·lyos

🔊 LISTEN FOR

¡Es peligroso!	es pe·lee·*gro*·so	It's dangerous!

62a Call the police!	¡Llame a la policía! *lya*·me a la po·lee·*thee*·a
62b Call a doctor!	¡Llame a un médico! *lya*·me a oon *me*·dee·ko
62c Call an ambulance!	¡Llame a una ambulancia! *lya*·me a *oo*·na am·boo·*lan*·thya
62d Could you help me, please?	¿Me puede ayudar, por favor? me *pwe*·de a·yoo·*dar* por fa·*vor*
63a I have to use the telephone.	Necesito usar el teléfono. ne·the·*see*·to oo·*sar* el te·*le*·fo·no
63b I'm lost.	Estoy perdido. **m** es·*toy* per·*dee*·do
63c I'm lost.	Estoy perdida. **f** es·*toy* per·*dee*·da
63d Where's the toilet?	¿Dónde están los servicios? *don*·de es·*tan* los ser·*vee*·thyos

Police

KEY PHRASES

Where's the police station?	¿Dónde está la comisaría?	don·de es·ta la ko·mee·sa·ree·a
I want to contact my embassy/ consulate.	Quiero ponerme en contacto con mi embajada/ consulado.	kye·ro po·ner·me en kon·tak·to kon mee em·ba·kha·da/ kon·soo·la·do
My money was stolen.	Mi dinero fue robado.	mee dee·ne·ro fwe ro·ba·do

In an emergency, call the police. They will then put you through to other emergency services (fire brigade and ambulance). For more on making a call, see **communications** (p85).

64a	**Where's the police station?**	¿Dónde está la comisaría? don·de es·ta la ko·mee·sa·ree·a
64b	**I want to report an offence.**	Quiero denunciar un delito. kye·ro de·noon·thyar oon de·lee·to
64c	**I've been robbed.**	Me han robado. me an ro·ba·do
64d	**I've been raped.**	He sido violado. m e see·do vee·o·la·do
64e	**I've been raped.**	He sido violada. f e see·do vee·o·la·da
	It was him/her.	Fue él/ella. fwe el/e·lya
	My (money) was stolen.	Mi (dinero) fue robado. mee (dee·ne·ro) fwe ro·ba·do

My (bags/suitcases) were stolen.	Mis (maletas) fueron robadas. mee (ma·*le*·tas) fwe·*ron* ro·*ba*·das
65a I've lost my passport.	He perdido mi pasaporte. e per·*dee*·do mee pa·sa·*por*·te
What am I accused of?	¿De qué me acusan? de ke me a·*ku*·san
I didn't realise I was doing anything wrong.	No sabía que estaba haciendo algo mal. no sa·*bee*·a ke es·*ta*·ba a·*thyen*·do al·go mal
I'm innocent.	Soy inocente. soy ee·no·*then*·te
65b I want to contact my embassy.	Quiero ponerme en contacto con mi embajada. *kye*·ro po·*ner*·me en kon·*tak*·to kon mee em·ba·*kha*·da
65c I want to contact my consulate.	Quiero ponerme en contacto con mi consulado. *kye*·ro po·*ner*·me en kon·*tak*·to kon mee kon·soo·*la*·do
I need a lawyer who speaks (English).	Necesito un abogado que hable (inglés). ne·the·*see*·to oon a·bo·*ga*·do ke *a*·ble (een·*gles*)
Can I have a copy, please?	¿Puede darme una copia, por favor? *pwe*·de *dar*·me oo·na *ko*·pya por fa·*vor*
65d I have insurance.	Tengo seguro. *ten*·go se·*goo*·ro
This drug is for personal use.	Esta droga es para uso personal. es·ta *dro*·ga es *pa*·ra oo·so per·so·*nal*
I have a prescription for this drug.	Tengo receta para esta droga. *ten*·go re·*the*·ta *pa*·ra es·ta *dro*·ga

Health

KEY PHRASES

Where's the nearest hospital?	¿Dónde está el hospital más cercano?	don·de es·ta el os·pee·tal mas ther·ka·no
I'm sick.	Estoy enfermo/a. **m/f**	es·toy en·fer·mo/a
I need a doctor.	Necesito un doctor.	ne·the·see·to oon dok·tor
I'm on regular medication for ...	Estoy bajo medicación para ...	es·toy ba·kho me·dee·ka·thyon pa·ra ...
I'm allergic to ...	Soy alérgico/a a... **m/f**	soy a·ler·khee·ko/a a ...

Doctor

66a	Where's the nearest doctor?	¿Dónde está el médico más cercano? don·de es·ta el me·dee·ko mas ther·ka·no
66b	Where's the nearest dentist?	¿Dónde está el dentista más cercano? don·de es·ta el den·tees·ta mas ther·ka·no
66c	Where's the nearest hospital?	¿Dónde está el hospital más cercano? don·de es·ta el os·pee·tal mas ther·ka·no
66d	I need a doctor.	Necesito un doctor. ne·the·see·to oon dok·tor

> **CULTURE TIP** **Etiquette Tip**
> A polite way to respond to someone sneezing is by
> saying *¡Salud!* sa·*loo* (health) or *¡Jesús!* khe·*soos*
> (lit: 'Jesus').

I need a doctor (who speaks English).	Necesito un doctor (que hable inglés). ne·the·*see*·to oon dok·*tor* (ke a·ble een·*gles*)
66e Could I see a female doctor?	¿Puede examinarme una doctora? pwe·de ek·sa·mee·*nar*·me oo·na dok·*to*·ra
67a I've run out of my medication.	Se me terminaron los medicamentos. se me ter·mee·*na*·ron los me·dee·ka·*men*·tos
This is my usual medicine.	Éste es mi medicamento habitual. es·te es mee me·dee·ka·*men*·to a·bee·too·*al*
I don't want a blood transfusion.	No quiero que me hagan una transfusión de sangre. no *kye*·ro ke me a·gan oo·na trans·foo·*syon* de san·gre
Please use a new syringe.	Por favor, use una jeringa nueva. por fa·*vor* oo·se oo·na khe·*reen*·ga nwe·va
I need new contact lenses.	Necesito lentes de contacto nuevas. ne·the·*see*·to *len*·tes de kon·*tak*·to nwe·vas
I need new glasses.	Necesito gafas nuevas. ne·the·*see*·to *ga*·fas nwe·vas

| I've been vaccinated for ... | Estoy vacunado/a contra ... m/f
es·*toy* va·koo·*na*·do/a *kon*·tra ... |
| He's/She's been vaccinated for ... | Está vacunado/a contra ... m/f
es·*ta* va·koo·*na*·do/a *kon*·tra ... |

tetanus	el tétano	el *te*·ta·no
typhoid	la tifus	la *tee*·foos
hepatitis A/B/C	la hepatitis A/B/C	la e·pa·*tee*·tees a/be/the
... fever	la fiebre ...	la *fye*·bre ...

For women's medical issues, see **women's health** (p162).

Symptoms & Conditions

67b I'm sick.	Estoy enfermo. m es·*toy* en·*fer*·mo
67c I'm sick.	Estoy enferma. f es·*toy* en·*fer*·ma
I have ...	Tengo ... *ten*·go ...
I've recently had ...	Hace poco he tenido ... a·the po·ko e te·*nee*·do ...
I'm on regular medication for ...	Estoy bajo medicación para ... es·*toy* ba·kho me·dee·ka·*thyon* pa·ra ...
67d It hurts here.	Me duele aquí. me *dwe*·le a·*kee*
I've been injured.	He sido herido/a. m/f e *see*·do e·*ree*·do/a

🔊 LISTEN FOR

¿Qué le pasa?	ke le *pa*·sa What's the problem?
¿Dónde le duele?	*don*·de le *dwe*·le Where does it hurt?
¿Tiene fiebre?	*tye*·ne *fye*·bre Do you have a temperature?
¿Desde cuándo se siente así?	*des*·de *kwan*·do se *syen*·te a·*see* How long have you been like this?
¿Ha tenido esto antes?	a te·*nee*·do *es*·to *an*·tes Have you had this before?

I've been vomiting.	He estado vomitando. e es·*ta*·do vo·mee·*tan*·do
I can't sleep.	No puedo dormir. no *pwe*·do dor·*meer*
I have a rash.	Tengo una erupción cutánea. *ten*·go *oo*·na e·roop·*thyon* koo·*ta*·ne·a
I have an infection.	Tengo una infección. *ten*·go *oo*·na in·fek·*thyon*
I feel ...	Me siento ... me *syen*·to ...

better	mejor m&f	me·*khor*
depressed	deprimido/a m/f	de·pree·*mee*·do/a
dizzy	mareado/a m/f	ma·re·a·do/a
shivery	destemplado/a m/f	des·tem·*pla*·do/a
weak	débil m&f	*de*·beel
worse	peor m&f	pe·*or*

asthma	asma m
	as·ma
diarrhoea	diarrea f
	dee·a·*re*·a
fever	fiebre f
	fye·bre
headache	dolor m de cabeza
	do·*lor* de ka·*be*·tha
sprain	torcedura f
	tor·the·*doo*·ra

For more symptoms & conditions, see the **dictionary**.

Women's Health

(I think) I'm pregnant.	(Creo que) Estoy embarazada.
	(*kre*·o ke) es·*toy* em·ba·ra·*tha*·da
I haven't had my period for ... weeks.	Hace ... semanas que no me viene la regla.
	a·the ... se·*ma*·nas ke no me *vye*·ne la *reg*·la
I'm on the Pill.	Tomo la píldora.
	to·mo la *peel*·do·ra
I've noticed a lump here.	He notado un bulto aquí.
	e no·*ta*·do oon *bool*·to a·*kee*
I have period pain.	Tengo dolor menstrual.
	ten·go do·*lor* mens·troo·*al*
contraception	anticonceptivos m pl
	an·tee·kon·thep·*tee*·vos
pregnancy test	prueba f de embarazo
	prwe·ba de em·ba·*ra*·tho
the morning-after pill	píldora f del día siguiente
	peel·do·ra del *dee*·a see·*gyen*·te

🔊 LISTEN FOR

¿Usted bebe?	oos·*te be*·be Do you drink?
¿Usted fuma?	oos·*te foo*·ma Do you smoke?
¿Usted toma drogas?	oos·*te to*·ma *dro*·gas Do you take drugs?
¿Tiene Usted alergias?	*tye*·ne oos·*te a·ler*·khyas Are you allergic to anything?
¿Se encuentra bajo medicación?	se en·*kwen*·tra *ba*·kho me·dee·ka·*thyon* Are you on medication?

Allergies

68a	I'm allergic to antibiotics.	Soy alérgico a los antibióticos. m soy a·*ler*·khee·ko a los an·tee·*byo*·tee·kos
68b	I'm allergic to antibiotics.	Soy alérgica a los antibióticos. f soy a·*ler*·khee·ka a los an·tee·*byo*·tee·kos
68c	I'm allergic to anti-inflammatories.	Soy alérgico a los anti-inflamatorios. m soy a·*ler*·khee·ko a los an·tee· een·fla·ma·*to*·ryos
68d	I'm allergic to anti-inflammatories.	Soy alérgica a los anti-inflamatorios. f soy a·*ler*·khee·ka a los an·tee· een·fla·ma·*to*·ryos
68e	I'm allergic to aspirin.	Soy alérgico a la aspirina. m soy a·*ler*·khee·ko a la as·pee·*ree*·na

68f	I'm allergic to aspirin.	Soy alérgica a la aspirina. f
		soy a·ler·khee·ka a la as·pee·ree·na
69a	I'm allergic to bees.	Soy alérgico a las abejas. m
		soy a·ler·khee·ko a las a·be·khas
69b	I'm allergic to bees.	Soy alérgica a las abejas. f
		soy a·ler·khee·ka a las a·be·khas
69c	I'm allergic to codeine.	Soy alérgico a la codeina. m
		soy a·ler·khee·ko a la ko·de·ee·na
69d	I'm allergic to codeine.	Soy alérgica a la codeina. f
		soy a·ler·khee·ka a la ko·de·ee·na
69e	I'm allergic to penicillin.	Soy alérgico a la penicilina. m
		soy a·ler·khee·ko a la pe·nee·thee·lee·na
69f	I'm allergic to penicillin.	Soy alérgica a la penicilina. f
		soy a·ler·khee·ka a la pe·nee·thee·lee·na

He/She is allergic to ...	Es alérgico/a ... m/f
	es a·ler·khee·ko/a ...
I have a skin allergy.	Tengo una alergia en la piel.
	ten·go oo·na a·ler·khya en la pyel
I'm on a special diet.	Estoy a régimen especial.
	es·toy a re·khee·men es·pe·thyal
antihistamines	antihistamínicos m pl
	an·tee·ees·ta·mee·nee·kos
inhaler	inhalador m
	een·a·la·dor
sulphur-based drugs	drogas con base de azufre f pl
	dro·gas kon ba·se de a·thoo·fre

For food-related allergies, see **vegetarian & special meals** (p187).

70g
head
cabeza f
ka·be·tha

70j
nose
nariz f
na·reeth

70i
mouth
boca f
bo·ka

70b
chest
pecho m
pe·cho

70k
stomach
estómago m
es·to·ma·go

70h
leg
pierna f
pyer·na

70d
eye
ojo m
o·kho

70c
ear
oreja f
o·re·kha

70a
arm
brazo m
bra·tho

70f
hand
mano f
ma·no

bum
culo m
koo·lo

70e
foot
pie m
pee·e

Parts of the Body

My ... hurts.	Me duele ...
	me dwe·le ...
I can't move my ...	No puedo mover ...
	no pwe·do mo·ver ...
I have a cramp in my ...	Tengo calambres en ...
	ten·go ka·lam·bres en ...
My ... is swollen.	Mi ... está hinchado.
	mee ... es·ta een·cha·do

For more parts of the body, see the **dictionary**.

Chemist

I need something for ...	Necesito algo para ... ne·the·see·to al·go pa·ra ...
I have a prescription.	Tengo receta médica. ten·go re·the·ta me·dee·ka
Do I need a prescription for ...?	¿Necesito receta para ...? ne·the·see·to re·the·ta pa·ra ...
How many times a day?	¿Cuántas veces al día? kwan·tas ve·thes al dee·a

For pharmaceutical items, see the **dictionary**.

Dentist

I have a broken tooth.	Se me ha roto un diente. se me a ro·to oon dyen·te
I have a toothache.	Me duele una muela. me dwe·le oo·na mwe·la
I've lost a filling.	Se me ha caído un empaste. se me a ka·ee·do oon em·pas·te
My gums hurt.	Me duelen las encías. me dwe·len las en·thee·as
I don't want it extracted.	No quiero que me lo saquen. no kye·ro ke me lo sa·ken
I need an anaesthetic.	Necesito una anestesia. ne·the·see·to oo·ne a·nes·te·sya
I need a filling.	Necesito un empaste ne·the·see·to oon em·pas·te

Food

Eating Out

FOOD EATING OUT

KEY PHRASES

Can you recommend a restaurant?	¿Puede recomendar un restaurante?	pwe·de re·ko·men·dar oon res·tow·ran·te
I'd like a table for two, please.	Quisiera una mesa para dos, por favor.	kee·sye·ra oo·na me·sa pa·ra dos por fa·vor
I'd like the menu, please.	Quisiera el menú, por favor.	kee·sye·ra el me·noo por fa·vor
I'd like ...	Quisiera ...	kee·sye·ra ...

Basics

The main meal in Spain, 'lunchtime' is called *la hora de comer* la o·ra de ko·*mer*. It's served between 1.30pm and 4.30pm.

71a breakfast	desayuno m de·sa·yoo·no
71b lunch	comida f ko·mee·da
71c dinner	cena f the·na
71d snack	tentempié m ten·tem·pye
71e eat	comer ko·mer
71f drink	beber be·ber

I'd like ...	Quisiera ... kee·*sye*·ra ...
I'm starving!	¡Estoy hambriento/a! **m/f** es·*toy* am·*bryen*·to/a
Enjoy your meal!	¡Buen provecho! bwen pro·*ve*·cho

Finding a Place to Eat

72a Can you recommend a bar?	¿Puede recomendar un bar? *pwe*·de re·ko·men·*dar* oon bar
72b Can you recommend a cafe?	¿Puede recomendar un café? *pwe*·de re·ko·men·*dar* oon ka·*fe*
72c Can you recommend a restaurant?	¿Puede recomendar un restaurante? *pwe*·de re·ko·men·*dar* oon res·tow·*ran*·te
Are you still serving food?	¿Siguen sirviendo comida? *see*·gen seer·*vyen*·do ko·*mee*·da
How long is the wait?	¿Cuánto hay que esperar? *kwan*·to ai ke es·pe·*rar*
Where would you go for a cheap meal?	¿Adónde se va para comer barato? a·*don*·de se va *pa*·ra ko·*mer* ba·*ra*·to
Where would you go for local specialities?	¿Adónde se va para comer comida típica? a·*don*·de se va *pa*·ra ko·*mer* ko·*mee*·da *tee*·pee·ka

🔊 LISTEN FOR

Lo siento, hemos cerrado.	lo *syen*·to *e*·mos the·*ra*·do Sorry, we're closed.
No tenemos mesa.	no te·*ne*·mos *me*·sa We have no free tables.
Un momento.	oon mo·*men*·to One moment.

I'd like to reserve a table for (two) people.	Quisiera reservar una mesa para (dos) personas. kee·*sye*·ra re·ser·*var* oo·na *me*·sa *pa*·ra (dos) per·*so*·nas
I'd like to reserve a table for (eight) o'clock.	Quisiera reservar una mesa para las (ocho). kee·*sye*·ra re·ser·*var* oo·na *me*·sa *pa*·ra las (o·cho)

At the Restaurant

I'd like the (non)smoking section, please.	Quisiera el área de (no) fumadores, por favor. kee·*sye*·ra el *a*·re·a de (no) foo·ma·*do*·res por fa·*vor*
73a **I'd like a table for (two), please.**	Quisiera una mesa para (dos), por favor. kee·*sye*·ra oo·na *me*·sa *pa*·ra (dos) por fa·*vor*

✂ **For two, please.**	Para dos, por favor.	*pa*·ra dos por fa·*vor*

73b **I'd like the drink list, please.**	Quisiera la lista de bebidas, por favor. kee·*sye*·ra la *lees*·ta de be·*bee*·das por fa·*vor*

Eating Out

Can I see the menu, please?

¿Puedo ver el menú, por favor?
pwe·do ver el me·*noo* por fa·*vor*

What would you recommend for ...?

¿Qué me recomendaría para ...?
ke me re·ko·men·da·*ree*·a *pa*·ra ...

the main meal
el plato principal
el *pla*·to preen·thee·*pal*

dessert
postre
pos·tre

drinks
bebidas
be·*bee*·das

Can you bring me some ..., please?

Por favor me trae ...
por fa·*vor* me *tra*·e ...

I'd like the bill, please.

Quisiera la cuenta, por favor.
kee·*sye*·ra la *kwen*·ta por fa·*vor*

73c I'd like the menu, please.

Quisiera el menú, por favor.
kee·sye·ra el me·noo por fa·vor

✂ **The menu, please.**

El menú, por favor.

el me·noo por fa·vor

Do you have children's meals?

¿Tienen comidas para niños?
tye·nen ko·mee·das pa·ra nee·nyos

Do you have a menu in English?

¿Tienen un menú en inglés?
tye·nen oon me·noo en een·gles

Is service included in the bill?

¿La cuenta incluye servicio?
la kwen·ta een·kloo·ye ser·vee·thyo

73d What would you recommend?

¿Qué recomienda?
ke re·ko·myen·da

Can you tell me which traditional foods I should try?

¿Que platos típicos debería probar?
ke pla·tos tee·pee·kos de·be·ree·a pro·bar

◀)) LISTEN FOR

¿Le gusta ...?	le goos·ta ... Do you like ...?
Recomiendo ...	re·ko·myen·do ... I suggest the ...
¿Cómo lo quiere preparado?	ko·mo lo kye·re pre·pa·ra·do How would you like that cooked?

I'll have what they're having.	Tomaré lo mismo que ellos. to·ma·*re* lo *mees*·mo ke e·*lyos*
Does it take long to prepare?	¿Tarda mucho en prepararse? *tar*·da moo·cho en pre·pa·*rar*·se
What's in that dish?	¿Que lleva ese plato? ke *lye*·va e·se *pla*·to
Are these complimentary?	¿Éstos son gratis? es·tos son *gra*·tees
We're just having drinks.	Sólo queremos tomar algo. *so*·lo ke·*re*·mos to·*mar* al·go

✂ **Just drinks.**   Sólo bebidas.   *so*·lo be·*bee*·das

FOOD   EATING OUT

spoon
 cuchara f <br> koo·*cha*·ra

fork
 tenedor m <br> te·ne·*dor*

plate
 plato m
 pla·to

knife
 cuchillo m <br> koo·*chee*·lyo

wineglass
 copa de vino m
 ko·pa de *vee*·no

glass
 vaso m
 va·so

table
 mesa f
 me·sa

Requests

Please bring a glass.	Por favor nos trae un vaso.
	por fa·*vor* nos *tra*·e oon *va*·so
Please bring a serviette.	Por favor nos trae una servilleta.
	por fa·*vor* nos *tra*·e *oo*·na ser·vee·*lye*·ta
I'd like it ...	Lo quiero ...
	lo *kye*·ro ...
I don't want it ...	No lo quiero ...
	no lo *kye*·ro ...

deep fried	frito en aceite abundante	*free*·to en a·*they*·te a·boon·*dan*·te
medium	no muy hecho	no mooy e·cho
rare	vuelta y vuelta	*vwel*·ta ee *vwel*·ta
re-heated	recalentado	re·ka·len·*ta*·do
steamed	al vapor	al va·*por*
well-done	muy hecho	mooy e·cho
with the dressing on the side	con el aliño aparte	kon el a·*lee*·nyo a·*par*·te
without ...	sin ...	seen ...

For other specific meal requests, see **vegetarian & special meals** (p187).

Compliments & Complaints

I love this dish.	Me encanta este plato.
	me en·*kan*·ta *es*·te *pla*·to
I didn't order this.	Yo no he pedido esto.
	yo no e pe·*dee*·do *es*·to

🔍 LOOK FOR

Aperitivos	a·pe·ree·*tee*·vos	Appetisers
Cervezas	ther·*ve*·thas	Beers
Caldos	*kal*·dos	Soups
De Entrada	de en·*tra*·da	Entrees
Ensaladas	en·sa·*la*·das	Salads
Postres	*pos*·tres	Desserts
Refrescos	re·*fres*·kos	Soft Drinks
Segundos Platos	se·*goon*·dos *pla*·tos	Main Courses

That was delicious!	¡Estaba buenísimo! es·*ta*·ba bwe·*nee*·see·mo
My compliments to the chef.	Mi enhorabuena al cocinero. mee en·o·ra·*bwe*·na al ko·thee·*ne*·ro
I'm full.	Estoy lleno/a. **m/f** es·*toy lye*·no/a
This is burnt.	Esto está quemado. es·to es·*ta* ke·*ma*·do
This is (too) cold.	Esto está (demasiado) frío. es·to es·*ta* (de·ma·*sya*·do) *free*·o
This is superb.	Esto está exquisito. es·to es·*ta* eks·kee·*see*·to
We love the local cuisine.	Nos encanta la comida típica de la zona. nos en·*kan*·ta la ko·*mee*·da *tee*·pee·ka de la *tho*·na

Paying the Bill

74a	I'd like the bill please.	Quisiera la cuenta, por favor. kee·sye·ra la kwen·ta por fa·vor
✂	Bill, please.	La cuenta, por favor.	la kwen·ta por fa·vor

There's a mistake in the bill.	Hay un error en la cuenta. ai oon e·ror en la kwen·ta

For methods of payment, see **money & banking** (p91).

Nonalcoholic Drinks

	I don't drink alcohol.	No bebo alcohol. no be·bo al·kol
75a	I'd like a cup of coffee.	Quisiera un café. kee·sye·ra oon ka·fe
75b	I'd like a cup of tea.	Quisiera un té. kee·sye·ra oon te
75c	with milk	con leche kon le·che
75d	without sugar	sin azúcar seen a·thoo·kar
75e	soft drink	refrescos re·fres·kos
75f	boiled water	agua hervida a·gwa er·vee·da
75g	mineral water	agua mineral a·gwa mee·ne·ral
	sparkling mineral water	agua mineral con gas a·gwa mee·ne·ral kon gas

Alcoholic Drinks

... beer	cerveza f ... ther·ve·tha ...	
draught	de barril	de ba·ril
dark	negra	neg·ra
light	rubia	roo·bee·a
nonalcoholic	sin alcohol	sin al·kol

small bottle of beer (250 ml)	botellín m bo·te·lyin
litre bottle of beer	litrona f lee·tro·na
bottle of beer (300 ml)	mediana f me·dya·na

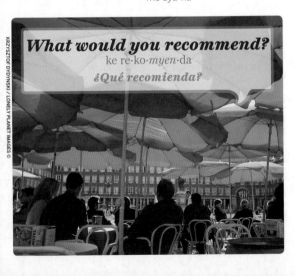

What would you recommend?
ke re·ko·myen·da
¿Qué recomienda?

FOOD EATING OUT

76a a glass of beer	una caña de cerveza	*oo*·na *ka*·nya de ther·*ve*·tha
a pint of beer	una pinta de cerveza	*oo*·na *peen*·ta de ther·*ve*·tha
a jug of beer	una jarra de cerveza	*oo*·na *kha*·ra de ther·*ve*·tha
brandy	coñac **m**	*ko*·nyak
Champagne	champán **m**	cham·*pan*
cocktail	combinado **m**	kom·bee·*na*·do
sangria (red-wine punch)	sangría **f**	san·*gree*·a
a shot of (rum)	un chupito de (ron)	oon choo·*pee*·to de (ron)
a shot of (gin)	un chupito de (ginebra)	oon choo·*pee*·to de (khee·*ne*·bra)
76b a shot of (whisky)	un chupito de (güisqui)	oon choo·*pee*·to de (*gwees*·kee)
76c a bottle of red wine	una botella de vino tinto	*oo*·na bo·*te*·lya de *vee*·no *teen*·to
76d a glass of red wine	una copa de vino tinto	*oo*·na *ko*·pa de *vee*·no *teen*·to
76e a bottle of white wine	una botella de vino blanco	*oo*·na bo·*te*·lya de *vee*·no *blan*·ko
76f a glass of white wine	una copa de vino blanco	*oo*·na *ko*·pa de *vee*·no *blan*·ko

CULTURE TIP

Tapas

Tapas are scrumptious cooked bar snacks, available pretty much around the clock at bars and some clubs. You'll find they're free in some places, laid out in the bar for you to choose from. Other venues will rotate the dishes.

banderilla f/ **moruno** m/ **pinchito** m	ban·de·*ree*·lya/ mo·*roo*·no/ peen·*chee*·to	small tapa serving on bread or a toothpick
ración f	ra·*thyon*	large tapa serving
montadito m	mon·ta·*dee*·to	bread-topped tapa
pan tumaca m	pan too·*ma*·ka	tapa of toasted bread rubbed with tomatoes and garlic, served with oil
queso m **en aceite**	*ke*·so en a·*they*·te	cheese in olive oil, served as a tapa

In the Bar

Excuse me!	¡Oiga! *oy*·ga
I'm next.	Ahora voy yo. a·*o*·ra voy yo
77a Q What would you like?	¿Qué desea tomar? ke de·*se*·a to·*mar*
A I'll have ...	Para mí ... *pa*·ra mee ...
Same again, please.	Otra de lo mismo. *o*·tra de lo *mees*·mo
No ice, thanks.	Sin hielo, gracias. seen *ye*·lo *gra*·thyas
77b I'll buy you a drink.	Te invito a una copa. te een·*vee*·to a *oo*·na *ko*·pa

FOOD EATING OUT

¿Dónde le gustaría sentarse?	*don·*de le gus·ta·*ree·*a sen·*tar·*se Where would you like to sit?
¿En qué le puedo servir?	en ke le *pwe·*do ser·*veer* What can I get for you?
¡Aquí tiene!	a·*kee tye·*ne Here you go!

It's my round.	Es mi ronda. es mee *ron·*da
You can get the next one.	La próxima la pagas tú. la *prok·*see·ma la *pa·*gas too
Do you serve meals here?	¿Sirven comidas aquí? *seer·*ven ko·*mee·*das a·*kee*

Drinking Up

77c Cheers!	¡Salud! sa·*loo*
Thanks, but I don't feel like it.	Lo siento, pero no me apetece. lo *syen·*to *pe·*ro no me a·pe·te·*the*
No thanks, I'm driving.	No gracias, tengo que conducir. no *gra·*thyas *ten·*go ke kon·doo·*theer*
This is hitting the spot.	Me lo estoy pasando muy bien. me lo es·*toy* pa·*san·*do mooy byen

CULTURE TIP

Minis

Many Spanish bars provide massive plastic beakers of beer to cater for young revellers. It's cut with water and average tasting – but cheap and free flowing! These fountains of froth are called *minis*.

I feel fantastic!	¡Me siento fenomenal! me *syen*·to fe·no·me·*nal*
I'm feeling drunk.	Esto me está subiendo mucho. es·to me es·*ta* soo·*byen*·do *moo*·cho
I think I've had one too many.	Creo que he tomado demasiado. *kre*·o ke e to·*ma*·do de·ma·*sya*·do
I'm tired, I'd better go home.	Estoy cansado/a, mejor me voy a casa. **m/f** es·*toy* kan·*sa*·do/a me·*khor* me voy a *ka*·sa
I don't think you should drive.	No creo que deberías conducir. no *kre*·o ke de·be·*ree*·as kon·doo·*theer*
Can you call a taxi for me?	¿Me puedes pedir un taxi? me *pwe*·des pe·*deer* oon *tak*·see

Self-Catering

KEY PHRASES

What's the local speciality?	¿Cuál es la especialidad de la zona?	kwal es la es·pe·thya·lee·*da* de la *tho*·na
Where can I find the ... section?	¿Dónde está la sección de ...?	*don*·de es·*ta* la sek·*thyon* de ...
I'd like ...	Póngame ...	*pon*·ga·me ...

Buying Food

Where can I find the ... section?	¿Dónde está la sección de ...? *don*·de es·*ta* la sek·*thyon* de ...

dairy	productos lácteos	pro·*dook*·tos *lak*·te·os
frozen goods	productos congelados	pro·*dook*·tos kon·khe·*la*·dos
fruit and vegetable	frutas y verduras	*froo*·tas ee ver·*doo*·ras
meat	carne	*kar*·ne

Where's the health-food section/store?	¿Dónde esta la sección/ tienda de comida dietética? *don*·de es·*ta* la sek·*thyon*/ *tyen*·da de ko·*mee*·da dye·*te*·tee·ka
78a What's that?	¿Qué es eso? ke es *e*·so

🔊 LISTEN FOR

¿En qué le puedo servir?	en ke le *pwe*·do ser·*veer*
	Can I help you?
¿Qué querías?	ke ke·*ree*·as
	What would you like?
No tengo.	no *ten*·go
	I don't have any.
No queda más.	no *ke*·da mas
	There's none left.

Can I taste it?	¿Puedo probarlo/a? **m/f**
	pwe·do pro·*bar*·lo/a
78b What's the local speciality?	¿Cuál es la especialidad de la zona?
	kwal es la es·pe·thya·lee·*da* de la *tho*·na
How much?	¿Cuánto?
	kwan·to
How many?	¿Cuántos/as? **m/f**
	kwan·tos/as
How much is (a kilo of cheese)?	¿Cuánto vale (un kilo de queso)?
	kwan·to *va*·le (oon *kee*·lo de *ke*·so)
Do you have anything cheaper?	¿Tiene algo más barato?
	tye·ne *al*·go mas ba·*ra*·to
Do you have any other kinds?	¿Tiene otros tipos?
	tye·ne *ot*·ros *tee*·pos
Do you sell locally produced food?	¿Se venden comestibles de la zona?
	se *ven*·den ko·mes·*tee*·bles de la *tho*·na

Do you sell organic produce?	¿Se venden productos agrícolas biológicos? se ven·den pro·*dook*·tos a·*gree*·ko·las bee·o·*lo*·khee·kos
79a I'd like ...	Póngame ... *pon*·ga·me ...
79b I'd like (three) pieces.	Póngame (tres) piezas. *pon*·ga·me (tres) *pye*·thas
79c I'd like (six) slices.	Póngame (seis) pedazos. *pon*·ga·me (seys) pe·*da*·thos
79d I'd like (two) kilos.	Póngame (dos) kilos. *pon*·ga·me (dos) *kee*·los
79e I'd like (200) grams.	Póngame (doscientos) gramos. *pon*·ga·me (dos·*thyen*·tos) *gra*·mos
half a dozen	una media docena oo·na *me*·dya do·*the*·na
half a kilo	un medio kilo oon *me*·dyo *kee*·lo
a kilo	un kilo oon *kee*·lo
a bottle (of ...)	una botella (de ...) oo·na bo·*te*·lya (de ...)
a jar	una jarra oo·na *kha*·ra
a packet	un paquete oon pa·*ke*·te
(just) a little	(sólo) un poquito (*so*·lo) oon po·*kee*·to
many	muchos/as **m/f** *moo*·chos/as
(a bit) more	(un poco) más (oon *po*·ko) mas

FOOD · SELF-CATERING

🔊 LISTEN FOR

Eso es (un manchego).	*e·so es (oon man·che·go)*	That's (a manchego).
Eso es (cinco euros).	*e·so es (theen·ko e·oo·ros)*	That's (five euros).
¿Algo más?	*al·go mas*	Anything else?

some	algunos/as m/f *al·goo·nos/as*
less	menos *me·nos*
that one	ése *e·se*
this	esto *es·to*
Enough!	¡Basta! *ba·sta*

For food items, see the **menu decoder** (p190) and the **dictionary**.

Cooking

cooked	cocido/a m/f *ko·thee·do/a*
dried	seco/a m/f *se·ko/a*
fresh	fresco/a m/f *fres·ko/a*
frozen	congelado/a m/f *kon·khe·la·do/a*
raw	crudo/a m/f *kroo·do/a*
smoked	ahumado/a m/f *a·oo·ma·do/a*

Could I please borrow a/an ...?	¿Me puede prestar un/una ...? m/f
	me *pwe*·de pres·*tar* oon/*oo*·na ...
Where's a/an ...?	¿Dónde hay un/una ...? m/f
	don·de ai oon/*oo*·na ...

bottle opener	abrebotellas m	a·bre·bo·*te*·lyas
can opener	abrelatas m	a·bre·*la*·tas
chopping board	tabla f para cortar	*tab*·la *pa*·ra kor·*tar*
corkscrew	sacacorchos m	sa·ka·*kor*·chos
cup	taza f	*ta*·tha
fork	tenedor m	te·ne·*dor*
frying pan	sartén f	sar·*ten*
glass	vaso m	*va*·so
knife	cuchillo m	koo·*chee*·lyo
plate	plato m	*pla*·to
saucepan	cazo m	*ka*·tho
spoon	cuchara f	koo·*cha*·ra
toaster	tostadora f	tos·ta·*do*·ra

For more cooking terminology, see the **dictionary**.

Vegetarian & Special Meals

KEY PHRASES

Do you have vegetarian food?	¿Tienen comida vegetariana?	*tye*·nen ko·*mee*·da ve·khe·ta·*rya*·na
Could you prepare a meal without ...?	¿Me puede preparar una comida sin ...?	me *pwe*·de pre·pa·*rar* oo·na ko·*mee*·da seen ...
I'm allergic to ...	Soy alérgico/a a ... m/f	soy a·*ler*·khee·ko/a a ...

Special Diets & Allergies

I'm vegetarian.	Soy vegetariano/a. m/f soy ve·khe·ta·*rya*·no/a
I'm on a special diet.	Estoy a régimen especial. es·*toy* a re·*khee*·men es·pe·*thyal*
80a I'm allergic to ...	Soy alérgico a ... m soy a·*ler*·khee·ko a ...
80b I'm allergic to ...	Soy alérgica a ... f soy a·*ler*·khee·ka a ...
80c I'm allergic to dairy produce.	Soy alérgico a los productos lácteos. m soy a·*ler*·khee·ko a los pro·*dook*·tos *lak*·te·os
80d I'm allergic to dairy produce.	Soy alérgica a los productos lácteos. f soy a·*ler*·khee·ka a los pro·*dook*·tos *lak*·te·os

81a	I'm allergic to MSG.	Soy alérgico al glutamato monosódico. m soy a·*ler*·khee·ko al gloo·ta·*ma*·to mo·no·so·dee·ko
81b	I'm allergic to MSG.	Soy alérgica al glutamato monosódico. f soy a·*ler*·khee·ka al gloo·ta·*ma*·to mo·no·so·dee·ko
81c	I'm allergic to nuts.	Soy alérgico a las nueces. m soy a·*ler*·khee·ko a las *nwe*·thes
81d	I'm allergic to nuts.	Soy alérgica a las nueces. f soy a·*ler*·khee·ka a las *nwe*·thes
81e	I'm allergic to seafood.	Soy alérgico a los mariscos. m soy a·*ler*·khee·ko a los ma·*rees*·kos
81f	I'm allergic to seafood.	Soy alérgica a los mariscos. f soy a·*ler*·khee·ka a los ma·*rees*·kos

Ordering Food

82a	Is there a vegetarian restaurant near here?	¿Hay un restaurante vegetariano por aquí? ai oon res·tow·*ran*·te ve·khe·ta·*rya*·no por a·*kee*
	Do you have vegetarian food?	¿Tienen comida vegetariana? *tye*·nen ko·*mee*·da ve·khe·ta·*rya*·na
	Do you have halal food?	¿Tienen comida halal? *tye*·nen ko·*mee*·da a·*lal*
	Do you have kosher food?	¿Tienen comida kosher? *tye*·nen ko·*mee*·da *ko*·sher

🔊 LISTEN FOR

¿Puede comer ...?	*pwe·de ko·mer ...* Can you eat ...?
Le preguntaré al cocinero.	*le pre·goon·ta·re al ko·thee·ne·ro* I'll check with the cook.
Todo lleva (carne).	*to·do lye·va (kar·ne)* It all has (meat) in it.

Do you have vegan food?	¿Tienen comida vegetariana estricta? *tye·nen ko·mee·da ve·khe·ta·rya·na es·trik·ta*
I don't eat red meat.	No como carne roja. *no ko·mo kar·ne ro·kha*
Is it cooked in/with butter?	¿Esta cocinado en/con mantequilla? *es·ta ko·thee·na·do en/kon man·te·kee·lya*
82b Could you prepare a meal without eggs?	¿Me puede preparar una comida sin huevo? *me pwe·de pre·pa·rar oo·na ko·mee·da seen we·vo*
82c Could you prepare a meal without meat stock?	¿Me puede preparar una comida sin caldo de carne? *me pwe·de pre·pa·rar oo·na ko·mee·da seen kal·do de kar·ne*
Could you prepare a meal without ...?	¿Me puede preparar una comida sin ...? *me pwe·de pre·pa·rar oo·na ko·mee·da seen ...*
Is this ...?	¿Esto es ...? *es·to es ...*

A

Menu
— DECODER —
léxico culinario

This miniguide to Spanish cuisine lists dishes and ingredients in Spanish alphabetical order (see **alphabet**, p12). Spanish nouns have their gender indicated by ⓜ or ⓕ. If it's a plural noun, you'll also see pl.

~ A ~

acebuche ⓜ a·the·*boo*·che wild olive
acedía ⓕ a·the·*dee*·a plaice/flounder
aceite ⓜ a·*they*·te oil
— de girasol de khee·ra·*sol* sunflower oil
— de oliva de o·*lee*·va olive oil
— de oliva virgen extra de o·*lee*·va *veer*·khen eks·tra extra virgin olive oil
aceituna ⓕ a·they·*too*·na olive
— negra *ne*·gra black olive
— verde *ver*·de green olive
ácido/a ⓜ/ⓕ a·*thee*·do/a tart (flavour)
adobo ⓜ a·*do*·bo marinade
agrios ⓜ pl a·gryos citrus fruits
aguacate ⓜ a·gwa·*ka*·te avocado
aguaturma ⓕ a·gwa·*toor*·ma Jerusalem artichoke
ajiaco ⓜ a·*khya*·ko spicy potato dish
ajoaceite ⓜ a·kho·a·*they*·te garlic & oil sauce • garlic mayonnaise
ajoharina ⓕ a·kho·a·*ree*·na potatoes stewed in garlic sauce
(al) ajoarriero (al) a·kho·a·*rye*·ro 'mule-driver's garlic' – anything cooked in a sauce of onions, garlic & chilli

ala ⓕ a·la (chicken) wing
alajú ⓜ a·la·*khoo* honey & almond cake
albaricoque ⓜ al·ba·ree·*ko*·ke apricot
— seco *se*·ko dried apricot
albóndigas ⓕ pl al·*bon*·dee·gas meatballs
— de pescado de pes·*ka*·do fish balls
alcachofas ⓕ pl al·ka·*cho*·fas artichokes
— guisadas a la española gee·*sa*·das a la es·pa·*nyo*·la artichokes in wine
— rellenas re·*lye*·nas stuffed artichokes
alcaparra ⓕ al·ka·*pa*·ra caper
alioli ⓕ a·lee·o·*lee* garlic mayonnaise
almejas ⓕ pl al·*me*·khas clams – superb eaten raw
— a la marinera a la ma·ree·*ne*·ra clams in white wine
— al horno al *or*·no baked clams
almendrado ⓜ al·men·*dra*·do almond cake or biscuit • chocolate covered ice cream bar
almendras ⓕ pl al·*men*·dras almonds
alubia ⓕ a·*loo*·bya haricot bean

B

anacardo ⓜ a·na·*kar*·do cashew nut
anchoas ⓕ pl an·*cho*·as anchovies – mostly eaten fresh, grilled or fried
angelote ⓜ an·khe·*lo*·te monkfish
anguila ⓕ an·*gee*·la adult eel
angulas ⓕ pl an·*goo*·las baby eels – prized as a delicacy, they resemble vermicelli
— en all i pebre en al ee *pe*·bre baby eels with pepper & garlic
apio ⓜ a·pyo celery
arándano a·*ran*·da·no blueberry
arenque ⓜ a·*ren*·ke herring
— ahumado a·oo·*ma*·do kipper
arroz ⓜ a·*roth* rice
— a la Alcireña a la al·thee·re·nya baked rice dish
— abanda (de València) a·*ban*·da (de va·*len*·thya) fish paella
— con leche kon *le*·che rice pudding
— con pollo kon *po*·lyo chicken & rice
— integral een·te·*gral* brown rice
— marinera ma·ree·*ne*·ra seafood & rice
— salvaje sal·*va*·khe wild rice
asadillo ⓜ a·sa·*dee*·lyo roasted red capsicums
asados ⓜ pl a·*sa*·dos roast meats
atún ⓜ a·*toon* tuna – often served marinated & raw
— al horno al or·no baked tuna
avellana ⓕ a·ve·*lya*·na hazelnut
aves ⓕ pl a·ves poultry
azúcar ⓜ a·*thoo*·kar sugar

~ B ~

bacalao ⓜ ba·ka·*low* cod – usually salted & dried
— a la vizcaína a la veeth·ka·ee·na cod with chillies & capsicums
— del convento del kon·*ven*·to cod with potatoes & spinach in broth
bacón ⓜ ba·*kon* bacon
barbo ⓜ *bar*·bo red mullet

barra ⓕ *ba*·ra long stick of bread
batata ⓕ ba·*ta*·ta sweet potato
beicon ⓜ *bey*·kon streaky bacon rashers
berberechos ⓜ pl ber·be·*re*·chos cockles
— en vinagre en vee·*na*·gre cockles in vinegar
berenjenas ⓕ pl be·ren·*khe*·nas eggplants
— a la mallorquina a la ma·lyor·*kee*·na eggplants with garlic mayonnaise
— con setas kon *se*·tas eggplants with mushrooms
berza ⓕ *ber*·tha cabbage
— a la andaluza a la an·da·*loo*·tha cabbage & meat hotpot
besugo ⓜ be·*soo*·go red bream
— a la Donostiarra a la do·nos·*tya*·ra barbecued red bream with garlic & paprika
— estilo San Sebastián es·*tee*·lo san se·bas·*tyan* barbecued red bream with garlic & paprika
bienmesabe ⓜ byen·me·*sa*·be sponge cake, egg & almond confection
bisbe ⓜ *bees*·be black & white blood sausage
bistec ⓜ bees·*tek* steak
— con patatas kon pa·*ta*·tas steak with chips
bizcocha ⓕ *manchega* beeth·*ko*·cha man·*che*·ga cake soaked in milk, sugar, vanilla & cinnamon
bizcocho ⓜ beeth·*ko*·cho sponge cake
— de almendra de al·*men*·dra almond cake
— de avellana de a·ve·*lya*·na hazelnut cake
bizcochos ⓜ pl **borrachos** beeth·*ko*·chos bo·*ra*·chos cake soaked in liqueur
bocadillo ⓜ bo·ka·*dee*·lyo bread roll with a filling

C

bocas ① pl **de la isla** *bo·*kas de la *ees·*la large crab claws
bogavante ⓜ bo·ga·*van·*te lobster
bollo ⓜ *bo·*lyo crusty bread roll
bonito ⓜ bo·*nee·*to white fleshy tuna
boquerón ⓜ bo·ke·*ron* whitebait
boquerones ⓜ pl bo·ke·*ro·*nes anchovies marinated in wine vinegar
— fritos *free·*tos fried anchovies
brama ① *bra·*ma sea bream
bróculi ⓜ *bro·*ko·lee broccoli
budín de atún boo·*deen* de a·*toon* baked tuna pudding
bull ⓜ **de atún** bool de a·*toon* rabbit with garlic & tuna boiled with potatoes
buñuelitos ⓜ pl boo·nywe·*lee·*tos small cheese or ham fritters
— de San José de san kho·*se* lemon & vanilla crepes
buñuelo ⓜ boo·*nywe·*lo fried pastry
burrida ① **de ratjada** boo·*ree·*da de rat·*kha·*da fish soup with almonds
butifarra ① **(blanca)** boo·tee·*fa·*ra (*blan·*ka) cured pork sausage
— con setas kon se·tas Catalan sausage with mushrooms

~ C ~

caballa ① ka·*ba·*lya mackerel
cabra ① *ka·*bra goat
cabracho ⓜ ka·*bra·*cho scorpion fish • mullet
cacahuete ⓜ ka·ka·*we·*te peanut
cachelos ⓜ pl ka·*che·*los potatoes with spicy sausage & pork
cádiz ⓜ *ka·*deeth fresh goats' milk cheese
calabacín ⓜ ka·la·ba·*theen* zucchini
calabaza ① ka·la·*ba·*tha pumpkin
calamares ⓜ pl ka·la·*ma·*res calamari – popular fried or stuffed
— fritos a la romana *free·*tos a la ro·*ma·*na squid rings fried in batter
— rellenos re·*lye·*nos stuffed squid

calçots ⓜ pl kal·*sots* spring onion-like vegetables chargrilled and eaten with a **romesco** dipping sauce
caldeirada ① kal·dey·*ra·*da salted cod & potatoes in a paprika sauce • fish soup
caldereta ① kal·de·*re·*ta stew
— asturiana as·too·*rya·*na fish stew
— de cordero de kor·*de·*ro lamb stew
caldillo ⓜ **de perro** kal·*dee·*lyo de pe·*rro* 'puppy dog soup' – stew of onions, fresh fish & orange juice
caldo ⓜ *kal·*do broth • clear soup • stock
— al estilo del Mar Menor al es·*tee·*lo del mar me·*nor* fish stew from the Mar Menor
— gallego ga·*lye·*go broth with haricot beans, ham & sausage
callos ⓜ pl *ka·*lyos tripe
camarones fritos ⓜ pl ka·ma·ro·nes *free·*tos deep-fried prawns
canagroc ka·na·*grok* mushroom
cañaillas ① pl **de la Isla** ka·*nyay·*lyas de la *ees·*la boiled sea snails
canelones ⓜ pl ka·na·*lo·*nes squares of pasta for making cannelloni
— con espinaca kon es·pee·*na·*ka cannelloni with spinach, anchovies & bechamel
— con pescado kon pes·*ka·*do cannelloni with cod, eggs & mushrooms
canapés ⓜ pl **de fiambres** ka·na·*pes* de fee·*am·*bres mini hors d'oeuvres with ham, anchovies or cheese
cangrejo ⓜ kan·*gre·*kho large-clawed crab usually eaten steamed or boiled
cantalupo ⓜ kan·ta·*loo·*po cantaloupe
canutillos ⓜ pl ka·noo·*tee·*lyos cream biscuits

capones ⓜ pl **de Villalba** ka·po·nes de vee·*lyal*·ba Christmas dish of chicken marinated in brandy

caracoles ⓕ ka·ra·ko·les snails

caramelos ⓜ pl ka·ra·me·los caramels • confection

cardos ⓜ pl **fritos** kar·dos free·tos fried thistles

carne ⓕ *kar*·ne meat

— de membrillo de mem·*bree*·lyo quince 'cheese'

— molida mo·lee·da minced meat

cassolada ⓕ ka·so·*la*·da potato & vegetable stew with bacon & ribs

castaña ⓕ kas·*ta*·nya chestnut

caviar ⓜ ka·*vyar* caviar

caza ⓕ *ka*·tha game

cazón ⓕ ka·*thon* dogfish or shark with a sweet scallop-like flavour

cazuelitas ⓕ pl **de langostinos San Rafael** ka·thwe·*lee*·tas de lan·gos·*tee*·nos san ra·fa·*el* baked rice with seafood

cebolla ⓕ the·*bo*·lya onion

cecina ⓕ the·*thee*·na cured meat

cerdo ⓜ *ther*·do pork

cereales ⓜ pl the·re·*a*·les cereal

cereza ⓕ the·*re*·tha cherry

— silvestre seel·*ves*·tre wild cherry

ciervo ⓜ *thyer*·vo deer

cigala ⓕ thee·*ga*·la crayfish

ciruela ⓕ thee·*rwe*·la plum

— pasa *pa*·sa prune

civet ⓜ **de llebre** see·*vet* de *le*·bre hare stew

cochifrito ⓜ **de cordero** ko·chee·*free*·to de kor·*de*·ro lamb fried with garlic & lemon

cochinillo ⓜ ko·chee·*nee*·lyo suckling pig

— asado a·*sa*·do roast suckling pig

— de pelotas de pe·*lo*·tas meatball stew

coco ⓜ *ko*·ko coconut

codornices ⓕ pl **a la plancha** ko·dor·*nee*·thes a la *plan*·cha grilled quail

codorniz ⓕ ko·dor·*neeth* quail

— con pimientos kon pee·*myen*·tos capsicums stuffed with quail

col ⓕ kol cabbage

— lombarda lom·*bar*·da red cabbage

coles ⓕ pl **de bruselas** *ko*·les de broo·*se*·las Brussels sprouts

coliflor ⓕ ko·lee·*flor* cauliflower

conejo ⓜ ko·*ne*·kho rabbit

— de monte de *mon*·te wild rabbit

coquina ⓕ ko·*kee*·na large clam

corazón ⓜ ko·ra·*thon* heart

cordero ⓜ kor·*de*·ro lamb

— al chilindrón al chee·leen·*dron* lamb in tomato & capsicum sauce

— con almendras kon al·*men*·dras lamb in almond sauce

costillas ⓕ pl kos·*tee*·lyas ribs

crema ⓕ *kre*·ma cream

— catalana ka·ta·*la*·na creme brulee

— de espinacas de es·pee·*na*·kas cream of spinach soup

— de naranja de na·*ran*·kha orange cream dessert

— de San José de san kho·*se* egg custard flavoured with cinnamon

— de verduras de ver·*doo*·ras cream of vegetable soup

crocante ⓜ kro·*kan*·te ice cream with chopped nuts & chocolate

~ CH ~

chalote ⓜ cha·*lo*·te shallot

champiñones ⓜ pl cham·pee·*nyo*·nes cultivated white mushrooms

chanquetes ⓜ pl chan·*ke*·tes whitebait • baby anchovies

(al) chilindrón (al) chee·leen·*dron* cooked in a tomato & red pepper sauce

chipirón ⓜ chee·pee·*ron* baby squid – very popular in the Basque Country

chocolate ⓜ cho·ko·*la*·te chocolate
— **caliente** ka·lee·*en*·te thick hot chocolate
chocos ⓜ pl *cho*·kos squid
chorizo ⓜ cho·*ree*·tho spicy red cooked sausage, similar to salami
— **de Pamplona** de pam·*plo*·na fine-textured, hard chorizo
— **de Salamanca** de sa·la·*man*·ka chunky chorizo from Salamanca
chuletas ⓕ pl choo·*le*·tas chops • cutlets
— **al sarmiento** al sar·*myen*·to chops prepared over wood from vines
— **de buey** de bwey ox chops
— **de cerdo a la aragonesa** de *ther*·do a la a·ra·go·*ne*·sa baked pork chops with wine & onion
churros ⓜ *choo*·ros fried doughnut strips bought from street-sellers or in cafes

~ D ~

de soja de so·kha of/with soya
despojos ⓜ pl des·*po*·khos offal
dorada ⓕ **a la sal** do·*ra*·da a la sal salted sea bream
dulce ⓜ *dool*·the sweet
— **de batata** de ba·*ta*·ta sweet potato pudding from Málaga
dulces ⓜ pl *dool*·thes sweets
— **de las monjas** *dool*·thes de las *mon*·khas confectionery made by nuns & sold in convents or cake shops

~ E ~

embutidos ⓜ pl em·boo·*tee*·dos generic name for cured sausages
empanada ⓕ em·pa·*na*·da savoury pie
— **de carne** de *kar*·ne spicy meat pie
— **de espinaca** de es·pee·*na*·ka spinach pie
empanadilla ⓕ em·pa·na·*dee*·lya small pie, either sweet or savoury

empanado ⓜ em·pa·*na*·do coated in bread crumbs
emparedado ⓜ em·pa·re·*da*·do sandwich
— **de jamón y espárragos** de kha·*mon* ee es·*pa*·ra·gos fried ham & asparagus rolls
empiñonado ⓜ em·pee·nyo·*na*·do small marzipan-filled pastry with pinenuts
en salsa verde en sal·sa ver·de in a parsley & garlic sauce
encurtidos ⓜ pl en·koor·*tee*·dos pickles
ensaimada ⓕ **mallorquina** en·sai·*ma*·da ma·lyor·*kee*·na spiral-shaped bun made with lard
ensalada ⓕ en·sa·*la*·da salad
— **de frutas** de *froo*·tas fruit salad
— **de patatas** de pa·*ta*·tas potato salad
— **del tiempo** del *tyem*·po seasonal salad
— **mixta** *meeks*·ta mixed salad
escaldadillas ⓕ pl es·kal·da·*dee*·lyas dough soaked in orange juice & fried
escalivada ⓕ es·ka·lee·*va*·da roasted red capsicums in olive oil
escalopes ⓜ pl **de ternera rellenos** es·ka·*lo*·pes de ter·*ne*·ra re·*lye*·nos deep fried veal cutlets stuffed with egg & cheese
espaguetis ⓜ pl es·pa·*ge*·tees spaghetti
espárragos ⓜ pl es·*pa*·ra·gos asparagus
— **con dos salsas** kon dos *sal*·sas asparagus & tomato or paprika mayonnaise
— **en vinagreta** en vee·na·*gre*·ta asparagus in vinaigrette
espinacas ⓕ pl es·pee·*na*·kas spinach
— **a la catalana** a la ka·ta·*la*·na spinach with pinenuts & raisins

F

esqueixada ① es·kee·*sha*·da cod dressed with olives, tomato & onion
etxeko kopa e·*che*·ko ko·pa ice cream dessert

~ **F** ~

fabada ① **asturiana** fa·ba·da as·too·*rya*·na stew made with pork, blood sausage & white beans
faisán ⓜ fai·*san* pheasant
faves ① pl **a la catalana** *fa*·ves a la ka·ta·*la*·na broad beans with ham
fiambres ⓜ pl fee·*am*·bres cold meats
— surtidos soor·*tee*·dos selection of cold meats
fideos ⓜ pl fee·de·os pasta noodles
fideua ① fee·de·wa rice or noodles with fish & shellfish
fideus ⓜ pl **a la cassola** fee·de·oos a la ka·so·la Catalan noodle dish
filete ⓜ fee·le·te steak • any boneless slice of meat
— a la parrilla a la pa·ree·lya grilled beef steak
— de ternera de ter·ne·ra veal steak
filloas ① pl fee·*lyo*·as Galician pancakes filled with cream
flan ⓜ flan creme caramel
flaó ① fla·o sweet cheese flan
flor manchega ① flor man·*che*·ga deep-fried sweet wafers
frambuesa ① fram·*bwe*·sa raspberry
frangellos ⓜ pl fran·*khe*·lyos sweet made from cornmeal, milk & honey
fresa ① *fre*·sa strawberry
fricandó ⓜ **de langostinos** free·kan·do de lan·gos·*tee*·nos shrimp in almond sauce
frite ① *free*·te lamb stew, served on festive occasions
fritos ⓜ pl *free*·tos fritters
— con miel kon myel honey-roasted fritters

fritura ① free·*too*·ra mixed fried fish
fruta ① *froo*·ta fruit
— variada va·ree·a·da selection of fresh fruit
frutas ① pl **en almíbar** *froo*·tas en al·*mee*·bar fruit in syrup
frutos ⓜ pl **secos** *froo*·tos se·kos nuts & dried fruit
fuet ① foo·*et* thin pork sausage

~ **G** ~

gachas ① pl **manchegas** ga·chas man·*che*·gas flavoured porridge
galleta ① ga·*lye*·ta biscuit
gambas ① pl *gam*·bas prawns
— a la plancha a la *plan*·cha grilled prawns
— en gabardina en ga·bar·*dee*·na prawns in batter
Gamonedo ⓜ ga·mo·ne·do sharp-tasting cheese, smoked & cured
garbanzos ⓜ pl gar·*ban*·thos chickpeas
— con cebolla kon the·bo·lya chickpeas in onion sauce
— tostados tos·*ta*·dos roasted chickpeas (sold as a snack)
garbure ① gar·boo·re green vegetable soup • pork & ham dish
garúm ① ga·*room* olive & anchovy dip
Gata-Hurdes ga·ta·*oor*·des cheese
gazpacho ⓜ gath·*pa*·cho cold tomato soup
— andaluz an·da·*looz* cold tomato soup with chopped salad vegetables
— pastoril pas·to·*reel* rabbit stew with tomato & garlic
gazpachos ⓜ pl **manchegos** gath·*pa*·chos man·*che*·gos game & vegetable hotpot
Gaztazarra ⓜ gath·ta·*tha*·ra cheese
gitano ⓜ khee·*ta*·no Andalusian chickpea & tripe stew

H

gofio ⓜ *go*-fyo toasted cornmeal or barley

granadilla ⓕ gra-na-*dee*-lya passion fruit

grano ⓜ *gra*-no grain

— largo *lar*-go long-grain (rice)

gratinado ⓜ **de berenjenas** gra-tee-*na*-do de be-ren-*khe*-nas eggplant gratin

Grazalema ⓕ gra-tha-*le*-ma semi-cured sheep's milk cheese

guindilla ⓕ geen-*dee*-lya mild green chilli

guisado ⓜ gee-*sa*-do stew

— de cordero de kor-*de*-ro lamb ragout

— de ternera de ter-*ne*-ra veal ragout

guisante ⓜ gee-*san*-te pea

— seco *se*-ko split pea

— mollar mo-*lyar* snow pea

guisantes ⓜ pl **con jamón a la española** gee-*san*-tes kon kha-*mon* a la es-pa-*nyo*-la pea & ham dish

guisat ⓜ **de marisco** gee-*sat* de ma-*rees*-ko stew made with seafood

guiso ⓜ **de conejo estilo canario** *gee*-so de ko-*ne*-kho es-*tee*-lo ka-*na*-ryo rabbit stew

guiso ⓜ **de rabo de toro** *gee*-so de *ra*-bo de *to*-ro stewed bull's tail with potatoes

~ H ~

habas ⓕ pl *a*-bas broad beans

— a la granadina a la gra-na-*dee*-na broad beans with eggs & ham

— fritas *free*-tas fried broad beans (sold as a snack)

habichuela ⓕ a-bee-*chwe*-la white bean

hamburguesa ⓕ am-boor-*ge*-sa hamburger

harina ⓕ a-*ree*-na flour

— integral een-te-*gral* wholemeal flour

helado ⓜ e-*la*-do ice cream

hígado ⓜ *ee*-ga-do liver

higo ⓜ *ee*-go fig

— seco *se*-ko dried fig

hogaza ⓕ o-*ga*-tha dense, thick-crusted bread

hoja ⓕ **de parra** o-*kha* de *pa*-ra vine leaf

hojaldres ⓜ pl o-*khal*-dres small flaky pastries covered in sugar

hojas ⓕ pl **verdes** o-*khas* *ver*-des green vegetables

hornazo ⓜ or-*na*-tho bread stuffed with sausage

hortalizas ⓕ pl or-ta-*lee*-thas vegetables

huevo ⓜ *we*-vo egg

— cocido ko-*thee*-do boiled egg

— de chocolate de cho-ko-*la*-te chocolate egg

— frito *free*-to fried egg

huevos ⓜ pl *we*-vos egg dishes

— a la flamenca a la fla-*men*-ka baked vegetables with egg & ham

— al estilo Sóller al es-*tee*-lo so-*lyer* fried eggs served with a milk & vegetable sauce

— en salsa agria en *sal*-sa *a*-grya boiled eggs in wine & vinegar

— escalfados es-kal-*fa*-dos poached eggs

— revueltos re-*vwel*-tos scrambled eggs

~ J ~

jabalí ⓜ kha-ba-*lee* wild boar

— con salsa de castaños kon *sal*-sa de kas-*ta*-nyos wild boar in chestnut sauce

jamón ⓜ kha-*mon* ham

— cocido ko-*thee*-do cooked ham

— ibérico ee-*ber*-ik-o ham from the Iberian pig, said to be the best in Spain

— serrano se-*ra*-no cured mountain ham

jengibre ⓜ khen·*gee*·bre ginger
jerez (al) khe·*reth* (al) in a sherry
sauce
judía ⓕ khoo·*dee*·a fresh green
bean • dried kidney bean
judías ⓕ pl **del tío Lucas**
khoo·*dee*·as del *tee*·o *loo*·kas bean
stew with garlic & bacon
judías ⓕ pl **verdes a la castellana**
khoo·*dee*·as *ver*·des a la kas·te·*lya*·na
fried capsicums, garlic & green beans
judiones ⓜ pl **de la granja**
kho·dee·o·nes de la *gran*·kha pork &
bean stew

~ K ~

kiskilla kees·*kee*·lya shrimp (also
spelled **quisquilla**)

~ L ~

langosta ⓕ lan·*gos*·ta lobster
— a la ibicenca a la ee·bee·*then*·ka
lobster with stuffed squid
langostinos ⓜ pl lan·gos·*tee*·nos
king prawns
— a la plancha a la *plan*·cha grilled
king prawns
lavanco ⓜ la·*van*·ko wild duck
lechuga ⓕ le·*choo*·ga lettuce
legumbres ⓕ pl le·*goom*·bres
pulses • vegetables • vegetable
dishes
— secas se·kas dried pulses
leguminosas ⓕ pl
le·goo·mee·*no*·sas legumes
lengua ⓕ *len*·gwa tongue
— a la aragonesa a la a·ra·go·*ne*·sa
tongue in tomato & capsicum sauce
lenguado ⓜ len·*gwa*·do sole
— al chacolí con hongos al
cha·ko·*lee* kon on·gos sole with white
wine & mushrooms
lenguados ⓜ pl **al plato**
len·*gwa*·dos al *pla*·to sole &
mushroom casserole

lenguas ⓕ pl **con salsa de
almendras** *len*·gwas kon *sal*·sa de
al·*men*·dras tongue in almond sauce
lentejas ⓕ pl len·*te*·khas lentils
liebre ⓕ *lye*·bre hare
— con castañas kon kas·*ta*·nyas
hare with chestnuts
— estofada es·to·*fa*·da stewed hare
lima ⓕ *lee*·ma lime
limón ⓜ lee·*mon* lemon
lomo ⓜ *lo*·mo fillet • loin • sirloin
— curado koo·*ra*·do cured pork
sausage
— de cerdo de *ther*·do loin of pork
longaniza ⓕ lon·ga·*nee*·tha chorizo,
long & skinny sausage
lubina ⓕ loo·*bee*·na sea bass
— a la marinera a la ma·ree·*ne*·ra
sea bass in parsley sauce
lucio ⓜ *loo*·thyo pike

~ LL ~

llagostí ⓜ **a l'allioli** lyan·*gos*·tee a
la·lyee·o·lee grilled prawns in garlic
mayonnaise
llenguado ⓜ **a la nyoca** lyen·*gwa*·do
a la *nyo*·ka sole with pine nuts & raisins

~ M ~

macedonia ⓕ **de frutas**
ma·the·*do*·nya de *froo*·tas fruit salad
macedonia ⓕ **de verduras**
ma·the·*do*·nya de ver·*doo*·ras mixed
vegetables
magdalena ⓕ ma·da·*le*·na small
fairy cake to dunk in coffee
magras ⓕ pl *ma*·gras fried eggs,
ham, cheese & tomato
maíz ⓜ ma·*eeth* maize • corn
— tierno *tyer*·no sweetcorn
mandarina ⓕ man·da·*ree*·na
tangerine • mandarin
mango ⓜ *man*·go mango
manitas ⓕ pl **de cerdo** ma·*nee*·tas
de *ther*·do pig's trotters

M

manitas ⓕ pl **de cordero** ma·nee·tas de kor·de·ro leg of lamb

manteca ⓕ man·te·ka lard

mantecado ⓜ man·te·ka·do a soft lard biscuit • dairy ice cream

mantequilla ⓕ man·te·kee·lya butter

— sin sal seen sal unsalted butter

manzana ⓕ man·tha·na apple

manzanas ⓕ **asadas** man·tha·nas a·sa·das baked apples

margarina ⓕ mar·ga·ree·na margarine

marinera (a la) ma·ree·ne·ra (a la) cooked or served in a white wine sauce

mariscos ⓜ ma·rees·kos shellfish • seafood

marmitako mar·mee·ta·ko fresh tuna & potato casserole

marrano ⓜ ma·ra·no pork

mar y cel ⓜ mar ee sel dish of sausages, rabbit, shrimp & angler fish

masa ⓕ ma·sa pastry (dough)

mayonesa ⓕ ma·yo·ne·sa mayonnaise

medallones ⓜ pl **de merluza** me·da·lyo·nes de mer·loo·tha hake steaks

mejillones ⓜ pl me·khee·lyo·nes mussels

— al vino blanco al vee·no blan·ko mussels in white wine

— con salsa kon sal·sa mussels with tomato sauce

mel ⓕ **i mató** mel ee ma·to dessert of curd cheese with honey

melocotón ⓜ me·lo·ko·ton peach

melocotones ⓜ pl **al vino** me·lo·ko·to·nes al vee·no peaches in red wine

melón ⓜ me·lon melon

membrillo ⓜ mem·bree·lyo quince

menestra ⓕ me·nes·tra mixed vegetable stew

— de pollo de po·lyo chicken & vegetable stew

merengue ⓜ me·ren·ge meringue

merluza ⓕ mer·loo·tha hake

mermelada ⓕ mer·me·la·da marmalade

mero ⓜ me·ro halibut • grouper • sea bass

miel ⓕ myel honey

— de azahar de a·tha·ar orange blossom honey

— de caña de ka·nya treacle

migas ⓕ pl mee·gas fried cubes of bread with capsicums

— a la aragonesa a la a·ra·go·ne·sa fried bread with bacon rashers in tomato sauce

— mulatas moo·la·tas cubes of bread soaked in chocolate & fried

mojarra ⓕ mo·kha·ra type of sea bream

moje ⓜ **manchego** mo·khe man·che·go cold broth with black olives

mojete ⓜ mo·khe·te dipping sauce for bread, made from potatoes, garlic, tomatoes & paprika

— murciano moor·thya·no fish & capsicum dish

mojo ⓜ mo·kho spicy capsicum sauce

mollejas ⓕ pl mo·lye·khas sweetbreads

mollete ⓜ mo·lye·te soft round bap roll

monas ⓕ pl **de pascua** mo·nas de pas·kwa Easter cakes • figures made of chocolate

mongetes ⓕ pl **seques i butifarra** mon·zhe·tes se·kes ee boo·tee·fa·ra haricot beans with roasted pork sausage

mora ⓕ mo·ra blackberry

moraga ⓕ **de sardina** mo·ra·ga de sar·dee·na fresh anchovies on a spit

morcilla ⓕ mor·thee·lya black pudding, often stewed with beans & vegetables

mortadela ⓕ mor·ta·*de*·la mortadella sausage

morteruelo ⓜ mor·te·*rwe*·lo pate dish containing offal, game & spices

mostachones ⓜ pl mos·ta·*cho*·nes small cakes for dipping in coffee or hot chocolate (also spelled **mostatxones**)

mostaza ⓕ mos·*ta*·tha mustard
— **en grano** en *gra*·no mustard seed

múgil ⓜ *moo*·kheel grey mullet

mujol ⓜ **guisado** moo·*khol* gee·*sa*·do red mullet

mus ⓜ **de chocolate** moos de cho·ko·*la*·te chocolate mousse

muslo ⓜ *moos*·lo (chicken) leg & thigh

N

nabo ⓜ *na*·bo root vegetable • turnip

naranja ⓕ na·*ran*·kha orange

nata ⓕ *na*·ta cream
— **agria** *a*·grya sour cream
— **montada** mon·*ta*·da whipped cream

natillas ⓕ pl na·*tee*·lyas creamy custard dessert
— **de chocolate** de cho·ko·*la*·te chocolate custard

navaja ⓕ na·*va*·kha razor clam

nécora ⓕ *ne*·ko·ra small crab

nueces ⓕ pl *new*·thes nuts

nuez ⓕ nweth nut
— **de América** de a·*me*·ree·ka pecan nut
— **de nogal** de no·*gal* walnut

~ Ñ ~

ñora ⓕ *nyo*·ra sweet red capsicum (usually dried)

~ O ~

oca ⓕ *o*·ka goose

olla ⓕ *o*·lya meat & vegetable stew • cooking pot

oreja ⓕ **de mar** o·*re*·kha de mar abalone

ostiones ⓜ pl **a la gaditana** os·*tyo*·nes a la ga·dee·*ta*·na Cádiz oysters with garlic, parsley & bread crumbs

ostra ⓕ *os*·tra oyster

oveja ⓕ o·*ve*·kha mutton

~ P ~

pá ⓜ **amb oli** pa amb o·*lee* toasted bread with garlic & olive oil

pacana ⓕ pa·*ka*·na pecan

paella ⓕ pa·*e*·lya rice dish which has many regional variations
— **marinera** ma·ree·*ne*·ra paella with fish & seafood
— **zamorana** tha·mo·*ra*·na paella with meat

palitos ⓜ pl **de queso** pa·*lee*·tos de *ke*·so cheese straws

palmera ⓕ pal·*me*·ra leaf-shaped flaky pastry, often coated in chocolate

palomitas ⓕ pl pa·lo·*mee*·tas popcorn

pan ⓜ pan bread
— **aceite** a·*they*·te flat round bread
— **árabe** *a*·ra·be pita bread
— **de Alá** de a·*la* 'Allah's Bread' – dessert
— **de boda** de *bo*·da sculpted bread traditionally made for weddings
— **de centeno** de then·*te*·no rye bread
— **duro** *doo*·ro stale bread, used for toasting & eating with olive oil
— **integral** een·te·*gral* wholemeal bread

panaché ⓜ pa·na·*che* mixed vegetable stew

panallets ⓜ pl pa·na·*lyets* marzipan sweets

panceta ⓕ pan·*the*·ta salt-cured, streaky bacon

panchineta ① pan·chee·*ne*·ta almond tart

panecillo ⑩ pa·ne·*thee*·lyo small bread roll

panojas ① pl **malagueñas** pa·*no*·khas ma·la·*ge*·nyas sardine dish

papas ① **arrugadas** *pa*·pas a·roo·*ga*·das potatoes boiled in their jackets

pargo ⑩ *par*·go sea bream

parrillada ① pa·ree·*lya*·da grilled meat

— de mariscos de ma·*rees*·kos seafood grill

pastel ⑩ pas·*tel* cake

— de boda de *bo*·da wedding cake

— de chocolate de cho·ko·*la*·te chocolate cake

— de cierva de *thyer*·va meat pie

— de cumpleaños de koom·ple·a·*nyos* birthday cake

pastelitos ⑩ pl **de miel** pas·te·*lee*·tos de myel honey fritters

pataco ⑩ pa·*ta*·ko tuna & potato stew

patatas ① pl pa·*ta*·tas potatoes

— a la riojana a la ree·o·*kha*·na potatoes with chorizo & paprika

— alioli a·lee·o·*lee* potatoes in garlic mayonnaise

— bravas *bra*·vas potatoes in spicy tomato sauce

— con chorizo kon cho·*ree*·tho potatoes with chorizo

— estofadas es·to·*fa*·das boiled potatoes

pato ⑩ *pa*·to duck

— a la sevillana a la se·vee·*lya*·na duck with orange sauce

— alcaparrada al·ka·pa·*ra*·da duck with capers & almonds

pavo ⑩ *pa*·vo turkey

pececillos ⑩ pl pe·the·*thee*·lyos small fish

pechina ① pe·*chee*·na scallop

pecho ⑩ *pe*·cho breast of lamb

pechuga ① pe·*choo*·ga breast of poultry

pepinillo ⑩ pe·pee·*nee*·lyo gherkin

pepino ⑩ pe·*pee*·no cucumber

pepitoria ① pe·pee·*to*·rya sauce made with egg & almond

pepitos ⑩ pl pe·*pee*·tos chocolate eclair cakes filled with custard

pera ① *pe*·ra pear

La Peral ① la pe·*ral* soft cheese

perca ① *per*·ka perch

perdices ① pl per·*dee*·thes partridges

— a la manchega a la man·*che*·ga partridge in red wine & capsicums

— con chocolate kon cho·ko·*la*·te partridge with chocolate

perdiz ① per·*deeth* partridge

peregrina ① pe·re·*gree*·na scallop

pericana ① pe·ree·*ka*·na dish of olives, cod oil, capsicums & garlic

perrito ⑩ **caliente** pe·*ree*·to ka·lee·*en*·te hot dog

pescada ① **á galega** pes·*ka*·da a ga·*le*·ga hake fried in olive oil & served with garlic & paprika sauce

pescadilla ① pes·ka·*dee*·lya whiting • young hake

pescaditos ⑩ pl **rebozados** pes·ka·*dee*·tos re·bo·*tha*·dos small fish fried in batter

pescado ⑩ pes·*ka*·do fish

— a l'all cremat a lal kre·*mat* fish in burnt garlic

pescaíto ⑩ **frito** pes·ka·*ee*·to *free*·to tiny fried fish

pestiños ⑩ pl pes·*tee*·nyos honey-coated aniseed pastries, fried with filling

pez ⑩ **espada** peth es·*pa*·da swordfish

— frito *free*·to fried swordfish steaks on a skewer

picada ① pee·*ka*·da mixture of garlic, parsley, toasted almonds & nuts, often used to thicken sauces

picadillo ⓜ pee·ka·*dee*·lyo salad consisting of diced vegetables
— de atún de a·*toon* salad made with diced tuna & capsicums
— de ternera de ter·*ne*·ra minced veal
pichón ⓜ pee·*chon* pigeon
pichones ⓜ pl **asados** pee·*cho*·nes a·*sa*·dos roast pigeons
pilotes ⓕ pl pee·*lo*·tes Catalan meatballs
pimiento ⓜ pee·*myen*·to capsicum
— amarillo a·ma·*ree*·lyo yellow capsicum
— rojo *ro*·kho red capsicum
— verde *ver*·de green capsicum
pimientos ⓜ pl pee·*myen*·tos capsicums (the ones from El Bierzo are especially good)
— a la riojana a la ree·o·*kha*·na roast red capsicum fried in oil & garlic
— al chilindrón al chee·leen·*dron* capsicum casserole
piña ⓕ *pee*·nya pineapple
pinchito ⓜ **moruno** peen·*chee*·to mo·*roo*·no lamb & chicken kebabs
piñón ⓜ pee·*nyon* pinenut
pinta ⓕ *peen*·ta pinto bean
pintada ⓕ peen·*ta*·da guinea fowl
piquillo ⓜ pee·*kee*·lyo sweet & spicy capsicums
pistacho ⓜ pees·*ta*·cho pistachio nut
pisto ⓜ **manchego** *pees*·to man·*che*·go zucchini with capsicum & tomato, fried or stewed
plátano ⓜ *pla*·ta·no banana
pochas ⓕ pl *po*·chas beans
— a la riojana a la ree·o·*kha*·na beans with chorizo in spicy paprika sauce
— con almejas kon al·*me*·khas beans with clams
pollo ⓜ *po*·lyo chicken
— asado a·*sa*·do roast chicken
— con samfaina kon sam·*fai*·na chicken with mixed vegetables

— en escabeche en es·ka·*be*·che marinated chicken
— en salsa de ajo en *sal*·sa de a·*kho* chicken in garlic sauce
— granadina gra·na·*dee*·na chicken with wine & ham
— y langosta ee lan·*gos*·ta chicken with crayfish
polvorón ⓜ pol·vo·*ron* almond shortbread, often eaten at Christmas
pomelo ⓜ po·*me*·lo grapefruit
postre ⓜ *pos*·tre dessert
— de naranja de na·*ran*·kha cream-filled oranges
potaje ⓜ po·*ta*·khe broth
— castellano kas·te·*lya*·no broth with beans & sausages
— de garbanzos de gar·*ban*·thos broth with chickpeas
— de lentejas de len·*te*·khas lentil broth
pote ⓜ **gallego** *po*·te ga·*lye*·go stew
potito ⓜ po·*tee*·to jar of baby food
pringada ⓕ preen·*ga*·da bread dipped in sauce • a marinated sandwich
productos ⓜ pl **biológicos** pro·*dook*·tos bee·o·*lo*·khee·kos organic produce
productos ⓜ pl **del mar** pro·*dook*·tos del mar seafood products
productos ⓜ pl **lácteos** pro·*dook*·tos *lak*·te·os dairy products
puchero ⓜ poo·*che*·ro casserole
pudin ⓜ poo·*din* pudding
puerco ⓜ *pwer*·ko pork
puerro ⓜ *pwe*·ro leek
pulpo ⓜ *pool*·po octopus
—ⓜ a feira *pool*·po a *fey*·ra spicy boiled octopus
punta ⓕ **de diamante** *poon*·ta de dya·*man*·te confection from Valencia
porrusalda ⓕ po·roo·*sal*·da cod & potato stew

Q

~ Q ~

queso ⓜ *ke*·so cheese
— **azul** *a·thool* blue cheese
— **crema** *kre*·ma cream cheese
quisquilla ⓕ kees·*kee*·lya shrimp (also spelled **kiskilla**)

~ R ~

rábano ⓜ *ra*·ba·no radish
rabas ⓕ **en salsa verde** *ra*·bas en *sal*·sa ver·de squid in green sauce
rabassola ⓕ ra·ba·so·la mushroom
rape ⓜ *ra*·pe monkfish
— **a la gallega** a la ga·*lye*·ga monkfish with potatoes & garlic sauce
— **a la Monistrol** a la mo·nees·*trol* monkfish with bechamel sauce
redondo ⓜ re·*don*·do round (of beef)
— **al horno** al or·no roast beef
regañaos ⓜ pl re·ga·*nya*·os pastry stuffed with sardines & red capsicum
relleno ⓜ re·*lye*·no stuffing
remolacha ⓕ re·mo·*la*·cha beetroot
reo ⓜ *re*·o sea trout
repollo ⓜ re·*po*·lyo cabbage
repostería ⓕ re·pos·te·*ree*·a confectionery
requesón ⓜ re·ke·*son* cottage cheese
riñón ⓜ ree·*nyon* kidney
róbalo ⓜ *ro*·ba·lo haddock • sea bass
rodaballo ⓜ ro·da·*ba*·lyo turbot • brill
romero ⓜ ro·*me*·ro rosemary
romesco ⓜ ro·*mes*·ko sweet red capsicum, almond & garlic sauce
rosca ⓕ **de carne** *ros*·ka de *kar*·ne meatloaf wrapped in bacon
rosco ⓜ *ros*·ko small sweet bun
rossejat ⓜ ro·se·*dyat* rice with fish & shellfish

rovellons ⓜ pl **a la plancha** ro·ve·*lyons* a la *plan*·cha garlic mushrooms
ruibarbo ⓜ roo·ee·*bar*·bo rhubarb

~ S ~

salchicha ⓕ sal·*chee*·cha pork sausage
salchichón ⓜ sal·chee·*chon* cured & peppery white sausage
salmón ⓜ sal·*mon* salmon
— **a la ribereña** a la ree·be·re·nya salmon in a cider sauce
— **ahumado** a·oo·*ma*·do smoked salmon
salmonete ⓜ sal·mo·*ne*·te red mullet
salmorejo ⓜ sal·mo·re·kho thick gazpacho soup made from tomato, bread, olive oil, vinegar, garlic & green capsicum
— **de Córdoba** de *kor*·do·ba gazpacho soup made with more vinegar than usual
salpicón ⓜ sal·pee·*kon* fish or meat salad
salsa ⓕ *sal*·sa sauce
— **alioli** a·lee·o·lee garlic & olive oil vinaigrette • garlic mayonnaise
— **de holandesa** de o·lan·*de*·sa hollandaise sauce
— **de mayonesa** de ma·yo·*ne*·sa mayonnaise sauce
— **de tomate** de to·*ma*·te tomato sauce
— **inglesa** een·*gle*·sa Worcestershire sauce
— **tártara** *tar*·ta·ra tartar sauce
— **verde** *ver*·de parsley & garlic sauce
samfaina ⓕ sam·*fai*·na grilled vegetable sauce
sancocho ⓜ san·*ko*·cho fish dish served with potatoes
sandía ⓕ san·*dee*·a watermelon

sándwich ⓜ *san*·weech sandwich
— **mixto** *meeks*·to toasted ham &
cheese sandwich
sanocho ⓜ **canario** sa·*no*·cho
ka·*na*·ryo baked monkfish with
potatoes
sardinas ⓕ sar·*dee*·nas sardines
— **a la parrilla** a la pa·*ree*·lya
sardines grilled
— **en cazuela** en ka·*thwe*·la sardines
served in a clay pot
sargo ⓜ *sar*·go bream
sepia ⓕ *se*·pya cuttlefish
sesos ⓜ pl *se*·sos brains
setas ⓕ pl *se*·tas wild mushrooms
— **a la kashera** a la ka·*she*·ra
sauteed wild mushrooms
— **rellenas** re·*lye*·nas mushrooms
stuffed
sofrit pagés ⓜ so·*freet* pa·*zhes*
vegetable stew
sofrito ⓜ so·*free*·to fried tomato
sauce
soja ⓕ *so*·kha soya bean
soldaditos ⓜ pl **de Pavía**
sol·da·*dee*·tos de pa·*vee*·a cod
fritters
solomillo ⓜ so·lo·*mee*·lyo fillet
sopa ⓕ *so*·pa soup
— **del día** del *dee*·a soup of the day
sopas ⓕ pl **de leche** *so*·pas de
le·che pieces of bread soaked in milk
& cinnamon
sopas ⓕ pl **engañadas** *so*·pas
en·ga·*nya*·das soup made from
capsicum, onion shoots, vinegar, figs
& grapes
sorbete ⓜ sor·*be*·te sorbet
sorroputún ⓜ so·ro·poo·*toon* tuna
casserole
suizo ⓜ *swee*·tho sugared bun
sukaldi soo·*kal*·dee beef stew
suquet ⓜ soo·*ket* clams in almond
sauce
suquet de peix ⓜ soo·*ket* de peysh
fish stew

suspiros ⓜ pl **de monja**
soos·*pee*·ros de mon·*kha* 'nun's
sighs' – custard sweets

~ T ~

tallarines ⓜ pl ta·lya·*ree*·nes pasta
noodles
tarta ⓕ *tar*·ta cake • tart
— **de almendra** de al·*men*·dra
almond tart
— **de manzana** de man·*tha*·na
apple tart
tartaleta ⓕ tar·ta·*le*·ta tartlet
tartaletas ⓕ pl **de huevos**
revueltos tar·ta·*le*·tas de *we*·vos
re·*vwel*·tos scrambled egg tartlets
ternera ⓕ ter·*ne*·ra veal
— **a la sevillana** a la se·vee·*lya*·na
veal served with wine & olives
— **en cazuela con berenjenas** en
ka·*thwe*·la kon be·ren·*khe*·nas veal &
eggplant casserole
tocino ⓜ to·*thee*·no salted pork •
bacon
— **del cielo** del *thye*·lo creamy
dessert made with egg yolk & sugar,
with a caramel topping
tocrudo ⓜ to·*kroo*·do 'everything
raw'– salad of meat, garlic, onion &
green capsicum
tomate ⓜ to·*ma*·te tomatoes
— **(de) pera** (de) *pe*·ra plum tomato
— **frito** *free*·to tinned tomato sauce
tomates ⓜ pl to·*ma*·tes
— **enteros y pelados** en·*te*·ros ee
pe·*la*·dos tinned whole tomatoes
— **rellenos de atún** re·*lye*·nos de
a·*toon* tomatoes stuffed with tuna
toro ⓜ *to*·ro bull meat
torrefacto ⓜ to·re·*fak*·to
dark-roasted coffee beans
torrija ⓕ to·*ree*·kha French toast
torta ⓕ *tor*·ta pie • tart • flat bread
— **de aceite** de a·*they*·te sweet, flat
cake or biscuit made with oil

U

— **pascualina** pas·kwa·*lee*·na spinach & egg pie, eaten at Easter

tortilla ① tor·*tee*·lya omelette

— **española** es·pa·*nyo*·la potato & onion omelette

— **francesa** fran·*the*·sa plain omelette

tortillas ① pl **de camarones** tor·*tee*·lyas de ka·ma·*ro*·nes shrimp fritters

tortita ① tor·*tee*·ta waffle

tostada ① tos·*ta*·da toasted bread

tocino ⓜ to·*thee*·no bacon

tripas ① pl *tree*·pas intestines • guts

trucha ① *troo*·cha trout

— **a la marinera** a la ma·ree·*ne*·ra trout in a white wine sauce

truchas ① pl *troo*·chas trout

— **a la navarra** a la na·*va*·ra trout with ham

— **con vino y romero** kon *vee*·no ee ro·*me*·ro trout with red wine & rosemary

trufa ① *troo*·fa truffle

— **tarta** *tar*·ta chocolate truffle cake

tumbet (de peix) ⓜ toom·*bet* (de peysh) vegetable souffle, sometimes containing fish

turrón ⓜ too·*ron* Spanish nougat

~ U ~

uva ① *oo*·va grape

— **de corinto** de ko·*reen*·to currant

— **pasa** *pa*·sa raisin

— **sultana** sool·*ta*·na sultana

~ V ~

vacuno ⓜ va·*koo*·no beef

venado ⓜ ve·*na*·do venison

verduras ① ver·*doo*·ras vegetables

vieira ① vee·*ey*·ra scallop

villagodio ⓜ vee·*lya*·go·dyo large steak

vinagre ⓜ vee·*na*·gre vinegar

visita ① vee·*see*·ta almond cake

~ Y ~

yemas ① pl *ye*·mas small round cakes • egg whites

yogur ⓜ yo·*goor* yoghurt

~ Z ~

zanahoria ① tha·na·o·*rya* carrot

zarangollo ⓜ tha·ran·go·*lyo* fried zucchini

zarzamora ① thar·tha·*mo*·ra blackberry

zarzuela ① **de mariscos** thar·*thwe*·la de ma·*rees*·kos spicy shellfish stew

zarzuela ① **de pescado** thar·*thwe*·la de pes·*ka*·do fish in almond sauce

zurrukutano ⓜ thoo·roo·koo·*ta*·no cod & green capsicum soup

Dictionary

ENGLISH *to* SPANISH

inglés–español

Nouns in the dictionary have their gender indicated by ⓜ or ⓕ. If it's a plural noun, you'll also see pl. Where a word that could be either a noun or a verb has no gender indicated, it's a verb.

A

(to be) able poder po·*der*
aboard a bordo a·*bor*·do
abortion aborto ⓜ a·*bor*·to
about sobre *so*·bre
above arriba a·*ree*·ba
abroad en el extranjero en el eks·tran·*khe*·ro
accept aceptar a·thep·*tar*
accident accidente ⓜ ak·thee·*den*·te
accommodation alojamiento ⓜ a·lo·kha·*myen*·to
across a través a tra·*ves*
activist activista ⓜ&ⓕ ak·tee·*vees*·ta
acupuncture acupuntura ⓕ a·koo·poon·*too*·ra
adaptor adaptador ⓜ a·dap·ta·*dor*
address dirección ⓕ dee·rek·*thyon*
administration administración ⓕ ad·mee·nees·tra·*thyon*
admission price precio ⓜ de entrada *pre*·thyo de en·*tra*·da
admit admitir ad·mee·*teer*
adult adulto ⓜ a·*dool*·to
advertisement anuncio ⓜ a·*noon*·thyo
advice consejo ⓜ kon·*se*·kho
aerobics aeróbic ⓜ ai·ro·beek

Africa África ⓕ a·*free*·ka
after después de des·*pwes* de
aftershave bálsamo de aftershave *bal*·sa·mo de *ahf*·ter·sha·eev
again otra vez *o*·tra veth
age edad ⓕ e·*da*
aggressive agresivo/a ⓜ/ⓕ a·gre·*see*·vo/a
agree estar de acuerdo es·*tar* de a·*kwer*·do
agriculture agricultura ⓕ a·gree·kul·*too*·ra
AIDS SIDA ⓜ *see*·da
air aire ⓜ *ai*·re
air mail por vía aérea por *vee*·a a·*e*·re·a
air-conditioned con aire acondicionado kon *ai*·re a·kon·dee·thyo·*na*·do
air-conditioning aire ⓜ acondicionado *ai*·re a·kon·dee·thyo·*na*·do
airline aerolínea ⓕ ai·ro·*lee*·nya
airport aeropuerto ⓜ ai·ro·*pwer*·to
airport tax tasa ⓕ del aeropuerto *ta*·sa del ai·ro·*pwer*·to
alarm clock despertador ⓜ des·per·ta·*dor*
alcohol alcohol ⓜ al·*kol*
all todo *to*·do
allergy alergia ⓕ a·*ler*·khya

B

allow permitir per·mee·*teer*
almonds almendras ① pl al·*men*·dras
almost casi *ka*·see
alone solo/a ⑩/① *so*·lo/a
already ya ya
also también tam·*byen*
altar altar ⑩ al·*tar*
altitude altura ① al·*too*·ra
always siempre *syem*·pre
amateur amateur ⑩&① a·ma·*ter*
ambassador embajador/embajadora ⑩/① em·ba·kha·*dor*/em·ba·kha·*do*·ra
among entre *en*·tre
anarchist anarquista ⑩&① a·nar·*kees*·ta
ancient antiguo/a ⑩/① an·*tee*·gwo/a
and y ee
angry enfadado/a ⑩/① en·fa·*da*·do/a
animal animal ⑩ a·nee·*mal*
ankle tobillo ⑩ to·*bee*·lyo
answer respuesta ① res·*pwes*·ta
answering machine contestador ⑩ automático kon·tes·ta·*dor* ow·to·*ma*·tee·ko
ant hormiga ① or·*mee*·ga
anthology antología ① an·to·lo·*khee*·a
antibiotics antibióticos ⑩ pl an·tee·byo·*tee*·kos
antinuclear antinuclear an·tee·noo·kle·*ar*
antique antigüedad ① an·tee·gwe·*da*
antiseptic antiséptico ⑩ an·tee·*sep*·tee·ko
any alguno/a ⑩/① al·*goo*·no/a
appendix apéndice ⑩ a·*pen*·dee·the
apple manzana ① man·*tha*·na
appointment cita ① *thee*·ta
apricot albaricoque ⑩ al·ba·ree·*ko*·ke
archaeological arqueológico/a ⑩/① ar·keo·lo·khee·ko/a
architect arquitecto/a ⑩/① ar·kee·*tek*·to/a
architecture arquitectura ① ar·kee·tek·*too*·ra
argue discutir dees·koo·*teer*

arm brazo ⑩ *bra*·tho
army ejército ⑩ e·*kher*·thee·to
arrest detener de·te·*ner*
arrivals llegadas ① pl lye·*ga*·das
arrive llegar lye·*gar*
art arte ⑩ *ar*·te
art gallery museo ⑩ de arte moo·se·o de *ar*·te
artichoke alcachofa ① al·ka·*cho*·fa
artist artista ⑩&① ar·*tees*·ta
ashtray cenicero ⑩ the·nee·*the*·ro
Asia Asia ① *a*·sya
ask (a question) preguntar pre·goon·*tar*
ask (for something) pedir pe·*deer*
aspirin aspirina ① as·pee·*ree*·na
assault asalto ⑩ a·*sal*·to
asthma asma ⑩ *as*·ma
athletics atletismo ⑩ at·le·*tees*·mo
atmosphere atmósfera ① at·*mos*·fe·ra
aubergine berenjena ① be·ren·*khe*·na
aunt tía ① *tee*·a
Australia Australia ① ow·*stra*·lya
Australian Rules football fútbol ⑩ australiano *foot*·bol ow·stra·*lya*·no
automatic teller machine cajero ⑩ automático ka·*khe*·ro ow·to·ma·*tee*·ko
autumn otoño ⑩ o·*to*·nyo
avenue avenida ① a·ve·*nee*·da
avocado aguacate ⑩ a·gwa·*ka*·te

B

B&W (film) blanco y negro *blan*·ko ee *ne*·gro
baby bebé ⑩ be·*be*
baby food comida ① de bebé ko·*mee*·da de be·*be*
baby powder talco ⑩ *tal*·ko
babysitter canguro ⑩ kan·*goo*·ro
back (of body) espalda ① es·*pal*·da
back (of chair) respaldo ⑩ res·*pal*·do
backpack mochila ① mo·*chee*·la
bacon tocino ⑩ to·*thee*·no
bad malo/a ⑩/① *ma*·lo/a
bag bolso ⑩ *bol*·so

B

baggage equipaje ⓜ e·kee·*pa*·khe

baggage allowance ⓜ límite de equipaje *lee*·mee·te de e·kee·*pa*·khe

baggage claim recogida ① de equipajes re·ko·*khee*·da de e·kee·*pa*·khes

bakery panadería ① pa·na·de·*ree*·a

balance (account) saldo ⓜ *sal*·do

balcony balcón ⓜ bal·*kon*

ball pelota ① pe·*lo*·ta

ballet ballet ⓜ ba·*le*

banana plátano ⓜ *pla*·ta·no

band grupo ⓜ *groo*·po

bandage vendaje ⓜ ven·*da*·khe

band-aids tiritas ① pl tee·*ree*·tas

bank banco ⓜ *ban*·ko

bank account cuenta ① bancaria *kwen*·ta ban·*ka*·rya

banknotes billetes ⓜ pl (de banco) bee·*lye*·tes (de *ban*·ko)

baptism bautizo ⓜ bow·*tee*·tho

bar bar ⓜ bar

bar (with music) pub ⓜ poob

bar work trabajo ⓜ de camarero/a ⓜ/① tra·*ba*·kho de ka·ma·*re*·ro/a

basket canasta ① ka·*nas*·ta

basketball baloncesto ⓜ ba·lon·*thes*·to

bath bañera ① ba·*nye*·ra

bathing suit bañador ⓜ ba·nya·*dor*

bathroom baño ⓜ *ba*·nyo

battery (car) batería ① ba·te·*ree*·a

battery (small) pila ① *pee*·la

be ser ser · estar es·*tar*

beach playa ① *pla*·ya

bean sprouts brotes ⓜ pl de soja *bro*·tes de *so*·kha

beans judías khoo·*dee*·as

beautiful hermoso/a ⓜ/① er·*mo*·so/a

beauty salon salón ⓜ de belleza sa·*lon* de be·*lye*·tha

because porque *por*·ke

bed cama ① *ka*·ma

bedding ropa ① de cama *ro*·pa de *ka*·ma

bedroom habitación ① a·bee·ta·*thyon*

bee abeja ① a·*be*·kha

beef carne ① de vaca *kar*·ne de *va*·ka

beer cerveza ① ther·*ve*·tha

beetroot remolacha ① re·mo·*la*·cha

before antes *an*·tes

beggar mendigo/a ⓜ/① men·*dee*·go/a

begin comenzar ko·men·*thar*

behind detrás de de·*tras* de

Belgium Bélgica ① *bel*·khee·ka

below abajo a·*ba*·kho

best lo mejor lo me·*khor*

bet apuesta ① a·*pwes*·ta

better mejor me·*khor*

between entre *en*·tre

bible biblia ① *bee*·blya

bicycle bicicleta ① bee·thee·*kle*·ta

big grande *gran*·de

bike bici ① *bee*·thee

bike chain cadena ① de bici ka·*de*·na de *bee*·thee

bike path camino ⓜ de bici ka·*mee*·no de *bee*·thee

bill cuenta ① *kwen*·ta

biodegradable biodegradable bee·o·de·gra·*da*·ble

biography biografía ① bee·o·gra·*fee*·a

bird pájaro ⓜ *pa*·kha·ro

birth certificate partida ① de nacimiento par·*tee*·da de na·thee·*myen*·to

birthday cumpleaños ⓜ koom·ple·a·*nyos*

birthday cake pastel ⓜ de cumpleaños pas·*tel* de koom·ple·a·*nyos*

biscuit ① galleta ga·*lye*·ta

bite (dog) mordedura ① mor·de·*doo*·ra

bite (food) bocado ⓜ bo·*ka*·do

bite (insect) picadura ① pee·ka·*doo*·ra

black negro/a ⓜ/① *ne*·gro/a

blanket manta ① *man*·ta

bleed sangrar san·*grar*

blind ciego/a ⓜ/① *thye*·go/a

B

blister ampolla ⓕ am·po·lya
blocked atascado/a ⓜ/ⓕ
a·tas·ka·do/a
blood sangre ⓕ san·gre
blood group grupo ⓜ sanguíneo
groo·po san·gee·neo
blood pressure presión ⓕ arterial
pre·syon ar·te·ryal
blood test análisis ⓜ de sangre
a·na·lee·sees de san·gre
blue azul a·thool
board (ship, etc) embarcarse
em·bar·kar·se
boarding house pensión ⓕ pen·syon
boarding pass tarjeta ⓕ de em·
barque tar·khe·ta de em·bar·ke
bone hueso ⓜ we·so
book libro ⓜ lee·bro
book (make a reservation) reservar
re·ser·var
booked out lleno/a ⓜ/ⓕ lye·no/a
bookshop librería ⓕ lee·bre·ree·a
boots botas ⓕ pl bo·tas
border frontera ⓕ fron·te·ra
boring aburrido/a ⓜ/ⓕ
a·boo·ree·do/a
borrow tomar prestado to·mar
pres·ta·do
botanic garden jardín ⓜ botánico
khar·deen bo·ta·nee·ko
both ambos/as ⓜ/ⓕ pl am·bos/bas
bottle botella ⓕ bo·te·lya
bottle opener abrebotellas ⓜ
a·bre·bo·te·lyas
bowl bol ⓜ bol
box caja ⓕ ka·kha
boxer shorts calzones ⓜ pl
kal·tho·nes
boxing boxeo ⓜ bo·se·o
boy chico ⓜ chee·ko
boyfriend novio ⓜ no·vyo
bra sujetador ⓜ soo·khe·ta·dor
brakes frenos ⓜ pl fre·nos
branch (office) sucursal ⓕ
soo·koor·sal
brandy coñac ⓜ ko·nyak

brave valiente va·lyen·te
bread pan ⓜ pan
bread (brown) pan moreno pan
mo·re·no
bread rolls bollos bo·lyos
bread (rye) pan de centeno pan de
then·te·no
bread (sourdough) pan de masa fer·
mentada pan de ma·sa fer·men·ta·da
bread (white) pan blanco pan blan·ko
bread (wholemeal) pan integral pan
een·te·gral
break romper rom·per
break down descomponerse
des·kom·po·ner·se
breakfast desayuno ⓜ des·a·yoo·no
breasts senos ⓜ pl se·nos
breathe respirar res·pee·rar
brewery fábrica ⓕ de cerveza
fab·ree·ka de ther·ve·tha
bribe soborno ⓜ so·bor·no
bribe sobornar so·bor·nar
bridge puente ⓜ pwen·te
briefcase maletín ⓜ ma·le·teen
brilliant cojonudo/a ⓜ/ⓕ
ko·kho·noo·do/a
bring traer tra·er
brochure folleto ⓜ fo·lye·to
broken roto/a ⓜ/ⓕ ro·to/a
bronchitis bronquitis ⓜ
bron·kee·tees
brother hermano ⓜ er·ma·no
brown marrón ma·ron
bruise cardenal ⓜ kar·de·nal
brussels sprouts coles ⓜ pl de
Bruselas ko·les de broo·se·las
bucket cubo ⓜ koo·bo
Buddhist budista ⓜ&ⓕ boo·dees·ta
buffet buffet ⓜ boo·fe
bug bicho ⓜ bee·cho
build construir kons·troo·eer
building edificio ⓜ e·dee·fee·thyo
bull toro ⓜ to·ro
bullfight corrida ⓕ ko·ree·da
bullring plaza ⓕ de toros pla·tha de
to·ros
bum (of body) culo ⓜ koo·lo

burn quemadura ① ke·ma·*doo*·ra
bus autobús ⓜ ow·to·*boos*
bus (intercity) autocar ⓜ ow·to·*kar*
bus station estación de autobuses/autocares ① es·ta·*thyon* de ow·to·*boo*·ses/ow·to·*ka*·res
bus stop parada ① de autobús pa·*ra*·da de ow·to·*boos*
business negocios ⓜ pl ne·*go*·thyos
business class clase ① preferente *kla*·se pre·fe·*ren*·te
business person comerciante ⓜ&① ko·mer·*thyan*·te
busker artista callejero/a ⓜ/① ar·*tees*·ta ka·lye·*khe*·ro/a
busy ocupado/a ⓜ/① o·koo·*pa*·do/a
but pero *pe*·ro
butcher's shop carnicería ① kar·nee·the·*ree*·a
butter mantequilla ① man·te·*kee*·lya
butterfly mariposa ① ma·ree·*po*·sa
buttons botones ⓜ pl bo·*to*·nes
buy comprar kom·*prar*

C

cabbage col kol
cable cable ⓜ *ka*·ble
cable car teleférico ⓜ te·le·*fe*·ree·ko
cafe café ⓜ ka·*fe*
cake pastel ⓜ pas·*tel*
cake shop pastelería ① pas·te·le·*ree*·a
calculator calculadora ① kal·koo·la·*do*·ra
calendar calendario ⓜ ka·len·*da*·ryo
calf ternero ⓜ ter·*ne*·ro
camera cámara ① (fotográfica) *ka*·ma·ra (fo·to·*gra*·fee·ka)
camera shop tienda ① de fotografía *tyen*·da de fo·to·gra·*fee*·a
camp acampar a·kam·*par*
camping store tienda ① de cámping *tyen*·da de *kam*·peen
campsite cámping ⓜ *kam*·peen
can lata ① *la*·ta
can (be able) poder po·*der*

can opener abrelatas ⓜ a·bre·*la*·tas
Canada Canadá ① ka·na·*da*
cancel cancelar kan·the·*lar*
cancer cáncer ⓜ *kan*·ther
candle vela ① *ve*·la
cantaloupe cantalupo ⓜ kan·ta·*loo*·po
capsicum (red/green) pimiento ⓜ rojo/verde pee·*myen*·to *ro*·kho/*ver*·de
car coche ⓜ *ko*·che
car hire alquiler ⓜ de coche al·kee·*ler* de *ko*·che
car owner's title papeles ⓜ pl del coche pa·*pe*·les del *ko*·che
car registration matrícula ① ma·*tree*·koo·la
caravan caravana ① ka·ra·*va*·na
cards cartas ① pl *kar*·tas
care (about something) preocuparse por pre·o·koo·*par*·se por
care (for someone) cuidar de kwee·*dar* de
caring bondadoso/a ⓜ/① bon·da·*do*·so/a
carpark aparcamiento ⓜ a·par·ka·*myen*·to
carpenter carpintero/a ⓜ/① kar·peen·*te*·ro/a
carrot zanahoria ① tha·na·o·rya
carry llevar lye·*var*
carton cartón ⓜ kar·*ton*
cash dinero ⓜ en efectivo dee·*ne*·ro en e·fek·*tee*·vo
cash (a cheque) cambiar (un cheque) kam·*byar* (oon *che*·ke)
cash register caja ① registradora *ka*·kha re·khees·tra·*do*·ra
cashew nut anacardo ⓜ a·na·*kar*·do
cashier caja ① *ka*·kha
casino casino ⓜ ka·*see*·no
cassette casete ⓜ ka·*se*·te
castle castillo ⓜ kas·*tee*·lyo
casual work trabajo ⓜ eventual tra·*ba*·kho e·ven·*twal*
cat gato/a ⓜ/① *ga*·to/a
cathedral catedral ① ka·te·*dral*

Catholic católico/a ⓜ/ⓕ ka·to·lee·ko/a
cauliflower coliflor ⓕ ko·lee·*flor*
caves cuevas ⓕ pl *kwe*·vas
CD cómpact ⓜ *kom*·pakt
celebrate (an event) celebrar the·le·*brar*
celebration celebración ⓕ the·le·bra·*thyon*
cemetery cementerio ⓜ the·men·*te*·ryo
cent centavo ⓜ then·*ta*·vo
centimetre centímetro ⓜ then·*tee*·me·tro
central heating calefacción ⓕ central ka·le·fak·*thyon* then·*tral*
centre centro ⓜ *then*·tro
ceramic cerámica ⓕ the·*ra*·mee·ka
cereal cereales ⓜ pl the·re·*a*·les
certificate certificado ⓜ ther·tee·fee·*ka*·do
chair silla ⓕ *see*·lya
champagne champán ⓜ cham·*pan*
chance oportunidad ⓕ o·por·too·nee·*da*
change (money) cambio ⓜ *kam*·byo
change cambiar kam·*byar*
changing rooms vestuarios ⓜ pl ves·*twa*·ryos
charming encantador/encantadora ⓜ/ⓕ en·kan·ta·*dor*/en·kan·ta·*do*·ra
chat up ligar lee·*gar*
cheap barato/a ⓜ/ⓕ ba·*ra*·to/a
cheat tramposo/a ⓜ/ⓕ tram·po·*so*/a
check revisar re·vee·*sar*
check (bank) cheque ⓜ *che*·ke
check-in facturación ⓕ de equipajes fak·too·ra·*thyon* de e·kee·pa·khes
checkpoint control ⓜ kon·*trol*
cheese queso ⓜ *ke*·so
chef cocinero ⓜ ko·thee·*ne*·ro
chemist (person) farmacéutico/a ⓜ/ⓕ far·ma·the·oo·ti·ko/a
chemist (shop) farmacia ⓕ far·*ma*·thya
chess ajedrez ⓜ a·khe·*dreth*
chess board tablero ⓜ de ajedrez ta·*ble*·ro de a·khe·*dreth*

chest pecho ⓜ *pe*·cho
chewing gum chicle ⓜ *chee*·kle
chicken pollo ⓜ *po*·lyo
chicken breast pechuga ⓕ pe·*choo*·ga
chickpeas garbanzos ⓜ pl gar·*ban*·thos
child niño/a ⓜ/ⓕ *nee*·nyo/a
child seat asiento ⓜ de seguridad para bebés a·*syen*·to de se·goo·ree·*da* pa·ra be·*bes*
childminding service guardería ⓕ gwar·de·*ree*·a
children hijos ⓜ pl ee·khos
chilli guindilla ⓕ geen·*dee*·lya
chilli sauce salsa ⓕ de guindilla *sal*·sa de geen·*dee*·lya
chocolate chocolate ⓜ cho·ko·*la*·te
choose escoger es·ko·*kher*
Christian cristiano/a ⓜ/ⓕ krees·*tya*·no/a
Christian name nombre ⓜ de pila *nom*·bre de *pee*·la
Christmas Navidad ⓕ na·vee·*da*
Christmas Eve Nochebuena ⓕ no·che·*bwe*·na
church iglesia ⓕ ee·*gle*·sya
cider sidra ⓕ *see*·dra
cigar cigarro ⓜ thee·*ga*·ro
cigarette cigarillo ⓜ thee·ga·*ree*·lyo
cigarette lighter mechero ⓜ me·*che*·ro
cigarette machine máquina ⓕ de tabaco *ma*·kee·na de ta·*ba*·ko
cigarette paper papel ⓜ de fumar pa·*pel* de foo·*mar*
cinema cine ⓜ *thee*·ne
circus circo ⓜ *theer*·ko
citizenship ciudadanía ⓕ thyu·da·da·*nee*·a
city ciudad ⓕ thyu·*da*
city centre centro ⓜ de la ciudad *then*·tro de la thyu·*da*
city walls murallas ⓕ pl moo·*ra*·lyas
civil rights derechos civiles ⓜ pl de·*re*·chos thee·*vee*·les
classical clásico/a ⓜ/ⓕ *kla*·see·ko/a

clean limpio/a ⓜ/ⓕ *leem*·pyo/a
cleaning limpieza ⓕ leem·*pye*·tha
client cliente/a ⓜ/ⓕ klee·*en*·te/a
cliff acantilado ⓜ a·kan·tee·*la*·do
climb subir soo·*beer*
cloak capote ⓜ ka·*po*·te
cloakroom guardarropa ⓜ
gwar·da·*ro*·pa
clock reloj ⓜ re·*lokh*
close cerrar the·*rar*
closed cerrado/a ⓜ/ⓕ the·*ra*·do/a
clothes line cuerda ⓕ para tender la
ropa *kwer*·da *pa*·ra ten·*der* la *ro*·pa
clothing ropa ⓕ *ro*·pa
clothing store tienda ⓕ de ropa
tyen·da de *ro*·pa
cloud nube ⓕ *noo*·be
cloudy nublado noo·*bla*·do
clove (garlic) diente ⓜ (de ajo)
dyen·te (de a·*kho*)
cloves clavos ⓜ pl *kla*·vos
clutch embrague ⓕ em·*bra*·ge
coach entrenador/entrenadora ⓜ/ⓕ
en·tre·na·*dor*/en·tre·na·*do*·ra
coast costa ⓕ *kos*·ta
cocaine cocaína ⓕ ko·ka·*ee*·na
cockroach cucaracha ⓕ koo·ka·*ra*·cha
cocoa cacao ⓜ ka·*kow*
coconut coco ⓜ *ko*·ko
codeine codeína ⓕ ko·de·*ee*·na
coffee café ⓜ ka·*fe*
coins monedas ⓕ pl mo·*ne*·das
cold frío/a ⓜ/ⓕ *free*·o/a
cold (illness) resfriado ⓜ
res·*free*·a·do
colleague colega ⓜ&ⓕ ko·*le*·ga
collect call llamada ⓕ a cobro revertido lya·*ma*·da a *ko*·bro re·ver·*tee*·do
college residencia ⓕ de estudiantes
re·see·*den*·thya de es·too·*dyan*·tes
colour color ⓜ ko·*lor*
colour (film) película ⓕ en color
pe·*lee*·koo·la en ko·*lor*
comb peine ⓜ *pey*·ne
come venir ve·*neer*
come (arrive) llegar lye·*gar*

comedy comedia ⓕ ko·*me*·dya
comfortable cómodo/a ⓜ/ⓕ
ko·mo·do/a
communion comunión ⓕ
ko·moo·*nyon*
communist comunista ⓜ&ⓕ
ko·moo·*nees*·ta
companion compañero/a ⓜ/ⓕ
kom·pa·*nye*·ro/a
company compañía ⓕ kom·pa·*nyee*·a
compass brújula ⓕ *broo*·khoo·la
complain quejarse ke·*khar*·se
computer ordenador ⓜ or·de·na·*dor*
computer game juegos ⓜ pl de
ordenador *khwe*·gos de or·de·na·*dor*
concert concierto ⓜ kon·*thyer*·to
conditioner acondicionador ⓜ
a·kon·dee·thyo·na·*dor*
condoms condones ⓜ pl kon·*do*·nes
confession confesión ⓕ kon·fe·*syon*
confirm confirmar kon·feer·*mar*
connection conexión ⓕ ko·ne·*ksyon*
conservative conservador/
conservadora ⓜ/ⓕ kon·ser·va·*dor*/
kon·ser·va·*do*·ra
constipation estreñimiento ⓜ
es·tre·nyee·*myen*·to
consulate consulado ⓜ kon·soo·*la*·do
contact lenses lentes ⓜ pl de contacto *len*·tes de kon·*tak*·to
contraceptives anticonceptivos ⓜ pl
an·tee·kon·thep·*tee*·vos
contract contrato ⓜ kon·*tra*·to
convenience store negocio ⓜ de
artículos básicos ne·*go*·thyo de
ar·*tee*·koo·los *ba*·see·kos
convent convento ⓜ kon·*ven*·to
cook cocinero ⓜ ko·thee·*ne*·ro
cook cocinar ko·thee·*nar*
cookie galleta ⓕ ga·*lye*·ta
corn maíz ⓜ ma·*eeth*
corn flakes copos ⓜ pl de maíz
ko·pos de ma·*eeth*
corner esquina ⓕ es·*kee*·na
corrupt corrupto/a ⓜ/ⓕ ko·*roop*·to/a
cost costar kos·*tar*

cottage cheese requesón ⓜ re·ke·*son*
cotton algodón ⓜ al·go·*don*
cotton balls bolas ① pl de algodón *bo*·las de al·go·*don*
cough tos ① tos
cough medicine jarabe ⓜ kha·*ra*·be
count contar kon·*tar*
counter mostrador ⓜ mos·tra·*dor*
country país ⓜ pa·*ees*
countryside campo ⓜ *kam*·po
coupon cupón ⓜ koo·*pon*
courgette calabacín ⓜ ka·la·ba·*theen*
court (tennis) pista ① *pees*·ta
cous cous cus cus ⓜ koos koos
cover charge precio ⓜ del cubierto *pre*·thyo del koo·*byer*·to
cow vaca ① *va*·ka
crab cangrejo ⓜ kan·*gre*·kho
crackers galletas ① pl saladas ga·*lye*·tas sa·*la*·das
crafts artesanía ① ar·te·sa·*nee*·a
crash choque ⓜ *cho*·ke
crazy loco/a ⓜ/① *lo*·ko/a
cream (food) crema *kre*·ma
cream (moisturising) crema ① hidratante *kre*·ma ee·dra·*tan*·te
cream cheese queso ⓜ crema *ke*·so *kre*·ma
creche guardería ① gwar·de·*ree*·a
credit card tarjeta ① de crédito tar·*khe*·ta de *kre*·dee·to
cricket críquet ⓜ *kree*·ket
crop cosecha ① ko·*se*·cha
crowded abarrotado/a ⓜ/① a·ba·ro·*ta*·do/a
cucumber pepino ⓜ pe·*pee*·no
cuddle abrazo ⓜ a·*bra*·tho
cup taza ① *ta*·tha
cupboard armario ⓜ ar·*ma*·ryo
currency exchange cambio ⓜ (de dinero) *kam*·byo (de dee·*ne*·ro)
current (electricity) corriente ① ko·*ryen*·te
current affairs informativo ⓜ een·for·ma·*tee*·vo
curry curry ⓜ *koo*·ree

curry powder curry ⓜ en polvo *koo*·ree en *pol*·vo
customs aduana ① a·*dwa*·na
cut cortar kor·*tar*
cutlery cubiertos ⓜ pl koo·*byer*·tos
CV historial ⓜ profesional ees·to·*ryal* pro·fe·syo·*nal*
cycle andar en bicicleta an·*dar* en bee·thee·*kle*·ta
cycling ciclismo ⓜ thee·*klees*·mo
cyclist ciclista ⓜ&① thee·*klees*·ta
cystitis cistitis ① thees·*tee*·tees

D

dad papá ⓜ pa·*pa*
daily diariamente dya·rya·*men*·te
dance bailar bai·*lar*
dancing bailar ⓜ bai·*lar*
dangerous peligroso/a ⓜ/① pe·lee·*gro*·so/a
dark oscuro/a ⓜ/① os·*koo*·ro/a
date citarse thee·*tar*·se
date (a person) salir con sa·*leer* kon
date (time) fecha ① *fe*·cha
date of birth fecha ① de nacimiento *fe*·cha de na·thee·*myen*·to
daughter hija ① *ee*·kha
dawn alba ① *al*·ba
day día ⓜ *dee*·a
day after tomorrow pasado mañana pa·*sa*·do ma·*nya*·na
day before yesterday anteayer an·te·a·*yer*
dead muerto/a ⓜ/① *mwer*·to/a
deaf sordo/a ⓜ/① *sor*·do/a
deal (cards) repartir re·par·*teer*
decide decidir de·thee·*deer*
deep profundo/a ⓜ/① pro·*foon*·do/a
deforestation deforestación ① de·fo·res·ta·*thyon*
degree título ⓜ *tee*·too·lo
delay demora ① de·*mo*·ra
delirious delirante de·lee·*ran*·te
deliver entregar en·tre·*gar*
democracy democracia ① de·mo·*kra*·thya

demonstration manifestación ①
ma·nee·fes·ta·thyon

Denmark Dinamarca ①
dee·na·mar·ka

dental floss hilo ⓜ dental ee·lo
den·tal

dentist dentista ⓜ&① den·tees·ta

deny negar ne·gar

deodorant desodorante ⓜ
de·so·do·ran·te

depart salir de sa·leer de

department store grande almacen
ⓜ gran·de al·ma·then

departure salida ① sa·lee·da

deposit depósito ⓜ de·po·see·to

descendant descendiente ⓜ
des·then·dyen·te

desert desierto ⓜ de·syer·to

design diseño ⓜ dee·se·nyo

destination destino ⓜ des·tee·no

destroy destruir des·troo·eer

detail detalle de·ta·lye

diabetes diabetes ① dee·a·be·tes

diaper pañal ⓜ pa·nyal

diaphragm diafragma ⓜ
dee·a·frag·ma

diarrhoea diarrea ① dee·a·re·a

diary agenda ① a·khen·da

dice (die) dados ⓜ pl da·dos

dictionary diccionario ⓜ
deek·thyo·na·ryo

die morir mo·reer

diet régimen ⓜ re·khee·men

different diferente ⓜ/① dee·fe·ren·te

difficult difícil ⓜ/① dee·fee·theel

dining car vagón ⓜ restaurante
va·gon res·tow·ran·te

dinner cena ① the·na

direct directo/a ⓜ/① dee·rek·to/a

direct-dial marcar directo mar·kar
dee·rek·to

director director/directora ⓜ/①
dee·rek·tor/dee·rek·to·ra

dirty sucio/a ⓜ/① soo·thyo/a

disabled minusválido/a ⓜ/①
mee·noos·va·lee·do/a

disco discoteca ① dees·ko·te·ka

discount descuento ⓜ des·kwen·to

discover descubrir des·koo·breer

discrimination discriminación ①
dees·kree·mee·na·thyon

disease enfermedad ① en·fer·me·da

disk disco ⓜ dees·ko

dive bucear boo·the·ar

diving submarinismo ⓜ
soob·ma·ree·nees·mo

diving equipment equipo ⓜ de
inmersión ① e·kee·po de een·mer·syon

dizzy mareado/a ⓜ/① ma·re·a·do/a

do hacer a·ther

doctor doctor/doctora ⓜ/① dok·tor/
dok·to·ra

documentary documental ⓜ
do·koo·men·tal

dog perro/a ⓜ/① pe·ro/a

dole paro ⓜ pa·ro

doll muñeca ① moo·nye·ka

domestic flight vuelo ⓜ doméstico
vwe·lo do·mes·tee·ko

donkey burro ⓜ boo·ro

door puerta ① pwer·ta

dope droga ① dro·ga

double doble ⓜ/① do·ble

double bed cama ① de matrimonio
ka·ma de ma·tree·mo·nyo

double room habitación ① doble
a·bee·ta·thyon do·ble

down abajo a·ba·kho

downhill cuesta abajo kwes·ta a·ba·kho

dozen docena ① do·the·na

draw dibujar dee·boo·khar

dream soñar so·nyar

dress vestido ⓜ ves·tee·do

dried fruit fruto ⓜ seco froo·to se·ko

drink bebida ① be·bee·da

drink beber be·ber

drive conducir kon·doo·theer

drivers licence carnet ⓜ de conducir
kar·ne de kon·doo·theer

drug droga ① dro·ga

drug addiction drogadicción ①
dro·ga·deek·thyon

E

drug dealer traficante ⓜ de drogas
tra·fee·*kan*·te de *dro*·gas
drums batería ⓕ ba·te·*ree*·a
drumstick (chicken) muslo *moos*·lo
drunk borracho/a ⓜ/ⓕ bo·*ra*·cho/a
dry secar se·*kar*
duck pato ⓜ *pa*·to
dummy (pacifier) chupete ⓜ
choo·*pe*·te

E

each cada *ka*·da
ear oreja ⓕ o·*re*·kha
early temprano tem·*pra*·no
earn ganar ga·*nar*
earplugs tapones ⓜ pl para los oídos
ta·*po*·nes *pa*·ra los o·*ee*·dos
earrings pendientes ⓜ pl pen·*dyen*·tes
Earth Tierra ⓕ *tye*·ra
earthquake terremoto ⓜ te·re·*mo*·to
east este *es*·te
Easter Pascua ⓕ *pas*·kwa
Easter Week Semana ⓕ Santa
se·*ma*·na *san*·ta
easy fácil *fa*·theel
eat comer ko·*mer*
economy class clase ⓕ turística
kla·se too·*rees*·tee·ka
eczema eczema ⓕ ek·*the*·ma
editor editor/editora ⓜ/ⓕ e·dee·*tor*/
e·dee·*to*·ra
education educación ⓕ
e·doo·ka·*thyon*
eggplant berenjenas ⓕ pl
be·ren·*khe*·nas
egg huevo ⓜ *we*·vo
elections elecciones ⓕ pl
e·lek·*thyo*·nes
electrical store tienda ⓕ de productos eléctricos *tyen*·da de pro·*dook*·tos
e·*lek*·tree·kos
electricity electricidad ⓕ
e·lek·tree·thee·*da*
elevator ascensor ⓜ as·then·*sor*
embarrassed avergonzado/a ⓜ/ⓕ
a·ver·gon·*tha*·do/a

embassy embajada ⓕ em·ba·*kha*·da
emergency emergencia ⓕ
e·mer·*khen*·thya
emotional emocional e·mo·thyo·*nal*
employee empleado/a ⓜ/ⓕ
em·ple·*a*·do/a
employer jefe/a ⓜ/ⓕ *khe*·fe/a
empty vacío/a ⓜ/ⓕ va·*thee*·o/a
end fin ⓜ feen
end acabar a·ka·*bar*
endangered species especies ⓕ pl
en peligro de extinción es·*pe*·thyes en
pe·*lee*·gro de eks·teen·*thyon*
engagement compromiso ⓜ
kom·pro·*mee*·so
engine motor ⓜ mo·*tor*
engineer ingeniero/a ⓜ/ⓕ
een·khe·*nye*·ro/a
engineering ingeniería ⓕ
een·khe·nye·*ree*·a
England Inglaterra ⓕ een·gla·*te*·ra
English inglés ⓜ een·*gles*
enjoy (oneself) divertirse
dee·ver·*teer*·se
enough suficiente ⓜ/ⓕ
soo·fee·*thyen*·te
enter entrar en·*trar*
entertainment guide guía ⓕ del ocio
gee·a del o·*thyo*
envelope sobre ⓜ *so*·bre
environment medio ⓜ ambiente
me·dyo am·*byen*·te
epilepsy epilepsia ⓕ e·pee·*lep*·sya
equal opportunity igualdad ⓕ
de oportunidades ee·gwal·*da* de
o·por·too·nee·*da*·des
equality igualdad ⓕ ee·gwal·*da*
equipment equipo ⓜ e·*kee*·po
escalator escaleras ⓕ pl mecánicas
es·ka·*le*·ras me·*ka*·nee·kas
euro euro ⓜ e·*oo*·ro
Europe Europa ⓕ e·oo·*ro*·pa
euthanasia eutanasia ⓕ
e·oo·ta·*na*·sya
evening noche ⓕ *no*·che
everything todo *to*·do

example ejemplo ⓜ e·*khem*·plo

excellent excelente ⓜ/ⓕ
eks·the·*len*·te

exchange cambio ⓜ *kam*·byo

exchange (money) cambiar kam·*byar*

exchange rate tipo ⓜ de cambio
tee·po de *kam*·byo

exchange (give gifts) regalar
re·ga·*lar*

excluded no incluido no
een·*kloo*·ee·do

exhaust tubo ⓜ de escape *too*·bo de
es·*ka*·pe

exhibit exponer eks·po·*ner*

exhibition exposición ⓕ
eks·po·see·*thyon*

exit salida ⓕ sa·*lee*·da

expensive caro/a ⓜ/ⓕ *ka*·ro/a

experience experiencia ⓕ
eks·pe·*ryen*·thya

express expreso/a ⓜ/ⓕ eks·*pre*·so/a

express mail correo ⓜ urgente
ko·*re*·o oor·*khen*·te

extension (visa) prolongación ⓕ
pro·lon·ga·*thyon*

eye ojo ⓜ o·*kho*

eye drops gotas ⓕ pl para los ojos
go·tas *pa*·ra los o·*khos*

F

fabric tela ⓕ *te*·la

face cara ⓕ *ka*·ra

face cloth toallita ⓕ to·a·*lyee*·ta

factory fábrica ⓕ *fa*·bree·ka

factory worker obrero/a ⓜ/ⓕ
o·*bre*·ro/a

fall caída ⓕ ka·*ee*·da

family familia ⓕ fa·*mee*·lya

family name apellido ⓜ a·pe·*lyee*·do

famous famoso/a ⓜ/ⓕ fa·*mo*·so/a

fan (hand held) abanico ⓜ
a·ba·*nee*·ko

fan (electric) ventilador ⓜ
ven·tee·la·*dor*

fanbelt correa ⓕ del ventilador
ko·*re*·a del ven·tee·la·*dor*

far lejos le·*khos*

farm granja ⓕ *gran*·kha

farmer agricultor/agricultora ⓜ/ⓕ
a·gree·kool·*tor*/a·gree·kool·*to*·ra

fast rápido/a ⓜ/ⓕ *ra*·pee·do/a

fat gordo/a ⓜ/ⓕ *gor*·do/a

father padre ⓜ *pa*·dre

father-in-law suegro ⓜ *swe*·gro

fault falta ⓕ *fal*·ta

faulty defectuoso/a ⓜ/ⓕ
de·fek·*two*·so/a

feed dar de comer dar de ko·*mer*

feel sentir sen·*teer*

feelings sentimientos ⓜ pl
sen·tee·*myen*·tos

fence cerca ⓕ *ther*·ka

fencing esgrima ⓕ es·*gree*·ma

festival festival ⓜ fes·tee·*val*

fever fiebre ⓕ *fye*·bre

few pocos/as ⓜ/ⓕ *po*·kos/as

fiance prometido ⓜ pro·me·*tee*·do

fiancee prometida ⓕ pro·me·*tee*·da

fiction ficción ⓕ feek·*thyon*

field campo ⓜ *kam*·po

fig higo ⓜ *ee*·go

fight pelea ⓕ pe·*le*·a

fight luchar loo·*char*

fill llenar lye·*nar*

fillet filete ⓜ fee·*le*·te

film película ⓕ pe·*lee*·koo·la

film speed sensibilidad ⓕ
sen·see·bee·lee·*da*

filtered con filtro kon *feel*·tro

find encontrar en·kon·*trar*

fine multa ⓕ *mool*·ta

finger dedo ⓜ *de*·do

finish terminar ter·mee·*nar*

fire fuego ⓜ *fwe*·go

firewood leña ⓕ *le*·nya

first primero/a ⓜ/ⓕ pree·*me*·ro/a

first class primera clase pree·*me*·ra
kla·se

first-aid kit maletín ⓜ de primeros
auxilios ma·le·*teen* de pree·*me*·ros
ow·*ksee*·lyos

fish pez ⓜ peth

G

fish (as food) pescado ⓜ pes·ka·do
fish shop pescadería ⓕ
pes·ka·de·ree·a
fishing pesca ⓕ pes·ka
flag bandera ⓕ ban·de·ra
flannel franela ⓕ fra·ne·la
flashlight linterna ⓕ leen·ter·na
flat llano/a ⓜ/ⓕ lya·no/a
flea pulga ⓕ pool·ga
flooding inundación ⓕ
ee·noon·da·thyon
floor suelo ⓜ swe·lo
florist florista ⓜ&ⓕ flo·rees·ta
flour harina ⓕ a·ree·na
flower flor ⓕ flor
flower seller vendedor/vend-
edora ⓜ/ⓕ de flores ven·de·dor/
ven·de·do·ra de flo·res
fly volar vo·lar
foggy brumoso/a ⓜ/ⓕ broo·mo·so
follow seguir se·geer
food comida ⓕ ko·mee·da
food supplies víveres ⓜ pl vee·ve·res
foot pie ⓜ pye
football fútbol ⓜ foot·bol
footpath acera ⓕ a·the·ra
foreign extranjero/a ⓜ/ⓕ
eks·tran·khe·ro/a
forest bosque ⓜ bos·ke
forever para siempre pa·ra syem·pre
forget olvidar ol·vee·dar
forgive perdonar per·do·nar
fork tenedor ⓜ te·ne·dor
fortnight quincena ⓕ keen·the·na
foul sucio/a ⓜ/ⓕ soo·thyo/a
foyer vestíbulo ⓜ ves·tee·boo·lo
fragile frágil fra·kheel
France Francia ⓕ fran·thya
free (not bound) libre lee·bre
free (of charge) gratis gra·tees
freeze helarse e·lar·se
friend amigo/a ⓜ/ⓕ a·mee·go/a
frost escarcha ⓕ es·kar·cha
frozen foods productos congelados
ⓜ pl pro·dook·tos kon·khe·la·dos
fruit fruta ⓕ froo·ta

fruit picking recolección ⓕ de fruta
re·ko·lek·thyon de froo·ta
fry freír fre·eer
frying pan sartén ⓕ sar·ten
full lleno/a ⓜ/ⓕ lye·no/a
full-time a tiempo completo a
tyem·po kom·ple·to
fun diversión ⓕ dee·ver·syon
funeral funeral ⓜ foo·ne·ral
funny gracioso/a ⓜ/ⓕ gra·thyo·so/a
furniture muebles ⓜ pl mwe·bles
future futuro ⓜ foo·too·ro

G

gay gay gai
general general khe·ne·ral
Germany Alemania ⓕ a·le·ma·nya
gift regalo ⓜ re·ga·lo
gig bolo ⓜ bo·lo
gin ginebra ⓕ khee·ne·bra
ginger jengibre ⓜ khen·khee·bre
girl chica ⓕ chee·ka
girlfriend novia ⓕ no·vya
give dar dar
glandular fever fiebre ⓕ glandular
fye·bre glan·doo·lar
glass (material) vidrio ⓜ vee·dryo
glass (drinking) vaso ⓜ va·so
glasses gafas ⓕ pl ga·fas
gloves guantes ⓜ pl gwan·tes
go ir eer
go out with salir con sa·leer kon
go shopping ir de compras eer de
kom·pras
goal gol ⓜ gol
goalkeeper portero/a ⓜ/ⓕ por·te·ro/a
goat cabra ⓕ ka·bra
goat's cheese queso ⓜ de cabra
ke·so de ka·bra
god Dios ⓜ dyos
goggles gafas ⓕ pl de submarinismo
ga·fas de soob·ma·ree·nees·mo
golf ball pelota ⓕ de golf pe·lo·ta
de golf
golf course campo ⓜ de golf kam·po
de golf

good bueno/a ⓜ/ⓕ *bwe*·no/a

government gobierno ⓜ
go·*byer*·no

gram gramo ⓜ *gra*·mo

grandchild nieto/a ⓜ/ⓕ *nye*·to/a

grandfather abuelo ⓜ a·*bwe*·lo

grandmother abuela ⓕ a·*bwe*·la

grapefruit pomelo ⓜ po·*me*·lo

grapes uvas ⓕ pl *oo*·vas

graphic art arte ⓜ gráfico *ar*·te
gra·fee·ko

grass hierba ⓕ *yer*·ba

grave tumba ⓕ *toom*·ba

gray gris grees

great fantástico/a ⓜ/ⓕ
fan·*tas*·tee·ko/a

green verde *ver*·de

greengrocery (shop) verdulería ⓕ
ver·doo·le·*ree*·a

grocer (shopkeeper) verdulero/a
ⓜ/ⓕ ver·doo·le·*ro*/a

grey gris grees

grocery tienda ⓕ de comestibles
tyen·da de ko·mes·*tee*·bles

grow crecer kre·*ther*

g-string tanga ⓕ *tan*·ga

guess adivinar a·dee·vee·*nar*

guide (audio) guía ⓕ audio *gee*·a
ow·dyo

guide (person) guía ⓜ&ⓕ *gee*·a

guide dog perro lazarillo ⓜ *pe*·ro
la·tha·*ree*·lyo

guidebook guía ⓕ *gee*·a

guided tour recorrido ⓜ guiado
re·ko·*ree*·do gee·*a*·do

guilty culpable kool·*pa*·ble

guitar guitarra ⓕ gee·*ta*·ra

gum chicle ⓜ *chee*·kle

gymnastics gimnasia ⓕ rítmica
kheem·*na*·sya *reet*·mee·ka

gynaecologist ginecólogo ⓜ
khee·ne·*ko*·lo·go

H

hair pelo ⓜ *pe*·lo

hairbrush cepillo ⓜ the·*pee*·lyo

hairdresser peluquero/a ⓜ/ⓕ
pe·loo·*ke*·ro/a

halal halal a·*lal*

half medio/a ⓜ/ⓕ *me*·dyo/a

half a litre medio litro ⓜ *me*·dyo
lee·tro

hallucinate alucinar a·loo·thee·*nar*

ham jamón ⓜ kha·*mon*

hammer martillo ⓜ mar·*tee*·lyo

hammock hamaca ⓕ a·*ma*·ka

hand mano ⓕ *ma*·no

handbag bolso ⓜ *bol*·so

handicrafts artesanía ⓕ
ar·te·sa·*nee*·a

handlebar manillar ⓜ ma·nee·*lyar*

handmade hecho a mano *e*·cho a
ma·no

handsome hermoso ⓜ er·*mo*·so

happy feliz fe·*leeth*

harassment acoso ⓜ a·*ko*·so

harbour puerto ⓜ *pwer*·to

hard duro/a ⓜ/ⓕ *doo*·ro/a

hardware store ferretería ⓕ
fe·re·te·*ree*·a

hash hachís ⓜ a·*chees*

hat sombrero ⓜ som·*bre*·ro

have tener te·*ner*

have a cold estar constipado/a ⓜ/ⓕ
es·*tar* kons·tee·*pa*·do/a

have fun divertirse dee·ver·*teer*·se

hay fever alergia ⓕ al polen a·*ler*·khya
al *po*·len

he él el

head cabeza ⓕ ka·*be*·tha

headache dolor ⓜ de cabeza do·*lor*
de ka·*be*·tha

headlights faros ⓜ pl *fa*·ros

health salud ⓕ sa·*loo*

hear oír o·*eer*

hearing aid audífono ⓕ ow·*dee*·fo·no

heart corazón ⓜ ko·ra·*thon*

heart condition condición ⓕ
cardíaca kon·dee·*thyon* kar·*dee*·a·ka

heat calor ⓜ ka·*lor*

heater estufa ⓕ es·*too*·fa

heavy pesado/a ⓜ/ⓕ pe·*sa*·do/a

I

helmet casco ⓜ *kas*·ko
help ayudar a·yoo·*dar*
hepatitis hepatitis ⓕ e·pa·*tee*·tees
her su soo
herbalist herbolario/a ⓜ/ⓕ
er·bo·*la*·ree·o/a
herbs hierbas ⓕ pl *yer*·bas
here aquí a·*kee*
heroin heroína ⓕ e·ro·ee·na
herring arenque ⓜ a·*ren*·ke
high alto/a ⓜ/ⓕ *al*·to/a
high school instituto ⓜ
eens·tee·*too*·to
hike ir de excursión eer de
eks·koor·*syon*
hiking excursionismo ⓜ
eks·koor·syo·*nees*·mo
hiking boots botas ⓕ pl de montaña
bo·tas de mon·*ta*·nya
hiking routes caminos ⓜ pl rurales
ka·*mee*·nos roo·*ra*·les
hill colina ⓕ ko·*lee*·na
Hindu hindú ⓜ&ⓕ een·*doo*
hire alquilar al·kee·*lar*
his su soo
historical histórico/a ⓜ/ⓕ
ees·*to*·ree·ko/a
hitchhike hacer dedo a·*ther* de·do
HIV positive seropositivo/a ⓜ/ⓕ
se·ro·po·see·*tee*·vo/a
hockey hockey ⓜ *kho*·kee
holiday día festivo ⓜ *dee*·a fes·*tee*·vo
holidays vacaciones ⓕ pl
va·ka·*thyo*·nes
homeless sin hogar seen o·*gar*
homemaker ama ⓕ de casa *a*·ma
de *ka*·sa
homosexual homosexual ⓜ&ⓕ
o·mo·sek·*swal*
honey miel ⓕ myel
honeymoon luna ⓕ de miel *loo*·na
de myel
horoscope horóscopo ⓜ
o·*ros*·ko·po
horse caballo ⓜ ka·*ba*·lyo
horse riding equitación ⓕ
e·kee·ta·*thyon*

horseradish rábano ⓜ picante
ra·ba·no pe·*kan*·te
hospital hospital ⓜ os·pee·*tal*
hospitality hostelería ⓕ os·te·le·*ree*·a
hot caliente ka·*lyen*·te
hot water agua caliente ⓜ *a*·gwa
ka·*lyen*·te
hotel hotel ⓜ o·*tel*
house casa ⓕ *ka*·sa
housework trabajo ⓜ de casa
tra·*ba*·kho de *ka*·sa
how cómo *ko*·mo
how much cuánto *kwan*·to
hug abrazo ⓜ a·*bra*·tho
huge enorme e·*nor*·me
human rights derechos ⓜ pl humanos de·*re*·chos oo·*ma*·nos
humanities humanidades ⓕ pl
oo·ma·nee·*da*·des
hungry hambriento/a ⓜ/ⓕ
am·*bryen*·to/a
hungry tener hambre te·*ner* am·bre
hunting caza ⓕ *ka*·tha
hurt dañar da·*nyar*
husband marido ⓜ ma·*ree*·do

I

I yo yo
ice hielo ⓜ *ye*·lo
ice axe piolet ⓜ pyo·*le*
ice cream helado ⓜ e·*la*·do
ice cream parlour heladería ⓕ
e·la·de·*ree*·a
ice hockey hockey ⓜ sobre hielo
kho·kee so·bre *ye*·lo
identification identificación ⓕ
ee·den·tee·fee·ka·*thyon*
identification card carnet ⓜ de
identidad kar·*net* de ee·den·tee·*da*
idiot idiota ⓜ&ⓕ ee·*dyo*·ta
if si see
ill enfermo/a ⓜ/ⓕ en·*fer*·mo/a
immigration inmigración ⓕ
een·mee·gra·*thyon*
important importante eem·por·*tan*·te
in a hurry de prisa de *pree*·sa

in front of enfrente de en·fren·te de
included incluido een·kloo·ee·do
income tax impuesto ⓜ sobre la renta eem·pwes·to so·bre la ren·ta
India India ⓕ een·dya
indicator indicador ⓜ een·dee·ka·dor
indigestion indigestión ⓕ een·dee·khes·tyon
industry industria ⓕ een·doos·trya
infection infección ⓕ een·fek·thyon
inflammation inflamación ⓕ een·fla·ma·thyon
influenza gripe ⓕ gree·pe
ingredient ingrediente ⓜ een·gre·dyen·te
inject inyectarse een·yek·tar·se
injection inyección ⓕ een·yek·thyon
injury herida ⓕ e·ree·da
innocent inocente ee·no·then·te
inside adentro a·den·tro
instructor profesor/profesora ⓜ/ⓕ pro·fe·sor/pro·fe·sor·a
insurance seguro ⓜ se·goo·ro
interesting interesante een·te·re·san·te
intermission descanso ⓜ des·kan·so
international internacional een·ter·na·thyo·nal
internet internet een·ter·net
internet cafe cibercafé thee·ber·ka·fe
interpreter intérprete ⓜ&ⓕ een·ter·pre·te
interview entrevista ⓕ en·tre·vees·ta
invite invitar een·vee·tar
Ireland Irlanda ⓕ eer·lan·da
iron plancha ⓕ plan·cha
island isla ⓕ ees·la
IT informática ⓕ een·for·ma·tee·ka
Italy Italia ⓕ ee·ta·lya
itch picazón ⓕ pee·ka·thon
itemised detallado/a ⓜ/ⓕ de·ta·lya·do/a
itinerary itinerario ⓜ ee·tee·ne·ra·ryo
IUD DIU ⓜ de·ee·oo

J

jacket chaqueta ⓕ cha·ke·ta
jail cárcel ⓕ kar·thel
jam mermelada ⓕ mer·me·la·da
Japan Japón ⓜ kha·pon
jar jarra ⓕ kha·ra
jaw mandíbula ⓕ man·dee·boo·la
jealous celoso/a ⓜ/ⓕ the·lo·so/a
jeans vaqueros ⓜ pl va·ke·ros
jeep yip ⓜ yeep
jet lag jet lag ⓜ dyet lag
jewellery shop joyería ⓕ kho·ye·ree·a
Jewish judío/a ⓜ/ⓕ khoo·dee·o/a
job trabajo ⓜ tra·ba·kho
jockey jockey ⓜ dyo·kee
jogging footing ⓜ foo·teen
joke broma ⓕ bro·ma
joke bromear bro·me·ar
journalist periodista ⓜ&ⓕ pe·ryo·dees·ta
judge juez ⓜ&ⓕ khweth
juice jugo ⓜ khoo·go • zumo ⓜ thoo·mo
jump saltar sal·tar
jumper (sweater) jersey ⓜ kher·say
jumper leads cables ⓜ pl de arranque ka·bles de a·ran·ke

K

ketchup salsa ⓕ de tomate sal·sa de to·ma·te
key llave ⓕ lya·ve
keyboard teclado ⓜ te·kla·do
kick dar una patada dar oo·na pa·ta·da
kick (a goal) meter (un gol) me·ter (oon gol)
kill matar ma·tar
kilogram kilogramo ⓜ kee·lo·gra·mo
kilometre kilómetro ⓜ kee·lo·me·tro
kind amable a·ma·ble
kindergarten escuela ⓕ de párvulos es·kwe·la de par·voo·los
king rey ⓜ rey
kiss beso ⓜ be·so
kiss besar be·sar

L

kitchen cocina ⓕ ko·*thee*·na
kitten gatito/a ⓜ/ⓕ ga·*tee*·to/a
kiwifruit kiwi ⓜ *kee*·wee
knapsack mochila ⓕ mo·*chee*·la
knee rodilla ⓕ ro·*dee*·lya
knife cuchillo ⓜ koo·*chee*·lyo
know (someone) conocer ko·no·*ther*
know (something) saber sa·*ber*
kosher kosher *ko*·sher

L

labourer obrero/a ⓜ/ⓕ o·*bre*·ro/a
lace encaje ⓜ en·*ka*·khe
lager cerveza ⓕ rubia ther·*ve*·tha *roo*·bya
lake lago ⓜ *la*·go
lamb cordero ⓜ kor·*de*·ro
land tierra ⓕ *tye*·ra
landlady propietaria ⓕ pro·pye·*ta*·rya
landlord propietario ⓜ pro·pye·*ta*·ryo
languages idiomas ⓜ pl ee·*dyo*·mas
laptop ordenador ⓜ portátil or·de·na·*dor* por·*ta*·teel
lard manteca ⓕ man·*te*·ka
large grande *gran*·de
late tarde *tar*·de
laugh reírse re·*eer*·se
laundrette lavandería ⓕ la·van·de·*ree*·a
laundry lavadero ⓜ la·va·*de*·ro
law ley ⓕ ley
lawyer abogado/a ⓜ/ⓕ a·bo·*ga*·do/a
leader líder ⓜ&ⓕ *lee*·der
leaf hoja ⓕ o·kha
learn aprender a·pren·*der*
leather cuero ⓜ *kwe*·ro
leave dejar de·*khar*
leave (behind/over) quedar ke·*dar*
lecturer profesor/profesora ⓜ/ⓕ pro·fe·*sor*/pro·fe·*so*·ra
ledge saliente ⓜ sa·*lyen*·te
leek puerro ⓜ *pwe*·ro
left izquierda ⓕ eeth·*kyer*·da
left luggage consigna ⓕ kon·*seeg*·na
left-wing de izquierdas de eeth·*kyer*·das

leg pierna ⓕ *pyer*·na
legal legal le·*gal*
legislation legislación ⓕ le·khees·la·*thyon*
lemon limón ⓜ lee·*mon*
lemonade limonada ⓕ lee·mo·*na*·da
lens objetivo ⓜ ob·khe·*tee*·vo
Lent Cuaresma ⓕ kwa·res·ma
lentils lentejas ⓕ pl len·*te*·khas
lesbian lesbiana ⓕ les·bee·*a*·na
less menos *me*·nos
letter carta ⓕ *kar*·ta
lettuce lechuga ⓕ le·*choo*·ga
liar mentiroso/a ⓜ/ⓕ men·tee·ro·so/a
library biblioteca ⓕ bee·blyo·te·ka
lice piojos ⓜ pl *pyo*·khos
license plate number matrícula ⓕ ma·*tree*·koo·la
lie (not stand) tumbarse toom·*bar*·se
life vida ⓕ *vee*·da
lifejacket chaleco ⓜ salvavidas cha·*le*·ko sal·va·*vee*·das
lift ascensor ⓜ as·then·*sor*
light (weight) leve *le*·ve
light luz ⓕ looth
light bulb bombilla ⓕ bom·*bee*·lya
light meter fotómetro ⓜ fo·*to*·me·tro
lighter encendedor ⓜ en·then·de·*dor*
like gustar(le) goos·*tar*(le)
lime lima ⓕ *lee*·ma
line línea ⓕ *lee*·ne·a
lip balm bálsamo ⓜ de labios *bal*·sa·mo de *la*·byos
lips labios ⓜ pl *la*·byos
lipstick pintalabios ⓜ peen·ta·la·byos
liquor store bodega ⓕ bo·*de*·ga
listen escuchar es·koo·*char*
live (life) vivir vee·*veer*
live (somewhere) ocupar o·koo·*par*
liver hígado ⓜ *ee*·ga·do
lizard lagartija ⓕ la·gar·*tee*·kha
local de cercanías de ther·ka·*nee*·as
lock cerradura ⓕ the·ra·*doo*·ra
lock cerrar the·*rar*
locked cerrado/a ⓜ/ⓕ con llave the·*ra*·do/a kon *lya*·ve

M

lollies caramelos ⓜ pl ka·ra·me·los
long largo/a ⓜ/ⓕ lar·go·a
long-distance a larga distancia a lar·ga dees·tan·thya
look mirar mee·rar
look after cuidar kwee·dar
look for buscar boos·kar
lookout mirador ⓜ mee·ra·dor
lose perder per·der
lost perdido/a ⓜ/ⓕ per·dee·do/a
lost property office oficina ⓕ de objetos perdidos o·fee·thee·na de ob·khe·tos per·dee·dos
loud ruidoso/a ⓜ/ⓕ rwee·do·so/a
love querer ke·rer
lover amante ⓜ&ⓕ a·man·te
low bajo/a ⓜ/ⓕ ba·kho/a
lubricant lubricante ⓜ loo·bree·kan·te
luck suerte ⓕ swer·te
lucky afortunado/a ⓜ/ⓕ a·for·too·na·do/a
luggage equipaje ⓜ e·kee·pa·khe
luggage lockers consigna ⓕ automática kon·seeg·na ow·to·ma·tee·ka
luggage tag etiqueta ⓕ de equipaje e·tee·ke·ta de e·kee·pa·khe
lump bulto ⓜ bool·to
lunch almuerzo ⓜ al·mwer·tho
lungs pulmones ⓜ pl pool·mo·nes
luxury lujo ⓜ loo·kho

M

machine máquina ⓕ ma·kee·na
made of (cotton) hecho a de (algodón) e·cho a de (al·go·don)
magazine revista ⓕ re·vees·ta
magician mago/a ⓜ/ⓕ ma·go/a
mail correo ⓜ ko·re·o
mailbox buzón ⓜ boo·thon
main principal preen·thee·pal
make hacer a·ther
make fun of burlarse de boor·lar·se de
make-up maquillaje ⓜ ma·kee·lya·khe
mammogram mamograma ⓜ ma·mo·gra·ma

man hombre ⓜ om·bre
manager gerente ⓜ&ⓕ khe·ren·te
mandarin mandarina ⓕ man·da·ree·na
mango mango ⓜ man·go
manual worker obrero/a ⓜ/ⓕ o·bre·ro/a
many muchos/as ⓜ/ⓕ pl moo·chos/as
map mapa ⓜ ma·pa
margarine margarina ⓕ mar·ga·ree·na
marijuana marihuana ⓕ ma·ree·wa·na
marital status estado ⓜ civil es·ta·do thee·veel
market mercado ⓜ mer·ka·do
marmalade mermelada ⓕ mer·me·la·da
marriage matrimonio ⓜ ma·tree·mo·nyo
marry casarse ka·sar·se
martial arts artes ⓜ pl marciales ar·tes mar·thya·les
mass misa ⓕ mee·sa
massage masaje ⓜ ma·sa·khe
masseur/masseuse masajista ⓜ&ⓕ ma·sa·khees·ta
mat esterilla ⓕ es·te·ree·lya
match partido ⓜ par·tee·do
matches cerillas ⓕ pl the·ree·lyas
mattress colchón ⓜ kol·chon
maybe quizás kee·thas
mayonnaise mayonesa ⓕ ma·yo·ne·sa
mayor alcalde ⓜ&ⓕ al·kal·de
measles sarampión ⓜ sa·ram·pyon
meat carne ⓕ kar·ne
mechanic mecánico/a ⓜ/ⓕ me·ka·nee·ko
media medios ⓜ pl de comunicación me·dyos de ko·moo·nee·ka·thyon
medicine medicina ⓕ me·dee·thee·na
meditation meditación ⓕ me·dee·ta·thyon
meet encontrar en·kon·trar

melon melón ⓜ me·*lon*

member miembro ⓜ *myem*·bro

menstruation menstruación ⓕ mens·trwa·*thyon*

menu menú ⓜ me·*noo*

message mensaje ⓜ men·*sa*·khe

metal metal ⓜ me·*tal*

metre metro ⓜ me·tro

metro station estación ⓕ de metro es·ta·*thyon* de *me*·tro

microwave microondas ⓜ mee·kro·*on*·das

midnight medianoche ⓕ me·dya·*no*·che

migraine migraña ⓕ mee·*gra*·nya

military service servicio ⓜ militar ser·*vee*·thyo mee·lee·*tar*

milk leche ⓕ *le*·che

millimetre milímetro ⓜ mee·*lee*·me·tro

million millón ⓜ mee·*lyon*

mince (meat) carne ⓜ molida *kar*·ne mo·*lee*·da

mind (object) cuidar kwee·*dar*

mineral water agua ⓜ mineral *a*·gwa mee·ne·*ral*

mints pastillas ⓕ pl de menta pas·*tee*·lyas de *men*·ta

minute minuto ⓜ mee·*noo*·to

mirror espejo ⓜ es·*pe*·kho

miscarriage aborto ⓜ natural a·*bor*·to na·too·*ral*

miss (feel sad) echar de menos e·*char* de *me*·nos

mistake error ⓜ e·*ror*

mix mezclar meth·*klar*

mobile phone teléfono ⓜ móvil te·*le*·fo·no *mo*·veel

modem módem ⓜ *mo*·dem

moisturiser crema ⓕ hidratante *kre*·ma ee·dra·*tan*·te

monastery monasterio ⓜ mo·nas·*te*·ryo

money dinero ⓜ dee·*ne*·ro

month mes ⓜ mes

monument monumento ⓜ mo·noo·*men*·to

(full) moon luna ⓕ (llena) *loo*·na (*lye*·na)

morning (6am–1pm) mañana ⓕ ma·*nya*·na

morning sickness náuseas ⓕ pl del embarazo *now*·se·as del em·ba·*ra*·tho

mosque mezquita ⓕ meth·*kee*·ta

mosquito mosquito ⓜ mos·*kee*·to

mosquito coil rollo ⓜ repelente contra mosquitos *ro*·lyo re·pe·*len*·te *kon*·tra mos·*kee*·tos

mosquito net mosquitera ⓕ mos·kee·*te*·ra

mother madre ⓕ *ma*·dre

mother-in-law suegra ⓕ *swe*·gra

motorboat motora ⓕ mo·*to*·ra

motorcycle motocicleta ⓕ mo·to·thee·*kle*·ta

motorway autovia ⓕ ow·to·*vee*·a

mountain montaña ⓕ mon·*ta*·nya

mountain bike bicicleta ⓕ de montaña bee·thee·*kle*·ta de mon·*ta*·nya

mountain path sendero ⓜ sen·*de*·ro

mountain range cordillera ⓕ kor·dee·*lye*·ra

mountaineering alpinismo ⓜ al·pee·*nees*·mo

mouse ratón ⓜ ra·*ton*

mouth boca ⓕ *bo*·ka

movie película ⓕ pe·*lee*·koo·la

mud lodo ⓜ *lo*·do

muesli muesli ⓜ *mwes*·lee

mum mamá ⓕ ma·*ma*

muscle músculo ⓜ *moos*·koo·lo

museum museo ⓜ moo·*se*·o

mushroom ⓜ champiñón cham·pee·*nyon*

music música ⓕ *moo*·see·ka

musician músico/a ⓜ/ⓕ *moo*·see·ko/a

Muslim musulmán/musulmana ⓜ/ⓕ moo·sool·*man*/moo·sool·*ma*·na

mussels mejillones ⓜ pl me·khee·*lyo*·nes

mustard mostaza ⓕ mos·*ta*·tha

mute mudo/a ⓜ/ⓕ *moo*·do/a
my mi mee

N

nail clippers cortauñas ⓜ pl kor·ta·*oo*·nyas
name nombre ⓜ *nom*·bre
napkin servilleta ⓕ ser·vee·*lye*·ta
nappy pañal ⓜ pa·*nyal*
nappy rash irritación ⓕ de pañal ee·ree·ta·*thyon* de pa·*nyal*
national park parque ⓜ nacional *par*·ke na·thyo·*nal*
nationality nacionalidad ⓕ na·thyo·na·lee·*da*
nature naturaleza ⓕ na·too·ra·*le*·tha
naturopathy naturopatia ⓕ na·too·ro·pa·*tya*
nausea náusea ⓕ *now*·se·a
near cerca *ther*·ka
nearby cerca *ther*·ka
nearest más cercano/a ⓜ/ⓕ mas *ther*·ka·no/a
necessary necesario/a ⓜ/ⓕ ne·the·*sa*·ryo/a
neck cuello ⓜ *kwe*·lyo
necklace collar ⓜ ko·*lyar*
need necesitar ne·the·see·*tar*
needle (sewing) aguja ⓕ a·*goo*·kha
needle (syringe) jeringa ⓕ khe·*reen*·ga
neither tampoco tam·*po*·ko
net red ⓕ red
Netherlands Holanda ⓕ o·*lan*·da
never nunca *noon*·ka
new nuevo/a ⓜ/ⓕ *nwe*·vo/a
New Year Año Nuevo ⓜ a·nyo *nwe*·vo
New Year's Eve Nochevieja ⓕ no·che·*vye*·kha
New Zealand Nueva Zelanda ⓕ *nwe*·va the·*lan*·da
news noticias ⓕ pl no·*tee*·thyas
news stand quiosco ⓜ *kyos*·ko
newsagency quiosco ⓜ *kyos*·ko
newspaper periódico ⓜ pe·*ryo*·dee·ko

next (month) el próximo (mes) el *prok*·see·mo (mes)
next to al lado de al la·do de
nice simpático/a ⓜ/ⓕ seem·*pa*·tee·ko/a
nickname apodo ⓜ a·*po*·do
night noche ⓕ *no*·che
no no no
noisy ruidoso/a ⓜ/ⓕ rwee·*do*·so/a
none nada *na*·da
nonsmoking no fumadores no foo·ma·*do*·res
noodles fideos ⓜ pl fee·*de*·os
noon mediodía ⓜ me·dyo·*dee*·a
north norte ⓜ *nor*·te
nose nariz ⓕ na·*reeth*
notebook cuaderno ⓜ kwa·*der*·no
nothing nada *na*·da
now ahora a·o·ra
nuclear energy energía ⓕ nuclear e·ner·*khee*·a noo·kle·*ar*
nuclear testing pruebas ⓕ pl nucleares *prwe*·bas noo·kle·*a*·res
nuclear waste desperdicios ⓜ pl nucleares des·per·*dee*·thyos noo·kle·*a*·res
number número ⓜ *noo*·me·ro
nun monja ⓕ *mon*·kha
nurse enfermero/a ⓜ/ⓕ en·fer·*me*·ro/a
nuts nueces ⓕ pl *nwe*·thes
nuts (raw) nueces ⓕ pl (crudas) *nwe*·thes (*kroo*·das)
nuts (roasted) nueces ⓕ pl (tostadas) *nwe*·thes (tos·*ta*·das)

O

oats avena ⓕ a·*ve*·na
ocean océano ⓜ o·*the*·a·no
off (food) pasado/a ⓜ/ⓕ pa·*sa*·do/a
office oficina ⓕ o·fee·*thee*·na
office worker oficinista ⓜ&ⓕ o·fee·thee·*nees*·ta
offside fuera de juego *fwe*·ra de *khwe*·go
often a menudo a me·*noo*·do
oil aceite ⓜ a·*they*·te

P

old viejo/a ⓜ/ⓕ *vye*·kho/a
olive oil aceite ⓜ de oliva a·*they*·te de o·*lee*·va
Olympic Games Juegos ⓜ pl Olímpicos *khwe*·gos o·*leem*·pee·kos
on en en
once vez ⓕ veth
one-way ticket billete ⓜ sencillo bee·*lye*·te sen·*thee*·lyo
onion ⓕ cebolla the·*bo*·lya
only sólo *so*·lo
open abierto/a ⓜ/ⓕ a·*byer*·to/a
open abrir a·*breer*
opening hours horas ⓕ pl de abrir *o*·ras de a·*breer*
opera ópera ⓕ *o*·pe·ra
opera house teatro ⓜ de la ópera te·*a*·tro de la o·pe·ra
operation operación ⓕ o·pe·ra·*thyon*
operator operador/operadora ⓜ/ⓕ o·pe·ra·*dor*/o·pe·ra·*do*·ra
opinion opinión ⓕ o·pee·*nyon*
opposite frente a *fren*·te a
or o o
orange (fruit) naranja ⓕ na·*ran*·kha
orange (colour) naranja na·*ran*·kha
orange juice zumo ⓜ de naranja *thoo*·mo de na·*ran*·kha
orchestra orquesta ⓕ or·*kes*·ta
order orden ⓜ *or*·den
order ordenar or·de·*nar*
ordinary corriente ko·*ryen*·te
orgasm orgasmo ⓜ or·*gas*·mo
original original ⓜ/ⓕ o·ree·khee·*nal*
other otro/a ⓜ/ⓕ *o*·tro/a
our nuestro/a ⓜ/ⓕ *nwes*·tro/a
outside exterior ⓜ eks·te·*ryor*
ovarian cyst quiste ⓜ ovárico *kees*·te o·*va*·ree·ko
oven horno ⓜ *or*·no
overcoat abrigo ⓜ a·*bree*·go
overdose sobredosis ⓕ so·bre·*do*·sees
owe deber de·*ber*
owner dueño/a ⓜ/ⓕ *dwe*·nyo/a
oxygen oxígeno ⓜ ok·*see*·khe·no
oyster ⓕ ostra *os*·tra

ozone layer capa ⓕ de ozono *ka*·pa de o·*tho*·no

P

pacemaker marcapasos ⓜ mar·ka·*pa*·sos
pacifier chupete ⓜ choo·*pe*·te
package paquete ⓜ pa·*ke*·te
packet paquete ⓜ pa·*ke*·te
padlock candado ⓜ kan·*da*·do
page página ⓕ *pa*·khee·na
pain dolor ⓜ do·*lor*
painful doloroso/a ⓜ/ⓕ do·lo·*ro*·so/a
painkillers analgésicos ⓜ pl a·nal·*khe*·see·kos
paint pintar peen·*tar*
painter pintor/pintora ⓜ/ⓕ peen·*tor*/peen·*to*·ra
painting pintura ⓕ peen·*too*·ra
pair (couple) pareja ⓕ pa·*re*·kha
palace palacio ⓜ pa·*la*·thyo
pan cazuela ⓕ ka·*thwe*·la
pants pantalones ⓜ pl pan·ta·*lo*·nes
panty liners salvaeslips ⓜ pl sal·va·e·*sleeps*
pantyhose medias ⓕ pl *me*·dyas
pap smear citología ⓕ thee·to·lo·*khee*·a
paper papel ⓜ pa·*pel*
paperwork trabajo ⓜ administrativo tra·*ba*·kho ad·mee·nees·tra·*tee*·vo
paraplegic parapléjico/a ⓜ/ⓕ pa·ra·*ple*·khee·ko/a
parasailing esqui ⓜ acuático con paracaídas es·*kee* a·*kwa*·tee·ko kon pa·ra·ka·*ee*·das
parcel paquete ⓜ pa·*ke*·te
parents padres ⓜ pl *pa*·dres
park parque ⓜ *par*·ke
park (car) estacionar es·ta·thyo·*nar*
parliament parlamento ⓜ par·la·*men*·to
parsley perejil ⓜ pe·re·*kheel*
part parte ⓕ *par*·te
part-time a tiempo parcial a *tyem*·po par·*thyal*

party fiesta ⓕ *fyes*·ta
party (political) partido ⓜ par·*tee*·do
pass pase ⓜ *pa*·se
passenger pasajero/a ⓜ/ⓕ pa·sa·*khe*·ro
passport pasaporte ⓜ pa·sa·*por*·te
passport number número ⓜ de pasaporte *noo*·me·ro de pa·sa·*por*·te
past pasado ⓜ pa·*sa*·do
pasta pasta ⓕ *pas*·ta
pate (food) paté ⓜ pa·*te*
path sendero ⓜ sen·*de*·ro
pay pagar pa·*gar*
payment pago ⓜ *pa*·go
peace paz ⓕ *path*
peach melocotón ⓜ me·lo·ko·*ton*
peak cumbre ⓕ *koom*·bre
peanuts cacahuetes ⓜ pl ka·ka·*we*·tes
pear pera ⓕ *pe*·ra
peas guisantes ⓜ pl gee·*san*·tes
pedal pedal ⓜ pe·*dal*
pedestrian peatón ⓜ&ⓕ pe·a·*ton*
pedestrian crossing paso ⓜ de cebra pa·so de *the*·bra
pen bolígrafo ⓜ bo·*lee*·gra·fo
pencil lápiz ⓜ *la*·peeth
penis pene ⓜ *pe*·ne
penknife navaja ⓕ na·*va*·kha
pensioner pensionista ⓜ&ⓕ pen·syo·*nees*·ta
people gente ⓕ *khen*·te
pepper (vegetable) pimiento ⓜ pee·*myen*·to
pepper (spice) pimienta ⓕ pee·*myen*·ta
per (day) por (dia) por (*dee*·a)
percent por ciento por *thyen*·to
performance actuación ⓕ ak·twa·*thyon*
perfume perfume ⓜ per·*foo*·me
period pain dolor ⓜ menstrual do·*lor* mens·*trwal*
permission permiso ⓜ per·*mee*·so
permit permiso ⓜ per·*mee*·so
permit permitir per·mee·*teer*

person persona ⓕ per·*so*·na
perspire sudar soo·*dar*
petition petición ⓕ pe·tee·*thyon*
petrol gasolina ⓕ ga·so·*lee*·na
pharmacy farmacia ⓕ far·*ma*·thya
phone book guía ⓕ telefónica *gee*·a te·le·*fo*·nee·ka
phone box cabina ⓕ telefónica ka·*bee*·ka te·le·*fo*·nee·ka
phone card tarjeta ⓕ de teléfono tar·*khe*·ta de te·*le*·fo·no
photo foto ⓕ *fo*·to
photographer fotógrafo/a ⓜ/ⓕ fo·*to*·gra·fo/a
photography fotografía ⓕ fo·to·gra·*fee*·a
phrasebook libro ⓜ de frases *lee*·bro de *fra*·ses
pick up ligar lee·*gar*
pickaxe piqueta ⓕ pee·*ke*·ta
pickles encurtidos ⓜ pl en·koor·*tee*·dos
picnic comida ⓕ en el campo ko·*mee*·da en el *kam*·po
pie pastel ⓜ pas·*tel*
piece pedazo ⓜ pe·*da*·tho
pig cerdo ⓜ *ther*·do
pill pastilla ⓕ pas·*tee*·lya
pill, the (contraceptive) píldora ⓕ *peel*·do·ra
pillow almohada ⓕ al·*mwa*·da
pillowcase funda ⓕ de almohada *foon*·da de al·*mwa*·da
pineapple piña ⓕ *pee*·nya
pink rosa *ro*·sa
pistachio pistacho ⓜ pees·*ta*·cho
place lugar ⓜ loo·*gar*
place of birth lugar ⓜ de nacimiento loo·*gar* de na·thee·*myen*·to
plane avión ⓜ a·*vyon*
planet planeta ⓜ pla·*ne*·ta
plant planta ⓕ *plan*·ta
plant sembrar sem·*brar*
plastic plástico ⓜ *plas*·tee·ko
plate plato ⓜ *pla*·to
plateau meseta ⓕ me·*se*·ta

P

platform plataforma ① pla·ta·*for*·ma
play obra ① o·*bra*
play (musical instrument) tocar
to·*kar*
play (sport/games) jugar khoo·*gar*
plug tapar ta·*par*
plum ciruela thee·*rwe*·la
pocket bolsillo ⓜ bol·*see*·lyo
poetry poesía ① po·e·*see*·a
point apuntar a·poon·*tar*
point (tip) punto ⓜ *poon*·to
poisonous venenoso/a ⓜ/①
ve·ne·*no*·so/a
poker póquer ⓜ *po*·ker
police policía ① po·lee·*thee*·a
police station comisaría ①
ko·mee·sa·*ree*·a
policy política ① po·*lee*·tee·ka
policy (insurance) póliza ①
po·lee·tha
politician político ⓜ po·*lee*·tee·ko
politics política ① po·*lee*·tee·ka
pollen polen ⓜ *po*·len
polls sondeos ⓜ pl son·*de*·os
pollution contaminación ①
kon·ta·mee·na·*thyon*
pool (swimming) piscina ①
pees·*thee*·na
poor pobre *po*·bre
popular popular po·poo·*lar*
pork cerdo ⓜ *ther*·do
pork sausage chorizo ⓜ cho·*ree*·tho
port puerto ⓜ *pwer*·to
port (wine) oporto ⓜ o·*por*·to
possible posible po·*see*·ble
post code código postal ⓜ *ko*·dee·go
pos·*tal*
post office correos ⓜ ko·*re*·os
postage franqueo ⓜ fran·*ke*·o
postcard postal ① pos·*tal*
poster póster ⓜ *pos*·ter
pot (kitchen) cazuela ① ka·*thwe*·la
pot (plant) tiesto ⓜ *tyes*·to
potato patata ① pa·*ta*·ta
pottery alfarería ① al·fa·re·*ree*·a
pound (money) libra ① *lee*·bra

poverty pobreza ① po·*bre*·tha
power poder ⓜ po·*der*
prawns gambas ① pl *gam*·bas
prayer oración ① o·ra·*thyon*
prayer book devocionario ⓜ
de·vo·thyo·*na*·ryo
prefer preferir pre·fe·*reer*
pregnancy test prueba ① del
embarazo *prwe*·ba del em·ba·*ra*·tho
pregnant embarazada ①
em·ba·ra·*tha*·da
premenstrual tension tensión ①
premenstrual ten·*syon* pre·mens·*trwal*
prepare preparar pre·pa·*rar*
president presidente/a ⓜ/①
pre·see·*den*·te/a
pressure presión ① pre·*syon*
pretty bonito/a ⓜ/① bo·*nee*·to/a
prevent prevenir pre·ve·*neer*
price precio ⓜ *pre*·thyo
priest sacerdote ⓜ sa·ther·*do*·te
prime minister primer ministro/
primera ministra ⓜ/① pree·*mer*
mee·*nees*·tro/pree·*me*·ra
mee·*nees*·tra
prison cárcel ① *kar*·thel
prisoner prisionero/a ⓜ/①
pree·syon·*ne*·ro/a
private privado/a ⓜ/① pree·*va*·do/a
private hospital clínica ① klee·*nee*·ka
produce producir pro·doo·*theer*
profit beneficio ⓜ be·ne·*fee*·thyo
programme programa ⓜ pro·*gra*·ma
projector proyector ⓜ pro·yek·*tor*
promise promesa ① pro·*me*·sa
protect proteger pro·te·*kher*
protected (species) protegido/a
ⓜ/① pro·te·*khee*·do/a
protest protesta ① pro·*tes*·ta
protest protestar pro·tes·*tar*
provisions provisiones ① pl
pro·vee·*syo*·nes
prune ciruela *pa*·sa thee·*rwe*·la *pa*·sa
pub pub ⓜ poob
public telephone teléfono ⓜ público
te·*le*·fo·no *poo*·blee·ko

public toilet servicios ⓜ pl ser·*vee*·thyos
pull tirar tee·*rar*
pump bomba ⓕ *bom*·ba
pumpkin calabaza ⓕ ka·la·*ba*·tha
puncture pinchar peen·*char*
punish castigar kas·tee·*gar*
puppy cachorro ⓜ ka·*cho*·ro
pure puro/a ⓜ/ⓕ *poo*·ro/a
purple lila *lee*·la
push empujar em·poo·*khar*
put poner po·*ner*

Q

qualifications cualificaciones ⓕ pl kwa·lee·fee·ka·*thyo*·nes
quality calidad ⓕ ka·lee·*da*
quarantine cuarentena ⓕ kwa·ren·*te*·na
quarrel pelea ⓕ pe·*le*·a
quarter cuarto ⓜ *kwar*·to
queen reina ⓕ *rey*·na
question pregunta ⓕ pre·*goon*·ta
question cuestionar kwes·tyo·*nar*
queue cola ⓕ *ko*·la
quick rápido/a ⓜ/ⓕ *ra*·pee·do/a
quiet tranquilo/a ⓜ/ⓕ tran·*kee*·lo/a
quiet tranquilidad ⓕ tran·kee·lee·*da*
quit dejar de·*khar*

R

rabbit conejo ⓜ ko·*ne*·kho
race (people) raza ⓕ *ra*·tha
race (sport) carrera ⓕ ka·*re*·ra
racetrack (bicycles) velódromo ⓜ ve·*lo*·dro·mo
racetrack (cars) circuito ⓜ de carreras theer·*kwee*·to de ka·*re*·ras
racetrack (horses) hipódromo ⓜ ee·*po*·dro·mo
racetrack (runners) pista ⓕ *pees*·ta
racing bike bicicleta ⓕ de carreras bee·thee·*kle*·ta de ka·*re*·ras
racquet raqueta ⓕ ra·*ke*·ta
radiator radiador ⓜ ra·dya·*dor*
radish rábano ⓜ *ra*·ba·no

railway station estación ⓕ de tren es·ta·*thyon* de tren
rain lluvia ⓕ *lyoo*·vya
raincoat impermeable ⓜ eem·per·me·*a*·ble
raisin uva ⓕ pasa *oo*·va *pa*·sa
rally concentración ⓕ kon·then·tra·*thyon*
rape violar vyo·*lar*
rare raro/a ⓜ/ⓕ *ra*·ro/a
rash irritación ⓕ ee·rre·ta·*thyon*
raspberry frambuesa ⓕ fram·*bwe*·sa
rat rata ⓕ *ra*·ta
rate of pay salario ⓜ sa·la·ryo
raw crudo/a ⓜ/ⓕ *kroo*·do/a
razor afeitadora ⓕ a·fey·ta·*do*·ra
razor blades cuchillas ⓕ pl de afeitar koo·*chee*·lyas de a·fey·*tar*
read leer le·*er*
ready listo/a ⓜ/ⓕ *lees*·to/a
real estate agent agente inmobiliario ⓜ a·*khen*·te een·mo·bee·*lya*·ryo
realise darse cuenta de *dar*·se *kwen*·ta de
realistic realista re·a·*lees*·ta
reason razón ⓕ ra·*thon*
receipt recibo ⓜ re·*thee*·bo
receive recibir re·thee·*beer*
recently recientemente re·thyen·te·*men*·te
recognise reconocer re·ko·no·*ther*
recommend recomendar re·ko·men·*dar*
recording grabación ⓕ gra·ba·*thyon*
recyclable reciclable re·thee·*kla*·ble
recycle reciclar re·thee·*klar*
red rojo/a ⓜ/ⓕ *ro*·kho/a
referee árbitro ⓜ *ar*·bee·tro
reference referencias ⓕ pl re·fe·*ren*·thyas
refrigerator nevera ⓕ ne·*ve*·ra • frigerífico ⓜ free·ge·*ree*·fee·ko
refugee refugiado/a ⓜ/ⓕ re·foo·*khya*·do/a
refund reembolso ⓜ re·em·*bol*·so
refund reembolsar re·em·bol·*sar*
refuse negar ne·*gar*

S

registered mail correo ⓜ certificado ko·*re*·o ther·tee·fee·*ka*·do

regret lamentar la·men·*tar*

relationship relación ⓕ re·la·*thyon*

relax relajarse re·la·*khar*·se

relic reliquia ⓕ re·*lee*·kya

religion religión ⓕ re·lee·*khyon*

religious religioso/a ⓜ/ⓕ re·lee·*khyo*·so/a

remember recordar re·kor·*dar*

remote remoto/a ⓜ/ⓕ re·*mo*·to/a

remote control mando ⓜ a distancia *man*·do a dees·*tan*·thya

rent alquiler ⓜ al·kee·*ler*

rent alquilar al·kee·*lar*

repair reparar re·pa·*rar*

repeat repetir re·pe·*teer*

republic república ⓕ re·*poo*·blee·ka

reservation reserva ⓕ re·*ser*·va

reserve reservar re·ser·*var*

rest descansar des·kan·*sar*

restaurant restaurante ⓜ res·tow·*ran*·te

retired jubilado/a ⓜ/ⓕ khoo·bee·*la*·do/a

return volver vol·*ver*

return ticket billete ⓜ de ida y vuelta bee·*lye*·te de ee·da ee *vwel*·ta

review crítica ⓕ *kree*·tee·ka

rhythm ritmo ⓜ *reet*·mo

rice arroz ⓜ a·*roth*

rich rico/a ⓜ/ⓕ *ree*·ko/a

ride paseo ⓜ pa·*se*·o

ride montar mon·*tar*

right (correct) correcto/a ⓜ/ⓕ ko·*rek*·to/a

right (not left) derecha de·*re*·cha

right-wing derechista de·re·*chees*·ta

ring (phone) llamada ⓕ lya·*ma*·da

ring llamar por telefono lya·*mar* por te·*le*·fo·no

rip-off estafa ⓕ es·*ta*·fa

risk riesgo ⓜ *ryes*·go

river río ⓜ *ree*·o

road carretera ⓕ ka·re·*te*·ra

rob robar ro·*bar*

rock (stone) roca ⓕ *ro*·ka

rock (music) rock ⓜ rok

rock climbing escalada ⓕ es·ka·*la*·da

rock group grupo ⓜ de rock *groo*·po de rok

rollerblading patinar pa·*tee*·nar

romantic romántico/a ⓜ/ⓕ ro·*man*·tee·ko/a

room habitación ⓕ a·bee·ta·*thyon*

room number número ⓜ de la habitación *noo*·me·ro de la a·bee·ta·*thyon*

rope cuerda ⓕ *kwer*·da

round redondo/a ⓜ/ⓕ re·*don*·do/a

roundabout glorieta ⓕ glo·*rye*·ta

route ruta ⓕ *roo*·ta

rowing remo ⓜ *re*·mo

rubbish basura ⓕ ba·*soo*·ra

rug alfombra ⓕ al·*fom*·bra

rugby rugby ⓜ *roog*·bee

ruins ruinas ⓕ pl *rwee*·nas

rules reglas ⓕ pl *re*·glas

rum ron ron

run correr ko·*rer*

run out of quedarse sin ke·*dar*·se seen

S

sad triste *trees*·te

saddle sillín ⓜ see·*lyeen*

safe seguro/a ⓜ/ⓕ se·*goo*·ro/a

safe caja ⓕ fuerte *ka*·kha *fwer*·te

safe sex sexo ⓜ seguro *sek*·so se·*goo*·ro

saint santo/a ⓜ/ⓕ *san*·to/a

salad ensalada ⓕ en·sa·*la*·da

salami (Spanish sausage) chorizo cho·*ree*·tho

salary salario ⓜ sa·*la*·ryo

sales tax IVA ⓜ *ee*·va

salmon salmón ⓜ sal·*mon*

salt sal ⓕ sal

same igual ee·*gwal*

sand arena ⓕ a·*re*·na

sandals sandalias ⓕ pl san·*da*·lyas

sanitary napkins compresas ⓕ pl kom·*pre*·sas

S

sauna sauna ① *sow*·na

sausage salchicha ① sal·*chee*·cha

save salvar sal·*var*

save (money) ahorrar a·o·*rar*

say decir de·*theer*

scale/climb trepar tre·*par*

scarf bufanda ① boo·*fan*·da

school escuela ① es·*kwe*·la

science ciencias ① pl *thyen*·thyas

scientist científico/a ⑩/①
thyen·*tee*·fee·ko/a

scissors tijeras ① pl tee·*khe*·ras

score marcar mar·*kar*

scoreboard marcador ⑩ mar·ka·*dor*

Scotland Escocia ① es·*ko*·thya

screen pantalla ① pan·*ta*·lya

script guión ⑩ gee·*on*

sculpture escultura ① es·kool·*too*·ra

sea mar ⑩ mar

seasick mareado/a ⑩/①
ma·re·a·do/a

seaside costa ① *kos*·ta

season estación ① es·ta·*thyon*

season (in sport) temporada ①
tem·po·*ra*·da

seat asiento ⑩ a·*syen*·to

seatbelt cinturón ⑩ de seguridad
theen·too·*ron* de se·goo·ree·*da*

second (place) segundo/a ⑩/①
se·*goon*·do/a

second (time) segundo ⑩ se·*goon*·do

secondhand de segunda mano de
se·*goon*·da *ma*·no

secretary secretario/a ⑩/①
se·kre·*ta*·ryo/a

see ver ver

selfish egoísta e·go·ees·ta

self-service autoservicio ⑩
ow·to·ser·*vee*·thyo

sell vender ven·*der*

send enviar en·vee·*ar*

sensible prudente proo·*den*·te

sensual sensual sen·*swal*

separate separado/a ⑩/①
se·pa·*ra*·do/a

separate separar se·pa·*rar*

series serie ① *se*·rye

serious serio/a ⑩/① *se*·ryo/a

service station gasolinera ①
ga·so·lee·*ne*·ra

service charge carga ① *kar*·ga

several varias/os ⑩/① *va*·ryas/os

sew coser ko·*ser*

sex sexo ⑩ *sek*·so

sexism machismo ⑩ ma·*chees*·mo

sexy sexy *sek*·see

shadow sombra ① *som*·bra

shampoo champú ⑩ cham·*poo*

shape forma ① *for*·ma

share (a dorm) compartir (un
dormitorio) kom·par·*teer* (oon
dor·mee·to·ryo)

share (with) compartir kom·par·*teer*

shave afeitarse a·fey·*tar*·se

shaving cream espuma ① de afeitar
es·*poo*·ma de a·fey·*tar*

she ella ① *e*·lya

sheep oveja ① o·*ve*·kha

sheet (bed) sábana ① *sa*·ba·na

sheet (of paper) hoja ① *o*·kha

shelf estante ⑩ es·*tan*·te

ship barco ⑩ *bar*·ko

ship enviar en·vee·*ar*

shirt camisa ① ka·*mee*·sa

shoe shop zapatería ①
tha·pa·te·*ree*·a

shoes zapatos ⑩ pl tha·*pa*·tos

shoot disparar dees·pa·*rar*

shop tienda ① *tyen*·da

shoplifting ratería ① ra·te·*ree*·a

shopping centre centro ⑩ comercial
then·tro ko·mer·*thyal*

short (height) bajo/a ⑩/① *ba*·kho/a

short (length) corto/a ⑩/① *kor*·to/a

shortage escasez ① es·ka·*seth*

shorts pantalones ⑩ pl cortos
kor·tos pan·ta·*lo*·nes

shoulders hombros ⑩ pl *om*·bros

shout gritar gree·*tar*

show espectáculo ⑩ es·pek·*ta*·koo·lo

show mostrar mos·*trar*

show enseñar en·se·*nyar*

shower ducha ① *doo*·cha

S

shrine capilla ① ka·*pee*·lya

shut cerrado/a ⓜ/① the·*ra*·do/a

shut cerrar the·*rar*

shy tímido/a ⓜ/① *tee*·mee·do/a

sick enfermo/a ⓜ/① en·*fer*·mo/a

side lado ⓜ *la*·do

sign señal ① se·*nyal*

sign firmar feer·*mar*

signature firma ① *feer*·ma

silk seda ① *se*·da

silver plateado/a ⓜ/① pla·te·*a*·do/a

silver plata ① *pla*·ta

similar similar see·mee·*lar*

simple sencillo/a ⓜ/① sen·*thee*·lyo/a

since (mayo) des·de (*ma*·yo)

sing cantar kan·*tar*

Singapore Singapur ⓜ seen·ga·*poor*

singer cantante ⓜ&① kan·*tan*·te

single soltero/a ⓜ/① sol·*te*·ro/a

single room habitación ① individual a·bee·ta·*thyon* een·dee·vee·*dwal*

singlet camiseta ① ka·mee·*se*·ta

sister hermana ① er·*ma*·na

sit sentarse sen·*tar*·se

size (clothes) talla ① *ta*·lya

skateboarding monopatinaje ⓜ mo·no·pa·tee·*na*·khe

ski esquiar es·kee·*ar*

skiing esquí ⓜ es·*kee*

skimmed milk leche ① desnatada *le*·che des·na·*ta*·da

skin piel ① pyel

skirt falda ① *fal*·da

sky cielo ⓜ *thye*·lo

skydiving paracaidismo ⓜ pa·ra·kai·*dees*·mo

sleep dormir dor·*meer*

sleeping bag saco ⓜ de dormir *sa*·ko de dor·*meer*

sleeping car coche cama ⓜ *ko*·che *ka*·ma

sleeping pills pastillas ① pl para dormir pas·*tee*·lyas *pa*·ra dor·*meer*

(to be) sleepy tener sueño te·*ner swe*·nyo

slide diapositiva ① dya·po·see·*tee*·va

slow lento/a ⓜ/① *len*·to/a

slowly despacio des·*pa*·thyo

small pequeño/a ⓜ/① pe·*ke*·nyo/a

smell olor ⓜ o·*lor*

smell oler o·*ler*

smile sonreír son·re·*eer*

smoke fumar foo·*mar*

snack tentempié ⓜ ten·tem·*pye*

snail caracol ⓜ ka·ra·*kol*

snake serpiente ① ser·*pyen*·te

snorkel tubos ⓜ pl respiratorios *too*·bos res·pee·*to*·ryos

snorkel buceo ⓜ boo·*the*·o

snow nieve ① *nye*·ve

snowboarding surf ⓜ sobre la nieve soorf *so*·bre la *nye*·ve

soap jabón ⓜ kha·*bon*

soap opera telenovela ① te·le·no·*ve*·la

soccer fútbol ⓜ *foot*·bol

social welfare estado ⓜ del bienestar es·*ta*·do del byen·es·*tar*

socialist socialista ⓜ&① so·thya·*lees*·ta

socks calcetines ⓜ pl kal·the·*tee*·nes

soft drink refresco ① re·*fres*·ko

soldier soldado ⓜ sol·*da*·do

some alguno/a ⓜ/① al·*goon*/al·*goo*·na

someone alguien al·*gyen*

something algo *al*·go

sometimes de vez en cuando de veth en *kwan*·do

son hijo ⓜ *ee*·kho

song canción ① kan·*thyon*

soon pronto *pron*·to

sore dolorido/a ⓜ/① do·lo·*ree*·do/a

soup sopa ① *so*·pa

sour cream nata ① agria *na*·ta *a*·grya

south sur ⓜ soor

souvenir recuerdo ⓜ re·*kwer*·do

souvenir shop tienda ① de recuerdos *tyen*·da de re·*kwer*·dos

soy milk leche ① de soja *le*·che de *so*·kha

soy sauce salsa ① de soja *sal*·sa de *so*·kha

space espacio ⓜ es·*pa*·thyo

Spain España ⓕ es·*pa*·nya

sparkling espumoso/a ⓜ/ⓕ es·poo·*mo*·so

speak hablar a·*blar*

special especial es·pe·*thyal*

specialist especialista ⓜ&ⓕ es·pe·thya·*lees*·ta

speed velocidad ⓕ ve·lo·thee·*da*

speeding exceso ⓜ de velocidad eks·*the*·so de ve·lo·thee·*da*

speedometer velocímetro ⓜ ve·lo·*thee*·me·tro

spider araña ⓕ a·*ra*·nya

spinach espinacas ⓕ pl es·pee·na·kas

spoon cuchara ⓕ koo·*cha*·ra

sport deportes ⓜ pl de·*por*·tes

sports store tienda ⓕ deportiva *tyen*·da de·por·tee·va

sportsperson deportista ⓜ&ⓕ de·por·*tees*·ta

sprain torcedura ⓕ tor·the·*doo*·ra

spring (wire) muelle ⓜ *mwe*·lye

spring (season) primavera ⓕ pree·ma·ve·ra

square (shape) cuadrado ⓜ *kwa*·dra·do

(main) square plaza ⓕ (mayor) *pla*·tha (ma·*yor*)

stadium estadio ⓜ es·*ta*·dyo

stage escenario ⓜ es·the·na·ryo

stairway escalera ⓕ es·ka·*le*·ra

stamp sello ⓜ *se*·lyo

standby ticket billete ⓜ de lista de espera bee·*lye*·te de *lees*·ta de es·*pe*·ra

stars estrellas ⓕ pl es·*tre*·lyas

start comenzar ko·men·*thar*

station estación ⓕ es·ta·*thyon*

statue estatua ⓕ es·*ta*·twa

stay (remain) quedarse ke·*dar*·se

stay (somewhere) alojarse a·lo·*khar*·se

steak (beef) bistec ⓜ bees·*tek*

steal robar ro·*bar*

steep escarpado/a ⓜ/ⓕ es·kar·*pa*·do/a

step paso ⓜ *pa*·so

stereo equipo ⓜ de música e·*kee*·po de *moo*·see·ka

stingy tacaño/a ⓜ/ⓕ ta·*ka*·nyo/a

stock caldo ⓜ *kal*·do

stockings medias ⓕ pl *me*·dyas

stomach estómago ⓜ es·*to*·ma·go

stomachache dolor ⓜ de estómago do·*lor* de es·*to*·ma·go

stone piedra ⓕ *pye*·dra

stoned colocado/a ⓜ/ⓕ ko·lo·*ka*·do/a

stop parada ⓕ pa·*ra*·da

stop parar pa·*rar*

storm tormenta ⓕ tor·*men*·ta

story cuento ⓜ *kwen*·to

stove cocina ⓕ ko·*thee*·na

straight recto/a ⓜ/ⓕ *rek*·to/a

strange extraño/a ⓜ/ⓕ ek·*stra*·nyo/a

stranger desconocido/a ⓜ/ⓕ des·ko·no·*thee*·do/a

strawberry fresa ⓕ *fre*·sa

stream arroyo ⓜ a·*ro*·yo

street calle ⓕ *ka*·lye

string cuerda ⓕ *kwer*·da

strong fuerte *fwer*·te

stubborn testarudo/a ⓜ/ⓕ tes·ta·*roo*·do/a

student estudiante ⓜ&ⓕ es·too·*dyan*·te

studio estudio ⓜ es·*too*·dyo

stupid estúpido/a ⓜ/ⓕ es·too·*pee*·do/a

style estilo ⓜ es·*tee*·lo

subtitles subtítulos ⓜ pl soob·*tee*·too·los

suburb barrio ⓜ *ba*·ryo

subway parada ⓕ de metro pa·*ra*·da de *me*·tro

suffer sufrir soo·*freer*

sugar azúcar ⓜ a·*thoo*·kar

suitcase maleta ⓕ ma·*le*·ta

summer verano ⓜ ve·*ra*·no

sun sol ⓜ sol

sunblock crema ⓕ solar *kre*·ma so·*lar*

sunburn quemadura ⓕ de sol ke·ma·*doo*·ra de sol

T

sun-dried tomato tomate ⓜ secado al sol to·ma·te se·ka·do al sol
sunflower oil aceite ⓜ de girasol a·they·te de khee·ra·sol
sunglasses gafas ⓕ pl de sol ga·fas de sol
(to be) sunny hace sol a·the sol
sunrise amanecer ⓜ a·ma·ne·ther
sunset puesta ⓕ del sol pwes·ta del sol
supermarket supermercado ⓜ soo·per·mer·ka·do
superstition superstición ⓕ soo·pers·tee·thyon
supporters hinchas ⓜ&ⓕ pl een·chas
surf hacer surf a·ther soorf
surface mail por vía terrestre por vee·a te·res·tre
surfboard tabla de surf ⓕ ta·bla de soorf
surname apellido ⓜ a·pe·lyee·do
surprise sorpresa ⓕ sor·pre·sa
survive sobrevivir so·bre·vee·veer
sweater jersey ⓜ kher·sey
Sweden Suecia ⓕ swe·thya
sweet dulce dool·the
sweets (candy) dulces ⓜ pl dool·thes
swim nadar na·dar
swimming pool piscina ⓕ pees·thee·na
swimsuit bañador ⓜ ba·nya·dor
Switzerland Suiza ⓕ swee·tha
synagogue sinagoga ⓕ see·na·go·ga
synthetic sintético/a ⓜ/ⓕ seen·te·tee·ko/a
syringe jeringa ⓕ khe·reen·ga

T

table mesa ⓕ me·sa
table tennis ping pong ⓜ peeng pong
tablecloth mantel ⓜ man·tel
tail rabo ⓜ ra·bo
tailor sastre ⓜ sas·tre
take (away) llevar lye·var

take (the train) tomar to·mar
take (photo) sacar sa·kar
take photographs sacar fotos sa·kar fo·tos
talk hablar a·blar
tall alto/a ⓜ/ⓕ al·to/a
tampons tampones ⓜ pl tam·po·nes
tanning lotion bronceador ⓜ bron·the·a·dor
tap grifo ⓜ gree·fo
tasty sabroso/a ⓜ/ⓕ sa·bro·so/a
taxes impuestos ⓜ pl eem·pwes·tos
taxi taxi ⓜ tak·see
taxi stand parada ⓕ de taxis pa·ra·da de tak·sees
tea té ⓜ te
teacher profesor/profesora ⓜ/ⓕ pro·fe·sor/pro·fe·so·ra
team equipo ⓜ e·kee·po
teaspoon cucharita ⓕ koo·cha·ree·ta
technique técnica ⓕ tek·nee·ka
teeth dientes ⓜ pl dyen·tes
telegram telegrama ⓜ te·le·gra·ma
telephone teléfono ⓜ te·le·fo·no
telephone llamar (por teléfono) lya·mar (por te·le·fo·no)
telephone centre central ⓕ telefónica then·tral te·le·fo·nee·ka
telescope telescopio ⓜ te·les·ko·pyo
television televisión ⓕ te·le·vee·syon
tell decir de·theer
temperature (fever) fiebre ⓕ fye·bre
temperature (weather) temperatura ⓕ tem·pe·ra·too·ra
temple templo ⓜ tem·plo
tennis tenis ⓜ te·nees
tennis court pista ⓕ de tenis pees·ta de te·nees
tent tienda ⓕ (de campaña) tyen·da (de kam·pa·nya)
tent pegs piquetas ⓕ pl pee·ke·tas
terrible terrible te·ree·ble
test prueba ⓕ prwe·ba
thank dar gracias dar gra·thyas
theatre teatro ⓜ te·a·tro
their su soo

they ellos/ellas ⓜ/ⓕ e·lyos/e·lyas

thief ladrón/ladrona ⓜ/ⓕ la·dron/la·dro·na

thin delgado/a ⓜ/ⓕ del·ga·do/a

think pensar pen·sar

third tercio ⓜ ter·thyo

thirst sed ⓕ se

this éste/a ⓜ/ⓕ es·te/a

this month este mes es·te mes

thread hilo ⓜ ee·lo

throat garganta ⓕ gar·gan·ta

ticket billete ⓜ bee·lye·te

ticket collector revisor/revisora ⓜ/ⓕ re·vee·sor/re·vee·so·ra

ticket machine máquina ⓕ de billetes ma·kee·na de bee·lye·tes

ticket office taquilla ⓕ ta·kee·lya

tide marea ⓕ ma·re·a

tight apretado/a ⓜ/ⓕ a·pre·ta·do/a

time (watch) hora ⓕ o·ra

time (passing) tiempo ⓜ tyem·po

time difference diferencia ⓕ de horas dee·fe·ren·thya de o·ras

timetable horario ⓜ o·ra·ryo

tin hojalata ⓕ o·kha·la·ta

tin opener abrelatas ⓜ a·bre·la·tas

tiny pequeñito/a ⓜ/ⓕ pe·ke·nyee·to/a

tip propina ⓕ pro·pee·na

tired cansado/a ⓜ/ⓕ kan·sa·do/a

tissues pañuelos ⓜ pl de papel pa·nywe·los de pa·pel

toast tostada ⓕ tos·ta·da

toaster tostadora ⓕ tos·ta·do·ra

tobacco tabaco ⓜ ta·ba·ko

tobacconist estanquero ⓜ es·tan·ke·ro

tobogganing ir en tobogán eer en to·bo·gan

today hoy oy

toe dedo ⓜ del pie de·do del pye

tofu tofú ⓜ to·foo

together juntos/as ⓜ/ⓕ khoon·tos/as

toilet servicio ⓜ ser·vee·thyo

toilet paper papel ⓜ higiénico pa·pel ee·khye·nee·ko

tomato tomate ⓜ to·ma·te

tomato sauce salsa ⓕ de tomate sal·sa de to·ma·te

tomorrow mañana ma·nya·na

tomorrow afternoon mañana por la tarde ma·nya·na por la tar·de

tomorrow evening mañana por la noche ma·nya·na por la no·che

tomorrow morning mañana por la mañana ma·nya·na por la ma·nya·na

tone tono ⓜ to·no

tonight esta noche es·ta no·che

too (expensive) demasiado (caro/a) ⓜ/ⓕ de·ma·sya·do (ka·ro/a)

tooth diente ⓜ dyen·te

tooth (back) muela ⓕ mwe·la

toothache dolor ⓜ de muelas do·lor de mwe·las

toothbrush cepillo ⓜ de dientes the·pee·lyo de dyen·tes

toothpaste pasta ⓕ dentífrica pas·ta den·tee·free·ka

toothpick palillo ⓜ pa·lee·lyo

torch linterna ⓕ leen·ter·na

touch tocar to·kar

tour excursión ⓕ eks·koor·syon

tourist turista ⓜ&ⓕ too·rees·ta

tourist (slang) guiri ⓜ gee·ree

tourist office oficina ⓕ de turismo o·fee·thee·na de too·rees·mo

towards hacia a·thya

towel toalla ⓕ to·a·lya

tower torre ⓕ to·re

toxic waste residuos ⓜ pl tóxicos re·see·dwos tok·see·kos

toyshop juguetería ⓕ khoo·ge·te·ree·a

track (car racing) autódromo ⓜ ow·to·dro·mo

track (footprints) rastro ⓜ ras·tro

trade comercio ⓜ ko·mer·thyo

traffic tráfico ⓜ tra·fee·ko

traffic lights semáforos ⓜ pl se·ma·fo·ros

trail camino ⓜ ka·mee·no

train tren ⓜ tren

train station estación ⓕ de tren es·ta·thyon de tren

tram tranvía ⓜ tran·*vee*·a

transit lounge sala ⓕ de tránsito *sa*·la de tran·*see*·to

translate traducir tra·doo·*theer*

transport medios ⓜ pl de transporte *me*·dyos de trans·*por*·te

travel viajar vya·*khar*

travel agency agencia ⓕ de viajes a·*khen*·thya de *vya*·khes

travel books libros ⓜ pl de viajes *lee*·bros de *vya*·khes

travel sickness mareo ⓜ ma·*re*·o

travellers cheque cheque ⓜ de viajero *che*·ke de vya·*khe*·ro

tree árbol ⓜ *ar*·bol

trip viaje ⓜ *vya*·khe

trousers pantalones ⓜ pl pan·ta·*lo*·nes

truck camión ⓜ ka·*myon*

trust confianza ⓕ kon·fee·*an*·tha

trust confiar kon·fee·*ar*

try probar pro·*bar*

try (to do something) intentar (hacer algo) een·ten·*tar* (a·*ther* al·go)

T-shirt camiseta ⓕ ka·mee·*se*·ta

tube (tyre) cámara ⓕ de aire *ka*·ma·ra de *ai*·re

tuna atún ⓜ a·*toon*

tune melodía ⓕ me·lo·*dee*·a

turkey pavo ⓜ *pa*·vo

turn doblar do·*blar*

TV tele ⓕ *te*·le

TV series serie ⓕ *se*·rye

tweezers pinzas ⓕ pl *peen*·thas

twice dos veces dos *ve*·thes

twin beds dos camas ⓕ pl dos *ka*·mas

twins gemelos ⓜ pl khe·*me*·los

type tipo ⓜ *tee*·po

type escribir a máquina es·kree·*beer* a *ma*·kee·na

typical típico/a ⓜ/ⓕ *tee*·pee·ko/a

tyre neumático ⓜ ne·oo·*ma*·tee·ko

U

ultrasound ecografía ⓕ e·ko·gra·*fee*·a

umbrella (rain) paraguas ⓜ pa·ra·*gwas*

umbrella (sun) parasol ⓜ pa·ra·*sol*

umpire árbitro ⓜ *ar*·bee·tro

uncomfortable incómodo/a ⓜ/ⓕ een·ko·mo·do/a

underpants (men) calzoncillos ⓜ pl kal·thon·*thee*·lyos

underpants (women) bragas ⓕ pl *bra*·gas

understand comprender kom·pren·*der*

underwear ropa interior ⓕ *ro*·pa een·te·*ryor*

unemployed en el paro en el *pa*·ro

unfair injusto een·*khoos*·to

uniform uniforme ⓜ oo·nee·*for*·me

universe universo ⓜ oo·nee·*ver*·so

university universidad ⓕ oo·nee·ver·see·*da*

unleaded sin plomo seen *plo*·mo

unsafe inseguro/a ⓜ/ⓕ een·se·*goo*·ro/a

until (June) hasta (junio) *as*·ta (*khoo*·nyo)

unusual extraño/a ⓜ/ⓕ eks·*tra*·nyo/a

up arriba a·*ree*·ba

uphill cuesta arriba *kwes*·ta a·*ree*·ba

urgent urgente oor·*khen*·te

USA Estados ⓜ pl Unidos es·*ta*·dos oo·*nee*·dos

useful útil oo·*teel*

V

vacant vacante va·*kan*·te

vacation vacaciones ⓕ pl va·ka·*thyo*·nes

vaccination vacuna ⓕ va·*koo*·na

vagina vagina ⓕ va·*khee*·na

validate validar va·lee·*dar*

valley valle ⓜ *va*·lye

valuable valioso/a ⓜ/ⓕ va·*lyo*·so/a

value valor ⓜ va·*lor*

van caravana ⓕ ka·ra·*va*·na

veal ternera ⓕ ter·*ne*·ra

vegetable verdura ⓕ ver·*doo*·ra

vegetables verduras ⓕ pl ver·*doo*·ras

W

vegetarian vegetariano/a ⓜ/ⓕ
ve·khe·ta·*rya*·no/a

vein vena ⓕ *ve*·na

venereal disease enfermedad ⓕ
venérea en·fer·me·*da* ve·ne·*re*·a

venue local ⓜ lo·*kal*

very muy mooy

video tape cinta ⓕ de vídeo *theen*·ta
de *vee*·de·o

view vista ⓕ *vees*·ta

village pueblo ⓜ *pwe*·blo

vine vid ⓕ veed

vinegar vinagre ⓜ vee·*na*·gre

vineyard viñedo ⓜ vee·*nye*·do

virus virus ⓜ *vee*·roos

visa visado ⓜ vee·*sa*·do

visit visitar vee·see·*tar*

vitamins vitaminas ⓕ pl
vee·ta·*mee*·nas

vodka vodka ⓕ *vod*·ka

voice voz ⓕ voth

volume volumen ⓜ vo·*loo*·men

vote votar vo·*tar*

W

wage sueldo ⓜ *swel*·do

wait esperar es·pe·*rar*

waiter camarero/a ⓜ/ⓕ ka·ma·*re*·ro/a

waiting room sala ⓕ de espera *sa*·la
de es·*pe*·ra

walk caminar ka·mee·*nar*

wall (inside) pared ⓕ pa·*re*

wallet cartera ⓕ kar·*te*·ra

want querer ke·*rer*

war guerra ⓕ *ge*·ra

wardrobe vestuario ⓜ ves·*twa*·ryo

warm templado/a ⓜ/ⓕ tem·*pla*·do/a

warn advertir ad·ver·*teer*

wash (oneself) lavarse la·*var*·se

wash (something) lavar la·*var*

wash cloth toallita ⓕ to·a·*lyee*·ta

washing machine lavadora ⓕ
la·va·*do*·ra

watch reloj ⓜ de pulsera re·*lokh* de
pool·*se*·ra

watch mirar mee·*rar*

water agua ⓕ *a*·gwa

— tap del grifo del *gree*·fo

— bottle cantimplora ⓕ
kan·teem·*plo*·ra

waterfall cascada ⓕ kas·*ka*·da

watermelon ⓕ sandía san·*dee*·a

waterproof impermeable
eem·per·me·*a*·ble

waterskiing esquí ⓜ acuático es·*kee*
a·*kwa*·tee·ko

wave ola ⓕ *o*·la

way camino ⓜ ka·*mee*·no

we nosotros/nosotras ⓜ/ⓕ
no·*so*·tros/no·*so*·tras

weak débil ⓜ&ⓕ *de*·beel

wealthy rico/a ⓜ/ⓕ *ree*·ko/a

wear llevar lye·*var*

weather tiempo ⓜ *tyem*·po

wedding boda ⓕ *bo*·da

wedding cake tarta ⓕ nupcial *tar*·ta
noop·*thyal*

wedding present regalo ⓜ de bodas
re·*ga*·lo de *bo*·das

weekend fin de semana ⓜ feen de
se·*ma*·na

weigh pesar pe·*sar*

weight peso ⓜ *pe*·so

weights pesas ⓕ pl *pe*·sas

welcome bienvenida ⓕ
byen·ve·*nee*·da

welcome dar la bienvenida dar la
byen·ve·*nee*·da

welfare bienestar ⓜ byen·es·*tar*

well bien byen

well pozo ⓜ *po*·tho

west oeste ⓜ o·*es*·te

wet mojado/a ⓜ/ⓕ mo·*kha*·do/a

what lo que lo ke

wheel rueda ⓕ *rwe*·da

wheelchair silla ⓕ de ruedas *see*·lya
de *rwe*·das

when cuando *kwan*·do

where donde *don*·de

whiskey güisqui ⓜ *gwees*·kee

white blanco/a ⓜ/ⓕ *blan*·ko/a

white-water rafting rafting ⓜ
rahf·teen

Y

who quien *kyen*

why por qué por *ke*

wide ancho/a ⓜ/ⓕ *an·cho/a*

wife esposa ⓕ es·*po·sa*

win ganar ga·*nar*

wind viento ⓜ *vyen·*to

window ventana ⓕ ven·*ta·na*

window-shopping mirar los escaparates mee·*rar* los es·ka·pa·*ra·*tes

windscreen parabrisas ⓜ pa·ra·*bree·*sas

windsurfing hacer windsurf a·*ther ween·*soorf

wine vino ⓜ *vee·no*

wineglass copa ⓕ de vino *ko·*pa de *vee·no*

winery bodega ⓕ bo·*de·ga*

wings alas ⓕ pl *a·las*

winner ganador/ganadora ⓜ/ⓕ ga·na·*dor/ga·na·*do·ra

winter invierno ⓜ een·*vyer·*no

wire alambre ⓜ a·*lam·bre*

wish desear de·se·*ar*

with con *kon*

within (an hour) dentro de (una hora) *den·*tro de (*oo·*na *o·*ra)

without sin seen

woman mujer ⓕ moo·*kher*

wonderful maravilloso/a ⓜ/ⓕ ma·ra·vee·*lyo·*so/a

wood madera ⓕ ma·*de·ra*

wool lana ⓕ *la·na*

word palabra ⓕ pa·*la·bra*

work trabajo ⓜ tra·*ba·*kho

work trabajar tra·ba·*khar*

work experience experiencia ⓕ laboral eks·pe·*ryen·*thya la·bo·*ral*

work permit permiso ⓜ de trabajo per·*mee·*so de tra·*ba·*kho

workout entreno ⓜ en·*tre·*no

workshop taller ⓜ ta·*lyer*

world mundo ⓜ *moon·*do

World Cup Copa ⓕ Mundial *ko·*pa moon·*dyal*

worms lombrices ⓕ pl lom·*bree·*thes

worried preocupado/a ⓜ/ⓕ pre·o·koo·*pa·*do/a

worship adoración ⓕ a·do·ra·*thyon*

wrist muñeca ⓕ moo·*nye·*ka

write escribir es·kree·*beer*

writer escritor/escritora ⓜ/ⓕ es·kree·*tor*/es·kree·*to·*ra

wrong equivocado/a ⓜ/ⓕ e·kee·vo·*ka·*do/a

Y

yellow amarillo/a ⓜ/ⓕ a·ma·*ree·lyo/a*

yes sí *see*

(not) yet todavía (no) to·da·*vee·a* (no)

yesterday ayer a·*yer*

yoga yoga ⓜ *yo·ga*

yogurt yogur ⓜ yo·*goor*

you inf sg tú *too*

you ⓜ/ⓕ inf pl vosotros/as vo·so·*tros/as*

you pol pl Ustedes oo·*ste·*des

you pol sg Usted oo·*ste*

young joven *kho·*ven

your pol sg su *soo*

your inf sg tu *too*

youth hostel albergue ⓜ juvenil al·*ber·*ge khoo·ve·*neel*

Z

zodiac zodíaco ⓜ tho·*dee·*a·ko

zoo zoológico ⓜ zo·o·*lo·*khee·ko

Dictionary
SPANISH *to* ENGLISH
español–inglés

Nouns in the dictionary have their gender indicated by ⓜ or ⓕ. If it's a plural noun, you'll also see pl. Where a word that could be either a noun or a verb has no gender indicated, it's a verb.

A

abajo a·ba·kho below
abanico ⓜ a·ba·nee·ko fan (hand held)
abarrotado a·ba·ro·ta·do crowded
abeja ⓕ a·be·kha bee
abierto/a ⓜ/ⓕ a·byer·to/a open
abogado/a ⓜ/ⓕ a·bo·ga·do/a lawyer
aborto ⓜ a·bor·to abortion
abrazo ⓜ a·bra·tho hug
abrebotellas ⓜ a·bre·bo·te·lyas bottle opener
abrelatas ⓜ a·bre·la·tas can opener • tin opener
abrigo ⓜ a·bree·go overcoat
abrir a·breer open
abuela ⓕ a·bwe·la grandmother
abuelo ⓜ a·bwe·lo grandfather
aburrido/a ⓜ/ⓕ a·boo·ree·do/a bored • boring
acabar a·ka·bar end
acampar a·kam·par camp
acantilado a·kan·tee·la·do cliff
accidente ⓜ ak·thee·den·te accident
aceite ⓜ a·they·te oil
aceptar a·thep·tar accept
acera ⓕ a·the·ra footpath

acondicionador ⓜ a·kon·dee·thyo·na·dor conditioner
acoso ⓜ a·ko·so harassment
activista ⓜ&ⓕ ak·tee·vees·ta activist
actuación ⓕ ak·twa·thyon performance
acupuntura ⓕ a·koo·poon·too·ra acupuncture
adaptador ⓜ a·dap·ta·dor adaptor
adentro a·den·tro inside
adivinar a·dee·vee·nar guess
administración ⓕ ad·mee·nees·tra·thyon administration
admitir ad·mee·teer admit
adoración ⓕ a·do·ra·thyon worship
aduana ⓕ a·dwa·na customs
adulto/a ⓜ/ⓕ a·dool·to/a adult
aeróbic ⓜ ai·ro·beek aerobics
aerolínea ⓕ ai·ro·lee·nya airline
aeropuerto ⓜ ai·ro·pwer·to airport
afeitadora ⓕ a·fey·ta·do·ra razor
afeitarse a·fey·tar·se shave
afortunado/a ⓜ/ⓕ a·for·too·na·do/a lucky
África ⓕ a·free·ka Africa
agencia ⓕ **de viajes** a·khen·thya de vya·khes travel agency
agenda ⓕ a·khen·da diary

A

agente ⓜ **inmobiliario** a·*khen*·te een·mo·bee·*lya*·ryo real estate agent

agresivo/a ⓜ/ⓕ a·gre·*see*·vo/a aggressive

agricultor(a) ⓜ/ⓕ a·gree·kool·*tor*/ a·gree·kool·*to*·ra farmer

agricultura ⓕ a·gree·kool·*too*·ra agriculture

agua ⓕ *a*·gwa water

— **caliente** ka·*lyen*·te hot water

— **mineral** mee·ne·*ral* mineral water

aguacate ⓜ a·gwa·*ka*·te avocado

aguja ⓕ a·*goo*·kha needle (sewing)

ahora a·*o*·ra now

ahorrar a·o·*rar* save (money)

aire ⓜ *ai*·re air

— **acondicionado** a·kon·dee·thyo·*na*·do air-conditioning

ajedrez ⓜ a·*khe*·dreth chess

al lado de al *la*·do de next to

alambre ⓜ a·*lam*·bre wire

alba ⓕ *al*·ba dawn

albaricoque ⓜ al·ba·ree·*ko*·ke apricot

albergue ⓜ **juvenil** al·*ber*·ge khoo·ve·*neel* youth hostel

alcachofa ⓕ al·ka·*cho*·fa artichoke

alcohol ⓜ al·*kol* alcohol

Alemania ⓕ a·le·*ma*·nya Germany

alérgia ⓕ a·*ler*·khya allergy

alérgia ⓕ a·*ler*·khya **al polen** *po*·len hay fever

alfarería ⓕ al·fa·re·*ree*·a pottery

alfombra ⓕ al·*fom*·bra rug

algo *al*·go something

algodón ⓜ al·go·*don* cotton

alguien *al*·gyen someone

algún al·*goon* some

alguno/a ⓜ/ⓕ al·*goo*·no/a any

almendras ⓕ pl al·*men*·dras almonds

almohada ⓕ al·*mwa*·da pillow

almuerzo ⓜ al·*mwer*·tho lunch

alojamiento ⓜ a·lo·kha·*myen*·to accommodation

alojarse a·lo·*khar*·se stay (somewhere)

alpinismo ⓜ al·pee·*nees*·mo mountaineering

alquilar al·kee·*lar* hire • rent

alquiler ⓜ al·kee·*ler* rent

— **de coche** de *ko*·che car hire

altar ⓜ al·*tar* altar

alto/a ⓜ/ⓕ *al*·to/a high • tall

altura ⓕ al·*too*·ra altitude

ama ⓕ **de casa** *a*·ma de *ka*·sa homemaker

amable a·*ma*·ble kind

amanecer ⓜ a·ma·ne·*ther* sunrise

amante ⓜ&ⓕ a·*man*·te lover

amarillo/a ⓜ/ⓕ a·ma·*ree*·lyo/a yellow

amigo/a ⓜ/ⓕ a·*mee*·go/a friend

ampolla ⓕ am·*po*·lya blister

anacardo ⓜ a·na·*kar*·do cashew nut

analgésicos ⓜ pl a·nal·*khe*·see·kos painkillers

análisis de sangre ⓜ a·*na*·lee·sees de *san*·gre blood test

anarquista ⓜ/ⓕ a·nar·*kees*·ta anarchist

ancho/a ⓜ/ⓕ *an*·cho/a wide

andar an·*dar* walk

animal ⓜ a·nee·*mal* animal

Año ⓜ **Nuevo** *a*·nyo *nwe*·vo New Year

antes *an*·tes before

antibióticos ⓜ pl an·tee·*byo*·tee·kos antibiotics

anticonceptivos ⓜ pl an·tee·kon·thep·*tee*·vos contraceptives

antigüedad ⓕ an·tee·gwe·*da* antique

antiguo/a ⓜ/ⓕ an·*tee*·gwo/a ancient

antiséptico ⓜ an·tee·*sep*·tee·ko antiseptic

antología ⓕ an·to·lo·*khee*·a anthology

anuncio ⓜ a·*noon*·thyo advertisement

aparcamiento ⓜ a·par·ka·*myen*·to carpark

apellido ⓜ a·pe·*lyee*·do surname

apéndice ⓜ *a·pen·dee·the* appendix
apodo ⓜ *a·po·do* nickname
aprender *a·pren·der* learn
apretado/a ⓜ/ⓕ *a·pre·ta·do/a* tight
apuesta ⓕ *a·pwes·ta* bet
apuntar *a·poon·tar* point
aquí *a·kee* here
araña ⓕ *a·ra·nya* spider
árbitro ⓜ *ar·bee·tro* referee
árbol ⓜ *ar·bol* tree
arena ⓕ *a·re·na* sand
armario ⓜ *ar·ma·ryo* cupboard
arqueológico/a ⓜ/ⓕ
ar·ke·o·lo·khee·ko/a archaeological
arquitecto/a ⓜ/ⓕ *ar·kee·tek·to/a*
architect
arquitectura ⓕ *ar·kee·tek·too·ra*
architecture
arriba *a·ree·ba* above • up
arroyo ⓜ *a·ro·yo* stream
arroz ⓜ *a·roth* rice
arte ⓜ *ar·te* art
— gráfico *gra·fee·ko* graphic art
artes ⓜ pl **marciales** *ar·tes
mar·thya·les* martial arts
artesanía ⓕ *ar·te·sa·nee·a* crafts
artista ⓜ&ⓕ *ar·tees·ta* artist
ascensor ⓜ *as·then·sor* elevator
Asia ⓕ *a·sya* Asia
asiento ⓜ *a·syen·to* seat
— de seguridad para bebés de
se·goo·ree·da pa·ra be·bes child seat
asma ⓜ *as·ma* asthma
aspirina ⓕ *as·pee·ree·na* aspirin
atascado/a ⓜ/ⓕ *a·tas·ka·do/a*
blocked
atletismo ⓜ *at·le·tees·mo* athletics
atmósfera ⓕ *at·mos·fe·ra* atmosphere
atún ⓜ *a·toon* tuna
audífono ⓜ *ow·dee·fo·no* hearing aid
Australia ⓕ *ow·stra·lya* Australia
autobús ⓜ *ow·to·boos* bus
autocar ⓜ *ow·to·kar* bus (intercity)
autódromo ⓜ *ow·to·dro·mo* track
(car racing)

autoservicio ⓜ *ow·to·ser·vee·thyo*
self-service
autovía ⓕ *ow·to·vee·a* motorway
avenida ⓕ *a·ve·nee·da* avenue
avergonzado/a ⓜ/ⓕ
a·ver·gon·tha·do/a embarrassed
avión ⓜ *a·vyon* plane
ayer *a·yer* yesterday
ayudar *a·yoo·dar* help
azúcar ⓜ *a·thoo·kar* sugar
azul *a·thool* blue

B

bailar *bai·lar* dance
bajo/a ⓜ/ⓕ *ba·kho/a* low • short
(height)
balcón ⓜ *bal·kon* balcony
ballet ⓜ *ba·le* ballet
baloncesto ⓜ *ba·lon·thes·to*
basketball
bálsamo ⓜ **de aftershave** *bal·sa·mo
de af·ter·sha·eev* aftershave
bálsamo ⓜ **de labios** *bal·sa·mo de
la·byos* lip balm
bañador ⓜ *ba·nya·dor* bathing suit
banco ⓜ *ban·ko* bank
bandera ⓕ *ban·de·ra* flag
bañera ⓕ *ba·nye·ra* bath
baño ⓜ *ba·nyo* bathroom
bar ⓜ *bar* bar
barato/a ⓜ/ⓕ *ba·ra·to/a* cheap
barco ⓜ *bar·ko* boat
barrio ⓜ *ba·ryo* suburb
basura ⓕ *ba·soo·ra* rubbish
batería ⓕ *ba·te·ree·a* battery (car) •
drums
bebé ⓜ *be·be* baby
béisbol ⓜ *beys·bol* baseball
beneficio ⓜ *be·ne·fee·thyo* profit
berenjenas ⓕ pl *be·ren·khe·nas*
aubergine • eggplant
besar *be·sar* kiss
beso ⓜ *be·so* kiss
biblia ⓕ *bee·blya* bible
biblioteca ⓕ *bee·blyo·te·ka* library

bicho ⓜ *bee*·cho bug
bici ⓕ *bee*·thee bike
bicicleta ⓕ bee·thee·*kle*·ta bicycle
— de carreras de ka·*re*·ras racing bike
— de montaña de mon·*ta*·nya mountain bike
bien byen well
bienestar ⓜ byen·*es*·tar welfare
bienvenida ⓕ byen·ve·*nee*·da welcome
billete ⓜ bee·*lye*·te ticket
— de ida y vuelta de *ee*·da ee vwel·ta return ticket
— de lista de espera de *lees*·ta de es·*pe*·ra standby ticket
billetes ⓜ pl **de banco** bee·*lye*·tes de *ban*·ko banknotes
biografía ⓕ bee·o·gra·*fee*·a biography
bistec ⓜ bees·*tek* steak (beef)
blanco y negro *blan*·ko ee *ne*·gro B&W (film)
blanco/a ⓜ/ⓕ *blan*·ko/a white
boca ⓕ *bo*·ka mouth
bocado ⓜ bo·*ka*·do bite (food)
boda ⓕ *bo*·da wedding
bodega ⓕ bo·*de*·ga winery • liquor store
bol ⓜ bol bowl
bolas ⓕ pl **de algodón** *bo*·las de al·go·*don* cotton balls
bolígrafo ⓜ bo·*lee*·gra·fo pen
bollos ⓜ pl *bo*·lyos rolls (bread)
bolo ⓜ *bo*·lo gig
bolsillo ⓜ bol·*see*·lyo pocket
bolso ⓜ *bol*·so bag • handbag
bomba ⓕ *bom*·ba bomb • pump
bombilla ⓕ bom·*bee*·lya light bulb
bondadoso/a ⓜ/ⓕ bon·da·*do*·so/a caring
bonito/a ⓜ/ⓕ bo·*nee*·to/a pretty
bordo ⓜ *bor*·do edge
a bordo a *bor*·do aboard
borracho/a ⓜ/ⓕ bo·*ra*·cho/a drunk
bosque ⓜ *bos*·ke forest
botas ⓕ pl *bo*·tas boots
— de montaña de mon·*ta*·nya hiking boots

botella ⓕ bo·*te*·lya bottle
botones ⓜ pl bo·*to*·nes buttons
boxeo ⓜ bo·*kse*·o boxing
bragas ⓕ pl *bra*·gas underpants (women)
brazo ⓜ *bra*·tho arm
broma ⓕ *bro*·ma joke
bronceador ⓜ bron·the·a·*dor* tanning lotion
bronquitis ⓜ bron·*kee*·tees bronchitis
brotes ⓜ pl **de soja** *bro*·tes de so·*kha* bean sprouts
brújula ⓕ *broo*·khoo·la compass
brumoso broo·*mo*·so foggy
buceo ⓜ boo·*the*·o snorkelling
budista ⓜ&ⓕ boo·*dees*·ta Buddhist
bueno/a ⓜ/ⓕ *bwe*·no/a good
bufanda ⓕ boo·*fan*·da scarf
buffet ⓜ boo·*fe* buffet
bulto ⓜ *bool*·to lump
burlarse de boor·*lar*·se de make fun of
burro ⓜ *boo*·ro donkey
buscar boos·*kar* look for
buzón ⓜ boo·*thon* mailbox

C

caballo ⓜ ka·*ba*·lyo horse
cabeza ⓕ ka·*be*·tha head
cabina ⓕ **telefónica** ka·*bee*·na te·le·*fo*·nee·ka phone box
cable ⓜ *ka*·ble cable
cables ⓜ pl **de arranque** *ka*·bles de a·*ran*·ke jumper leads
cabra ⓕ *ka*·bra goat
cacahuetes ⓜ pl ka·ka·*we*·tes peanuts
cacao ⓜ ka·*kow* cocoa
cachorro ⓜ ka·*cho*·ro puppy
cada *ka*·da each
cadena ⓕ **de bici** ka·*de*·na de *bee*·thee bike chain
café ⓜ ka·*fe* coffee • cafe
caída ⓕ ka·*ee*·da fall

caja ① ka·kha box • cashier

— fuerte fwer·te safe

— registradora re·khees·tra·do·ra cash register

cajero ⓜ **automático** ka·khe·ro ow·to·ma·tee·ko automatic teller machine

calabacín ⓜ ka·la·ba·theen zucchini • courgette

calabaza ① ka·la·ba·tha pumpkin

calcetines ⓜ pl kal·the·tee·nes socks

calculadora ① kal·koo·la·do·ra calculator

caldo ⓜ kal·do stock

calefacción ① **central** ka·le·fak·thyon then·tral central heating

calendario ⓜ ka·len·da·ryo calendar

calidad ① ka·lee·da quality

caliente ka·lyen·te hot

calle ① ka·lye street

calor ⓜ ka·lor heat

calzoncillos ⓜ pl kal·thon·thee·lyos underpants (men)

calzones ⓜ pl kal·tho·nes boxer shorts

cama ① ka·ma bed

— de matrimonio de ma·tree·mo·nyo double bed

cámara ① **(fotográfica)** ka·ma·ra (fo·to·gra·fee·ka) camera

cámara ① **de aire** ka·ma·ra de ai·re tube (tyre)

camarero/a ⓜ/① ka·ma·re·ro/a waiter

cambiar kam·byar change • exchange (money)

cambio kam·byo ⓜ loose change

— de dinero de dee·ne·ro currency exchange

caminar ka·mee·nar walk

camino ⓜ ka·mee·no trail • way

caminos ⓜ pl **rurales** ka·mee·nos roo·ra·les hiking routes

camión ⓜ ka·myon truck

camisa ① ka·mee·sa shirt

camiseta ① ka·mee·se·ta singlet • T-shirt

cámping ⓜ kam·peen campsite

campo ⓜ kam·po countryside • field

Canadá ⓜ ka·na·da Canada

canasta ① ka·nas·ta basket

cancelar kan·the·lar cancel

cáncer ⓜ kan·ther cancer

canción ① kan·thyon song

candado ⓜ kan·da·do padlock

cangrejo ⓜ kan·gre·kho crab

canguro ⓜ kan·goo·ro babysitter

cansado/a ⓜ/① kan·sa·do/a tired

cantalupo ⓜ kan·ta·loo·po cantaloupe

cantante ⓜ&① kan·tan·te singer

cantar kan·tar sing

cantimplora ① kan·teem·plo·ra water bottle

capa ① **de ozono** ka·pa de o·tho·no ozone layer

capilla ① ka·pee·lya shrine

capote ⓜ ka·po·te cloak

cara ① ka·ra face

caracol ⓜ ka·ra·kol snail

caramelos ⓜ pl ka·ra·me·los lollies

caravana ① ka·ra·va·na caravan • van • traffic jam

cárcel ① kar·thel prison

cardenal ⓜ kar·de·nal bruise

carne ① kar·ne meat

— de vaca de va·ka beef

— molida mo·lee·da mince meat

carnet ⓜ kar·ne licence

— de identidad de ee·den·tee·da identification card

— de conducir de kon·doo·theer drivers licence

carnicería ① kar·nee·the·ree·a butcher's shop

caro/a ⓜ/① ka·ro/a expensive

carpintero ⓜ kar·peen·te·ro carpenter

carrera ① ka·re·ra race (sport)

carta ① kar·ta letter

cartas ① pl *kar*·tas cards
cartón ⓜ kar·*ton* carton • cardboard
casa ① *ka*·sa house
(en) casa (en) *ka*·sa (at) home
casarse ka·*sar*·se marry
cascada ① kas·*ka*·da waterfall
casco ⓜ *kas*·ko helmet
casete ⓜ ka·*se*·te cassette
casi *ka*·see almost
casino ⓜ ka·*see*·no casino
castigar kas·tee·*gar* punish
castillo ⓜ kas·*tee*·lyo castle
catedral ① ka·te·*dral* cathedral
católico/a ⓜ/① ka·*to*·lee·ko/a
Catholic
caza ① *ka*·tha hunting
cazuela ① ka·*thwe*·la pot (kitchen)
cebolla ① the·*bo*·lya onion
celebración ① the·le·bra·*thyon*
celebration
celebrar the·le·*brar* celebrate (an event)
celoso/a ⓜ/① the·*lo*·so/a jealous
cementerio ⓜ the·men·*te*·ryo
cemetery
cena ① *the*·na dinner
cenicero ⓜ the·nee·*the*·ro ashtray
centavo ⓜ then·*ta*·vo cent
centímetro ⓜ then·*tee*·me·tro
centimetre
central ① **telefónica** then·*tral*
te·le·fo·nee·ka telephone centre
centro ⓜ *then*·tro centre
— comercial ko·mer·*thyal* shopping
centre
— de la ciudad de la thyu·*da* city
centre
cepillo ⓜ the·*pee*·lyo hairbrush
— de dientes de *dyen*·tes toothbrush
cerámica ① the·*ra*·mee·ka ceramic
cerca ① *ther*·ka fence
cerca *ther*·ka near • nearby
cerdo ⓜ *ther*·do pork • pig
cereales ⓜ pl the·re·*a*·les cereal
cerillas ① pl las the·*ree*·lyas matches
cerrado/a ⓜ/① the·*ra*·do/a closed
— con llave kon *lya*·ve locked

cerradura ① the·ra·*doo*·ra lock
(padlock)
cerrar the·*rar* close • lock • shut
certificado ⓜ ther·tee·fee·*ka*·do
certificate
cerveza ① ther·*ve*·tha beer
— rubia *roo*·bya lager
cibercafé ⓜ thee·ber·ka·*fe* internet
cafe
ciclismo ⓜ thee·*klees*·mo cycling
ciclista ⓜ&① thee·*klees*·ta cyclist
ciego/a ⓜ/① *thye*·go/a blind
cielo ⓜ *thye*·lo heaven • sky
ciencias ① pl *thyen*·thyas science
científico/a ⓜ/① thyen·*tee*·fee·ko/a
scientist
cigarrillo ⓜ thee·ga·*ree*·lyo cigarette
cigarro ⓜ thee·*ga*·ro cigarette
cine ⓜ *thee*·ne cinema
cinta ① **de vídeo** *theen*·ta de
vee·de·o video tape
cinturón ⓜ **de seguridad**
theen·too·*ron* de se·goo·ree·*da* seatbelt
circuito ⓜ **de carreras** theer·*kwee*·to
de ka·*re*·ras racetrack (cars)
ciruela ① thee·*rwe*·la plum
— pasa *pa*·sa prune
cistitis ① thees·*tee*·tees cystitis
cita ① *thee*·ta appointment
citarse thee·*tar*·se date
citología ① thee·to·lo·*khee*·a pap
smear
ciudad ① thyu·*da* city
ciudadanía ① thyu·da·da·*nee*·a
citizenship
clase ① **preferente** *kla*·se
pre·fe·*ren*·te business class
clase ① **turística** *kla*·se
too·*rees*·tee·ka economy class
clásico/a ⓜ/① *kla*·see·ko/a classical
clienta/e ⓜ/① klee·*en*·ta/e client
clínica ① *klee*·nee·ka private hospital
cobrar (un cheque) ko·*brar* (oon
che·ke) cash (a cheque)
coca ① *ko*·ka cocaine

cocaína ① ko·ka·ee·na cocaine
coche ⓜ ko·che car
— cama ka·ma sleeping car
cocina ① ko·thee·na kitchen • stove
cocinar ko·thee·nar cook
cocinero ⓜ ko·thee·ne·ro chef • cook
coco ⓜ ko·ko coconut
codeína ① ko·de·ee·na codeine
código postal ko·dee·go pos·tal
post code
cojonudo/a ⓜ/① ko·kho·noo·do/a
fantastic
col ⓜ kol cabbage
cola ① ko·la queue
colchón ⓜ kol·chon mattress
colega ⓜ&① ko·le·ga colleague • mate
coles ⓜ pl **de Bruselas** ko·les de
broo·se·las brussels sprouts
coliflor ⓜ ko·lee·flor cauliflower
colina ① ko·lee·na hill
collar ⓜ ko·lyar necklace
color ⓜ ko·lor colour
comedia ① ko·me·dya comedy
comenzar ko·men·thar begin • start
comer ko·mer eat
comerciante ⓜ&① ko·mer·thyan·te
business person
comercio ⓜ ko·mer·thyo trade
comezón ⓜ ko·me·thon itch
comida ① ko·mee·da food
— de bebé de be·be baby food
— en el campo en el kam·po picnic
comisaría ① ko·mee·sa·ree·a police
station
cómo ko·mo how
cómodo/a ⓜ/① ko·mo·do/a
comfortable
cómpact ⓜ kom·pak CD
compañero/a ⓜ/① kom·pa·nye·ro/a
companion
compañía ① kom·pa·nyee·a company
compartir kom·par·teer share (with)
comprar kom·prar buy
comprender kom·pren·der
understand

compresas ① pl kom·pre·sas
sanitary napkins
compromiso ⓜ kom·pro·mee·so
engagement
comunión ① ko·moo·nyon
communion
comunista ⓜ&① ko·moo·nees·ta
communist
con kon with
coñac ⓜ ko·nyak brandy
concentración ① kon·then·tra·thyon
rally
concierto ⓜ kon·thyer·to concert
condición ① **cardíaca** kon·dee·thyon
kar·dee·a·ka heart condition
condones ⓜ pl kon·do·nes condoms
conducir kon·doo·theer drive
conejo ⓜ ko·ne·kho rabbit
conexión ① ko·ne·ksyon connection
confesión ① kon·fe·syon confession
confianza ① kon·fee·an·tha trust
confiar kon·fee·ar trust
confirmar kon·feer·mar confirm
conocer ko·no·ther know (someone)
conocido/a ⓜ/① ko·no·thee·do/a
famous
consejo ⓜ kon·se·kho advice
conservador(a) ⓜ/① kon·ser·va·dor/
kon·ser·va·do·ra conservative
consigna ① kon·seeg·na left luggage
— automática ow·to·ma·tee·ka
luggage lockers
construir kons·troo·eer build
consulado ⓜ kon·soo·la·do consulate
contaminación ①
kon·ta·mee·na·thyon pollution
contar kon·tar count
contestador ⓜ **automático**
kon·tes·ta·dor ow·to·ma·tee·ko
answering machine
contrato ⓜ kon·tra·to contract
control ⓜ kon·trol checkpoint
convento ⓜ kon·ven·to convent
copa ① ko·pa drink
— de vino de vee·no wineglass

CH

Copa ① Mundial ko·pa moon·dyal World Cup

copos de maíz ko·pos de ma·eeth corn flakes

corazón ⓜ ko·ra·thon heart

cordero ⓜ kor·de·ro lamb

cordillera ① kor·dee·lye·ra mountain range

correcto/a ⓜ/① ko·rek·to/a right (correct)

correo ⓜ ko·re·o mail

— urgente oor·khen·te express mail

correos ko·re·os post office

correr ko·rer run

corrida ① **de toros** ko·ree·da de to·ros bullfight

corriente ① ko·ryen·te current (electricity)

corriente ko·ryen·te ordinary

corrupto/a ⓜ/① ko·roop·to/a corrupt

cortar kor·tar cut

cortauñas ⓜ pl kor·ta·oo·nyas nail clippers

corto/a ⓜ/① kor·to/a short (length)

cosecha ① ko·se·cha crop

coser ko·ser sew

costa ① kos·ta coast • seaside

costar kos·tar cost

crecer kre·ther grow

crema ① kre·ma cream

— hidratante ee·dra·tan·te moisturising cream

— solar so·lar sunblock

críquet ⓜ kree·ket cricket

cristiano/a ⓜ/① krees·tya·no/a Christian

crítica ① kree·tee·ka review

cruce ⓜ kroo·the intersection

crudo/a ⓜ/① kroo·do/a raw

cuaderno ⓜ kwa·der·no notebook • square

cualificaciones ① pl kwa·lee·fee·ka·thyo·nes qualifications

cuando kwan·do when

cuánto kwan·to how much

cuarentena ① kwa·ren·te·na quarantine

Cuaresma ① kwa·res·ma Lent

cuarto ⓜ kwar·to quarter

cubiertos ⓜ pl koo·byer·tos cutlery

cubo ⓜ koo·bo bucket

cucaracha ① koo·ka·ra·cha cockroach

cuchara ① koo·cha·ra spoon

cucharita ① koo·cha·ree·ta teaspoon

cuchillas ① pl **de afeitar** koo·chee·lyas de a·fey·tar razor blades

cuchillo ⓜ koo·chee·lyo knife

cuenta ① kwen·ta bill

— bancaria ban·ka·rya bank account

cuento ⓜ kwen·to story

cuerda ① kwer·da rope • string

— para tender la ropa pa·ra ten·der la ro·pa clothes line

cuero ⓜ kwe·ro leather

cuerpo ⓜ kwer·po body

cuesta abajo kwes·ta a·ba·kho downhill

cuesta arriba kwes·ta a·ree·ba uphill

cuestionar kwes·tyo·nar question

cuevas ① pl kwe·vas caves

cuidar kwee·dar care for • mind (an object)

cuidar de kwee·dar de care (for someone)

culo ⓜ koo·lo bum (of body)

culpable kool·pa·ble guilty

cumbre ① koom·bre peak

cumpleaños ⓜ koom·ple·a·nyos birthday

currículum ⓜ koo·ree·koo·loom resumé

curry ⓜ koo·ree curry

cus cus ⓜ koos koos cous cous

CH

chaleco ⓜ **salvavidas** cha·le·ko sal·va·vee·das lifejacket

champán ⓜ cham·pan Champagne

champiñón ⓜ cham·pee·nyon mushrooms

champú ⓜ cham·*poo* shampoo
chaqueta ⓕ cha·*ke*·ta jacket
cheque ⓜ *che*·ke check (bank)
cheques ⓜ pl **de viajero** *che*·kes de vya·*khe*·ro travellers cheque
chica ⓕ *chee*·ka girl
chicle ⓜ *chee*·kle chewing gum
chico ⓜ *chee*·ko boy
chocolate ⓜ cho·ko·*la*·te chocolate
choque ⓜ *cho*·ke crash
chorizo ⓜ cho·*ree*·tho salami (Spanish sausage)
chupete ⓜ choo·*pe*·te dummy • pacifier

D

dados ⓜ pl *da*·dos dice (die)
dañar da·*nyar* hurt
dar dar give
— **de comer** de ko·*mer* feed
— **gracias** *gra*·thyas thank
— **la bienvenida** la byen·ve·*nee*·da welcome
— **una patada** oo·na pa·*ta*·da kick
darse cuenta de *dar*·se *kwen*·ta de realise
de de from
— **(cuatro) estrellas** de (*kwa*·tro) es·*tre*·lyas (four-)star
— **izquierdas** de eeth·*kyer*·das left-wing
— **pena** de *pe*·na terrible
— **primera clase** de pree·*me*·ra *kla*·se first-class
— **segunda mano** de se·*goon*·da *ma*·no second-hand
— **vez en cuando** de veth en *kwan*·do sometimes
deber de·*ver* owe
débil *de*·beel weak
decidir de·thee·*deer* decide
decir de·*theer* say • tell
dedo ⓜ *de*·do finger
— **del pie** del pye toe
defectuoso/a ⓜ/ⓕ de·fek·*two*·so/a faulty

deforestación ⓕ de·fo·res·ta·*thyon* deforestation
dejar de·*khar* leave • quit
delgado/a ⓜ/ⓕ del·*ga*·do/a thin
delirante de·lee·*ran*·te delirious
demasiado caro/a ⓜ/ⓕ de·ma·sya·do *ka*·ro/a too (expensive)
democracia ⓕ de·mo·*kra*·thya democracy
demora ⓕ de·*mo*·ra delay
dentista ⓜ&ⓕ den·*tees*·ta dentist
dentro de (una hora) *den*·tro de (oo·na o·ra) within (an hour)
deportes ⓜ pl de·*por*·tes sport
deportista ⓜ&ⓕ de·por·*tees*·ta sportsperson
depósito ⓜ de·*po*·see·to deposit
derecha ⓕ de·*re*·cha right (not left)
derechista de·re·*chees*·ta right-wing
derechos ⓜ pl **civiles** de·re·chos *thee*·vee·les civil rights
derechos ⓜ pl **humanos** de·re·chos oo·*ma*·nos human rights
desayuno ⓜ des·a·*yoo*·no breakfast
descansar des·kan·*sar* rest
descanso ⓜ des·*kan*·so intermission
descendiente ⓜ des·then·*dyen*·te descendant
descomponerse des·kom·po·*ner*·se decompose
descubrir des·koo·*breer* discover
descuento ⓜ des·*kwen*·to discount
desde (mayo) *des*·de (*ma*·yo) since (may)
desear de·se·*ar* wish
desierto ⓜ de·*syer*·to desert
desodorante ⓜ de·so·do·*ran*·te deodorant
despacio des·*pa*·thyo slowly
desperdicios ⓜ pl **nucleares** des·per·*dee*·thyos noo·kle·a·res nuclear waste
despertador ⓜ des·per·ta·*dor* alarm clock
después de des·*pwes* de after

E

destino ⓜ des·tee·no destination

destruir des·troo·eer destroy

detallado/a ⓜ/ⓕ de·ta·lya·do/a itemised

detalle ⓜ de·ta·lye detail

detener de·te·ner arrest

detrás de de·tras de behind

devocionario ⓜ de·vo·thyo·na·ryo prayer book

día ⓜ dee·a day

— festivo fes·tee·vo holiday

diabetes ⓕ dee·a·be·tes diabetes

diafragma ⓜ dee·a·frag·ma diaphragm

diapositiva ⓕ dya·po·see·tee·va slide

diariamente dya·rya·men·te daily

diarrea ⓕ dee·a·re·a diarrhoea

dieta ⓕ dee·e·ta diet

dibujar dee·boo·khar draw

diccionario ⓜ deek·thyo·na·ryo dictionary

diente (de ajo) dyen·te (de a·kho) clove (garlic)

dientes ⓜ pl dyen·tes teeth

diferencia ⓕ **de horas** dee·fe·ren·thya de o·ras time difference

diferente dee·fe·ren·te different

difícil dee·fee·theel difficult

dinero ⓜ dee·ne·ro money

— en efectivo en e·fek·tee·vo cash

Dios dyos god

dirección ⓕ dee·rek·thyon address

directo/a ⓜ/ⓕ dee·rek·to/a direct

director(a) ⓜ/ⓕ dee·rek·tor/ dee·rek·to·ra director

disco ⓜ dees·ko disk

discoteca ⓕ dees·ko·te·ka disco

discriminación ⓕ dees·kree·mee·na·thyon discrimination

discutir dees·koo·teer argue

diseño ⓜ dee·se·nyo design

disparar dees·pa·rar shoot

DIU ⓜ de·ee·oo IUD

diversión ⓕ dee·ver·syon fun

divertirse dee·ver·teer·se enjoy (oneself)

doblar do·blar turn • bend

doble do·ble double

docena ⓕ do·the·na dozen

doctor(a) ⓜ/ⓕ dok·tor/dok·to·ra doctor

dólar ⓜ do·lar dollar

dolor ⓜ do·lor pain

— de cabeza de ka·be·tha headache

— de estómago de es·to·ma·go stomachache

— de muelas de mwe·las toothache

— menstrual mens·trwal period pain

dolorido/a ⓜ/ⓕ do·lo·ree·do/a sore

doloroso/a ⓜ/ⓕ do·lo·ro·so/a painful

donde don·de where

dormir dor·meer sleep

dos ⓜ/ⓕ pl dos two

— camas ka·mas twin beds

— veces ve·thes twice

drama ⓜ dra·ma drama

droga ⓕ dro·ga drug • dope

drogadicción ⓕ dro·ga·deek·thyon drug addiction

drogas ⓕ pl dro·gas drugs

ducha ⓕ doo·cha shower

dueño/a ⓜ/ⓕ dwe·nyo/a owner

dulce dool·the sweet

dulces ⓜ pl dool·thes sweets

duro/a ⓜ/ⓕ doo·ro/a hard

E

eczema ⓕ ek·the·ma eczema

edad ⓕ e·da age

edificio ⓜ e·dee·fee·thyo building

editor(a) ⓜ/ⓕ e·dee·tor/e·dee·to·ra editor

educación ⓕ e·doo·ka·thyon education ⓕ

egoísta e·go·ees·ta selfish

ejemplo ⓜ e·khem·plo example

ejército ⓜ e·kher·thee·to military

el ⓜ el the

él ⓜ el he

elecciones ⓕ pl e·lek·thyo·nes elections

electricidad ⓕ e·lek·tree·thee·da electricity

elegir e·le·*kheer* pick • choose

ella ① e·lya she

ellos/ellas ⑩/① e·lyos/e·lyas they

embajada ① em·ba·*kha*·da embassy

embajador(a) ⑩/① em·ba·kha·dor/
em·ba·kha·do·ra ambassador

embarazada em·ba·ra·*tha*·da
pregnant

embarcarse em·bar·*kar*·se board
(ship etc)

embrague ⑩ em·*bra*·ge clutch

emergencia ① e·mer·*khen*·thya
emergency

emocional e·mo·thyo·*nal* emotional

empleado/a ⑩/① em·ple·a·do/a
employee

empujar em·poo·*khar* push

en en on

— el extranjero el eks·tran·*khe*·ro
abroad

— el paro el *pa*·ro unemployed

encaje ⑩ en·*ka*·khe lace

encantador(a) ⑩/① en·kan·ta·dor/
en·kan·ta·do·ra charming

encendedor ⑩ en·then·de·*dor* lighter

encontrar en·kon·*trar* find • meet

encurtidos ⑩ pl en·koor·tee·dos
pickles

energía ① **nuclear** e·ner·*khee*·a
noo·kle·*ar* nuclear energy

enfadado/a ⑩/① en·fa·*da*·do/a
angry

enfermedad ① en·fer·me·da disease

— venérea ve·*ne*·re·a venereal disease

enfermero/a ⑩/① en·fer·*me*·ro/a
nurse

enfermo/a ⑩/① en·*fer*·mo/a sick

enfrente de en·*fren*·te de in front of

enorme e·*nor*·me huge

ensalada en·sa·*la*·da salad

enseñar en·se·*nyar* show • teach

entrar en·*trar* enter

entre *en*·tre among • between

entregar en·tre·*gar* deliver

entrenador(a) ⑩/① en·tre·na·dor/
en·tre·na·do·ra coach

entreno ⑩ en·*tre*·no workout

entrevista ① en·tre·vees·ta interview

enviar en·vee·*ar* send • ship off

epilepsia ① e·pee·*lep*·sya epilepsy

equipaje ⑩ e·kee·*pa*·khe luggage

equipo ⑩ e·*kee*·po equipment • team

— de inmersión de een·mer·*syon*
diving equipment

— de música ⑩ de *moo*·see·ka stereo

equitación ① e·kee·ta·*thyon* horse
riding

equivocado/a ⑩/① e·kee·vo·*ka*·do/a
wrong

error ⑩ e·*ror* mistake

escalada ① es·ka·*la*·da rock climbing

escalera ① es·ka·*le*·ra stairway

escaleras ① pl **mecánicas**
es·ka·*le*·ras me·*kan*·icas escalator

escarcha ① es·*kar*·cha frost

escarpado/a ⑩/① es·kar·*pa*·do/a
steep

escasez ① es·ka·*seth* shortage

escenario ⑩ es·the·*na*·ryo stage

Escocia ① es·*ko*·thya Scotland

escoger es·ko·*kher* choose

escribir es·kree·*beer* write

— a máquina a *ma*·kee·na type

escritor(a) ⑩/① es·kree·tor/
es·kree·to·ra writer

escuchar es·koo·*char* listen

escuela ① es·*kwe*·la school

— de párvulos de *par*·voo·los
kindergarten

escultura ① es·kool·*too*·ra sculpture

espacio ⑩ es·*pa*·thyo space

espalda ① es·*pal*·da back (body)

España ① es·*pa*·nya Spain

especial es·pe·*thyal* special

especialista ⑩&① es·pe·thya·*lees*·ta
specialist

especies ① pl **en peligro de
extinción** es·*pe*·thyes en pe·*lee*·gro de
eks·*teen*·thyon endangered species

espectáculo ⑩ es·pek·*ta*·koo·lo show

espejo ⑩ es·*pe*·kho mirror

esperar es·pe·*rar* wait

F

espinaca ⓕ es·pee·*na*·ka spinach
esposa ⓕ es·*po*·sa wife
espuma ⓕ **de afeitar** es·*poo*·ma de a·fey·*tar* shaving cream
espumoso/a ⓜ/ⓕ es·poo·*mo*·so/a sparkling • foamy
esquí ⓜ es·*kee* skiing
— acuático a·*kwa*·tee·ko waterskiing
esquiar es·kee·*ar* ski
esquina ⓕ es·*kee*·na corner
esta noche es·ta *no*·che tonight
éste/a ⓜ/ⓕ *es*·te/a this
estación ⓕ es·ta·*thyon* season • station
— de autobuses de ow·to·*boo*·ses bus station
— de metro de *me*·tro metro station
— de tren de tren railway station
estacionar es·ta·thyo·*nar* park (car)
estadio ⓜ es·*ta*·dyo stadium
estado ⓜ **civil** es·*ta*·do thee·*veel* marital status
estado ⓜ **del bienestar** es·*ta*·do del byen·es·*tar* social welfare • wellbeing
Estados ⓜ pl **Unidos** es·*ta*·dos oo·*nee*·dos USA
estafa ⓕ es·*ta*·fa rip-off
estanquero ⓜ es·tan·*ke*·ro tobacconist
estante ⓜ es·*tan*·te shelf
estar es·*tar* to be
— constipado/a ⓜ/ⓕ kons·tee·*pa*·do/a have a cold
— de acuerdo de a·*kwer*·do agree
estatua ⓕ es·*ta*·twa statue
este *es*·te east
esterilla ⓕ es·te·*ree*·lya mat
estilo ⓜ es·*tee*·lo style
estómago ⓜ es·*to*·ma·go stomach
estrellas ⓕ pl es·*tre*·lyas stars
estreñimiento ⓜ es·tre·nyee·*myen*·to constipation
estudiante ⓜ&ⓕ es·too·*dyan*·te student
estudio ⓜ es·*too*·dyo studio
estufa ⓕ es·*too*·fa heater

estúpido/a ⓜ/ⓕ es·*too*·pee·do/a stupid
etiqueta ⓕ **de equipaje** e·tee·*ke*·ta de e·kee·*pa*·khe luggage tag
euro ⓜ e·oo·ro euro
Europa ⓕ e·oo·ro·pa Europe
eutanasia ⓕ e·oo·ta·*na*·sya euthanasia
excelente eks·the·*len*·te excellent
excursión ⓕ eks·koor·*syon* tour
excursionismo ⓜ eks·koor·syo·*nees*·mo hiking
experiencia ⓕ eks·pe·*ryen*·thya experience
— laboral ⓕ la·bo·*ral* work experience
exponer eks·po·*ner* exhibit
exposición ⓕ eks·po·see·*thyon* exhibition
expreso eks·*pre*·so express
exterior ⓜ eks·te·*ryor* outside
extrañar eks·tra·*nyar* miss (feel sad)
extranjero/a ⓜ/ⓕ eks·tran·*khe*·ro/a foreign

F

fábrica ⓕ *fa*·bree·ka factory
fácil *fa*·theel easy
facturación ⓕ **de equipajes** fak·too·ra·*thyon* de e·kee·*pa*·khes check-in
falda ⓕ *fal*·da skirt
falta ⓕ *fal*·ta fault
familia ⓕ fa·*mee*·lya family
fantástico/a ⓜ/ⓕ fan·*tas*·tee·ko/a great
farmacia ⓕ far·*ma*·thya chemist (shop) • pharmacy
farmacéutico ⓜ far·ma·thee·oo·tee·ko chemist (person)
faros ⓜ pl *fa*·ros headlights
fecha ⓕ *fe*·cha date (time)
— de nacimiento de na·thee·*myen*·to date of birth
feliz fe·*leeth* happy

ferretería ① fe·re·te·ree·a hardware store

festival ⓜ fes·tee·val festival

ficción ① feek·thyon fiction

fideos ⓜ pl fee·de·os noodles

fiebre ① fye·bre fever

— glandular glan·doo·lar glandular fever

fiesta ① fyes·ta party

filete ⓜ fee·le·te fillet

film ⓜ feelm film

fin ⓜ feen end

— de semana de se·ma·na weekend

final ⓜ fee·nal end

firma ① feer·ma signature

firmar feer·mar sign

flor ① flor flower

florista ⓜ&① flo·rees·ta florist

folleto ⓜ fo·lye·to brochure

footing ⓜ foo·teen jogging

forma ① for·ma shape

fotografía ① fo·to·gra·fee·a photograph

fotógrafo/a ⓜ/① fo·to·gra·fo/a photographer

fotómetro ⓜ fo·to·me·tro light meter

frágil fra·kheel fragile

frambuesa ① fram·bwe·sa raspberry

franela ① fra·ne·la flannel

franqueo ⓜ fran·ke·o postage

freír fre·eer fry

frenos ⓜ pl fre·nos brakes

frente a fren·te a opposite

fresa ① fre·sa strawberry

frío/a ⓜ/① free·o/a cold

frontera ① fron·te·ra border

fruta ① froo·ta fruit

fruto ⓜ **seco** froo·to se·ko dried fruit

fuego ⓜ fwe·go fire

fuera de juego fwe·ra de khwe·go offside

fuerte fwer·te strong

fumar foo·mar smoke

funda ① **de almohada** foon·da de al·mwa·da pillowcase

funeral ⓜ foo·ne·ral funeral

fútbol ⓜ foot·bol football • soccer

— australiano ow·stra·lya·no Australian Rules football

futuro ⓜ foo·too·ro future

G

gafas ① pl ga·fas glasses

— de sol de sol sunglasses

— de submarinismo de soob·ma·ree·nees·mo goggles

galleta ① ga·lye·ta biscuit • cookie

galletas ① pl **saladas** ga·lye·tas sa·la·das biscuits • crackers

gambas ① pl gam·bas prawns

ganador(a) ⓜ/① ga·na·dor/ ga·na·do·ra winner

ganar ga·nar earn • win

garbanzos ⓜ pl gar·ban·thos chickpeas

garganta ① gar·gan·ta throat

gasolina ① ga·so·lee·na petrol

gasolinera ① ga·so·lee·ne·ra service station

gatito/a ⓜ/① ga·tee·to/a kitten

gato/a ⓜ/① ga·to/a cat

gay gai gay

gemelos ⓜ pl khe·me·los twins

general khe·ne·ral general

gente ① khen·te people

gimnasia ① **rítmica** kheem·na·sya reet·mee·ka gymnastics

ginebra ① khee·ne·bra gin

ginecólogo ⓜ khee·ne·ko·lo·go gynaecologist

gobierno ⓜ go·byer·no government

gol ⓜ gol goal

goma ① go·ma condom • rubber

gordo/a ⓜ/① gor·do/a fat

grabación ① gra·ba·thyon recording

gracioso/a ⓜ/① gra·thyo·so/a funny

gramo ⓜ gra·mo gram

grande gran·de big • large

grande almacene ⓜ gran·de al·ma·the·ne department store

granja ① gran·kha farm

gratis gra·tees free (of charge)

grifo ⓜ *gree*·fo tap
gripe ⓕ *gree*·pe influenza
gris grees grey
gritar gree·*tar* shout
grupo ⓜ *groo*·po group
— de rock de rok rock band
— sanguíneo san·*gee*·ne·o blood group
guantes ⓜ pl *gwan*·tes gloves
guardarropa ⓜ gwar·da·*ro*·pa cloakroom
guardería ⓕ gwar·de·*ree*·a childminding service • creche
guerra ⓕ *ge*·ra war
guía ⓜ&ⓕ *gee*·a guide (person)
guía ⓕ *gee*·a guidebook
— audio *ow*·dyo audioguide
— del ocio del o·*thyo* entertainment guide
— telefónica te·le·*fo*·nee·ka phone book
guindilla ⓕ geen·*dee*·lya chilli
guión ⓜ gee·*on* script
guiri ⓜ *gee*·ree tourist (slang)
guisantes gee·*san*·tes peas
güisqui *gwees*·kee whiskey
guitarra ⓕ gee·*ta*·ra guitar
gustar(le) goos·*tar*(·le) like

H

habitación ⓕ a·bee·ta·*thyon* bedroom • room
— doble *do*·ble double room
— individual een·dee·vee·*dwal* single room
hablar a·*blar* speak • talk
hace sol a·the sol sunny
hacer a·*ther* do • make
— dedo de·do hitchhike
— surf soorf surf
— windsurf ween·soorf windsurfing
hachís ⓜ a·*chees* hash
hacia a·thya towards
— abajo a·ba·kho down
halal a·*lal* halal

hamaca ⓕ a·*ma*·ka hammock
hambriento/a ⓜ/ⓕ am·*bryen*·to/a hungry
harina ⓕ a·*ree*·na flour
hasta (junio) *as*·ta (*khoo*·nyo) until (June)
hecho/a ⓜ/ⓕ e·cho/a made
— a mano a *ma*·no handmade
— de (algodón) de (al·go·*don*) made of (cotton)
heladería ⓕ e·la·de·*ree*·a ice cream parlour
helado ⓜ e·*la*·do ice cream
helar e·*lar* freeze
hepatitis ⓕ e·pa·*tee*·tees hepatitis
herbolario ⓜ er·bo·*la*·ryo herbalist (shop)
herida ⓕ e·*ree*·da injury
hermana ⓕ er·*ma*·na sister
hermano ⓜ er·*ma*·no brother
hermoso/a ⓜ/ⓕ er·*mo*·so/a beautiful
heroína ⓕ e·ro·*ee*·na heroin
hielo ⓜ *ye*·lo ice
hierba ⓕ *yer*·ba grass
hierbas ⓕ pl *yer*·bas herbs
hígado ⓜ *ee*·ga·do liver
higos ⓜ pl *ee*·gos figs
hija ⓕ *ee*·kha daughter
hijo ⓜ *ee*·kho son
hijos ⓜ pl *ee*·khos children
hilo thread *ee*·lo
— dental den·*tal* dental floss
hinchas ⓜ&ⓕ pl *een*·chas supporters
hindú een·*doo* Hindu
hipódromo ⓜ ee·*po*·dro·mo racetrack (horses)
historial profesional ees·to·*ryal* pro·fe·syo·*nal* CV
histórico/a ⓜ/ⓕ ees·*to*·ree·ko/a historical
hockey ⓜ *kho*·kee hockey
— sobre hielo so·bre *ye*·lo ice hockey
hoja ⓕ o·kha leaf • sheet (of paper)

hojalata ① o·kha·*la*·ta tin
Holanda ① o·*lan*·da Netherlands
hombre ⓜ *om*·bre man
hombros ⓜ pl *om*·bros shoulders
homosexual ⓜ&① o·mo·se·*kswal* homosexual
hora ① o·ra time
horario ⓜ o·*ra*·ryo timetable
horas ① pl **de abrir** o·ras de a·*breer* opening hours
hormiga ① or·*mee*·ga ant
horno ⓜ *or*·no oven
horóscopo ⓜ o·*ros*·ko·po horoscope
hospital ⓜ os·pee·*tal* hospital
hostelería ① os·te·le·*ree*·a hospitality
hotel ⓜ o·*tel* hotel
hoy oy today
hueso ⓜ *we*·so bone
huevo ⓜ *we*·vo egg
humanidades ① pl oo·ma·nee·*da*·des humanities

I

identificación ①
ee·den·tee·fee·ka·*thyon* identification
idiomas ⓜ pl ee·*dyo*·mas languages
idiota ⓜ/① ee·*dyo*·ta idiot
iglesia ① ee·*gle*·sya church
igual ee·*gwal* same
igualdad ① ee·gwal·*da* equality
impermeable ⓜ eem·per·me·*a*·ble raincoat
impermeable eem·per·me·*a*·ble waterproof
importante eem·por·*tan*·te important
impuesto ⓜ eem·*pwes*·to tax
— sobre la renta so·bre la *ren*·ta income tax
incluido een·kloo·ee·*do* included
incómodo/a ⓜ/① een·*ko*·mo·do/a uncomfortable
India ① *een*·dya India
indicador ⓜ een·dee·ka·*dor* indicator
indigestión ① een·dee·khes·*tyon* indigestion

industria ① een·*doos*·trya industry
infección ① een·fek·*thyon* infection
inflamación ① een·fla·ma·*thyon* inflammation
informática ① een·for·*ma*·tee·ka IT
ingeniería ① een·khe·nye·*ree*·a engineering
ingeniero/a ⓜ/① een·khe·*nye*·ro/a engineer
Inglaterra ① een·gla·*te*·ra England
inglés ⓜ een·*gles* English • English language
ingrediente ⓜ een·gre·*dyen*·te ingredient
injusto/a ⓜ/① een·*khoos*·to/a unfair
inmigración ① een·mee·gra·*thyon* immigration
inocente ee·no·*then*·te innocent
inseguro/a ⓜ/① een·se·*goo*·ro/a unsafe
instituto ⓜ eens·tee·*too*·to high school
intentar (hacer algo) een·ten·*tar* (a·*ther* al·go) try (to do something)
interesante een·te·re·*san*·te interesting
internacional een·ter·na·thyo·*nal* international
Internet ⓜ *een*·ter·net Internet
intérprete ⓜ&① een·*ter*·pre·te interpreter
inundación ① ee·noon·da·*thyon* flooding
invierno ⓜ een·*vyer*·no winter
invitar een·vee·*tar* invite
inyección ① een·yek·*thyon* injection
inyectar(se) een·yek·*tar*(·se) inject (oneself)
ir eer go
— de compras de *kom*·pras go shopping
— de excursión de eks·koor·*syon* hike
— en tobogán en to·bo·*gan* tobogganing
Irlanda ① eer·*lan*·da Ireland

J

irritación ① ee·ree·ta·*thyon* rash
— de pañal de pa·*nyal* nappy rash
isla ① *ees*·la island
itinerario ⓜ ee·tee·ne·*ra*·ryo itinerary
IVA ⓜ *ee*·va sales tax
izquierda ① eeth·*kyer*·da left

J

jabón ⓜ kha·*bon* soap
jamón ⓜ kha·*mon* ham
Japón ⓜ kha·*pon* Japan
jarabe ⓜ kha·*ra*·be cough medicine
jardín ⓜ **botánico** khar·*deen* bo·*ta*·nee·ko botanic garden
jarra ① *kha*·ra jar
jefe/a ⓜ/① *khe*·fe/a boss • leader
— de sección de sek·*thyon* manager
jengibre ⓜ khen·*khee*·bre ginger
jeringa ① khe·*reen*·ga syringe
jersey ⓜ kher·*sey* jumper • sweater
jet lag ⓜ dyet lag jet lag
jockey ⓜ *dyo*·kee jockey
joven *kho*·ven young
joyería ① kho·ye·*ree*·a jeweller (shop)
jubilado/a ⓜ/① khoo·bee·*la*·do/a retired
judías ① pl khoo·*dee*·as beans
judío/a ⓜ/① khoo·*dee*·o/a Jewish
juegos ⓜ pl **de ordenador** *khwe*·gos de or·de·na·*dor* computer games
juegos ⓜ pl **olímpicos** *khwe*·gos o·*leem*·pee·kos Olympic Games
juez ⓜ&① khweth judge
jugar khoo·*gar* play (sport/games)
jugo ⓜ *khoo*·go juice
juguetería ① khoo·ge·te·*ree*·a toyshop
juntos/as ⓜ/① pl *khoon*·tos/as together

K

kilogramo ⓜ kee·lo·*gra*·mo kilogram
kilómetro ⓜ kee·*lo*·me·tro kilometre

kiwi ⓜ *kee*·wee kiwifruit
kosher *ko*·sher Kosher

L

labios ⓜ pl *la*·byos lips
lado ⓜ *la*·do side
ladrón ⓜ la·*dron* thief
lagartija ① la·gar·*tee*·kha lizard
lago ⓜ *la*·go lake
lamentar la·men·*tar* regret
lana ① *la*·na wool
lápiz ⓜ *la*·peeth pencil
— de labios de *la*·byos lipstick
largo/a ⓜ/① *lar*·go/a long
lata ① *la*·ta can
lavadero de la·va·*de*·ro laundry
lavadora ① la·va·*do*·ra washing machine
lavandería ① la·van·de·*ree*·a laundrette
lavar la·*var* wash (something)
lavarse la·*var*·se wash (oneself)
leche ① *le*·che milk
— de soja de so·*kha* soy milk
— desnatada des·na·*ta*·da skimmed milk
lechuga ① le·*choo*·ga lettuce
leer le·*er* read
legal le·*gal* legal
legislación ① le·khees·la·*thyon* legislation
legumbre ① le·*goom*·bre legume
lejos *le*·khos far
leña ① *le*·nya firewood
lentejas ① pl len·*te*·khas lentils
lentes de contacto *len*·tes de kon·*tak*·to contact lenses
lento/a ⓜ/① *len*·to/a slow
lesbiana ① les·bee·*a*·na lesbian
leve *le*·ve light
ley ① ley law
libra ① *lee*·bra pound (money)
libre *lee*·bre free (not bound)
librería ① lee·bre·*ree*·a bookshop
libro ⓜ *lee*·bro book
— de frases de *fra*·ses phrasebook

libros m pl **de viajes** lee·bros de vya·khes travel books

líder m lee·der leader

ligar lee·gar pick up

lila lee·la purple

lima lee·ma lime

límite m **de equipaje** lee·mee·te de e·kee·pa·khe baggage allowance

limón m lee·mon lemon

limonada f lee·mo·na·da lemonade

limpio/a m/f leem·pyo/a clean

línea f lee·ne·a line

linterna f leen·ter·na flashlight • torch

listo/a m/f lees·to/a ready

lo que lo ke what

local m lo·kal venue

local lo·kal local

loco/a m/f lo·ko/a crazy

lodo m lo·do mud

lombrices f pl lom·bree·thes worms

los dos los dos both

lubricante m loo·bree·kan·te lubricant

luces f pl loo·thes lights

luchar contra loo·char kon·tra fight against

lugar m loo·gar place

— de nacimiento de na·thee·myen·to place of birth

lujo m loo·kho luxury

luna f loo·na moon

— llena lye·na full moon

— de miel de myel honeymoon

luz f looth light

llamada f lya·ma·da phone call

— a cobro revertido a ko·bro re·ver·tee·do collect call

llamar por telefono lya·mar por te·le·fo·no to make a phone call

llano/a m/f lya·no/a flat

llave f lya·ve key

llegadas f pl lye·ga·das arrivals

llegar lye·gar arrive

llenar lye·nar fill

lleno/a m/f lye·no/a full

llevar lye·var carry • wear

lluvia f lyoo·vya rain

M

machismo m ma·chees·mo sexism

madera f ma·de·ra wood

madre f ma·dre mother

madrugada f ma·droo·ga·da early morning

mago/a m/f ma·go/a magician

maíz m ma·eeth corn

maleta f ma·le·ta suitcase

maletín m ma·le·teen briefcase

— de primeros auxilios m de pree·me·ros ow·ksee·lyos first-aid kit

malo/a m/f ma·lo/a bad

mamá f ma·ma mum

mamograma m ma·mo·gra·ma mammogram

mañana f ma·nya·na tomorrow • morning (6am–1pm)

— por la mañana por la ma·nya·na tomorrow morning

— por la noche por la no·che tomorrow evening

— por la tarde por la tar·de tomorrow afternoon

mandarina f man·da·ree·na mandarin

mandíbula f man·dee·boo·la jaw

mando a distancia man·do a dees·tan·thya remote control

mango m man·go mango

manifestación f ma·nee·fes·ta·thyon demonstration

manillar m ma·nee·lyar handlebar

mano f ma·no hand

manta f man·ta blanket

manteca f man·te·ka lard

mantel m man·tel tablecloth

mantequilla f man·te·kee·lya butter

manzana f man·tha·na apple

mapa m ma·pa map

maquillaje ⓜ ma·kee·*lya*·khe make-up

máquina ⓕ ma·*kee*·na machine

— de billetes de bee·*lye*·tes ticket machine

— de tabaco de ta·*ba*·ko cigarette machine

mar ⓜ mar sea

marido ⓜ ma·*ree*·do husband

maravilloso/a ⓜ/ⓕ ma·ra·vee·*lyo*·so/a wonderful

marcador ⓜ mar·ka·*dor* scoreboard

marcapasos ⓜ mar·ka·*pa*·sos pacemaker

marcar mar·*kar* score

marea ⓕ ma·*re*·a tide

mareado/a ⓜ/ⓕ ma·re·a·do/a dizzy • seasick

mareo ⓜ ma·*re*·o travel sickness

margarina ⓕ mar·ga·*ree*·na margarine

marihuana ⓕ ma·ree·*wa*·na marijuana

mariposa ⓕ ma·ree·*po*·sa butterfly

marrón ma·*ron* brown

martillo ⓜ mar·*tee*·lyo hammer

más cercano/a ⓜ/ⓕ mas ther·*ka*·no/a nearest

masaje ⓜ ma·*sa*·khe massage

masajista ⓜ&ⓕ ma·sa·*khees*·ta masseur

matar ma·*tar* kill

matrícula ⓕ ma·*tree*·koo·la license plate number

matrimonio ⓜ ma·tree·*mo*·nyo marriage

mayonesa ⓕ ma·yo·*ne*·sa mayonnaise

mecánico ⓜ me·*ka*·nee·ko mechanic

mechero ⓜ me·*che*·ro lighter

medianoche ⓕ me·dya·*no*·che midnight

medias ⓕ pl *me*·dyas stockings • pantyhose

medicina ⓕ me·dee·*thee*·na medicine

medico/a ⓜ/ⓕ me·*dee*·co/a doctor

medio ⓜ **ambiente** *me*·dyo am·*byen*·te environment

medio/a ⓜ/ⓕ *me*·dyo/a half

mediodía ⓜ me·dyo·*dee*·a noon

medios ⓜ pl **de comunicación** *me*·dyos de ko·moo·nee·ka·*thyon* media

medios ⓜ pl **de transporte** *me*·dyos de trans·*por*·te means of transport

meditación ⓕ meditation me·dee·ta·*thyon*

mejillones ⓜ pl me·khee·*lyo*·nes mussels

mejor me·*khor* better • best

melocotón ⓜ me·lo·ko·*ton* peach

melodía ⓕ me·lo·*dee*·a tune

melón ⓜ me·*lon* melon

mendigo/a ⓜ/ⓕ men·*dee*·go/a beggar

menos *me*·nos less

mensaje ⓜ men·*sa*·khe message

menstruación ⓕ mens·trwa·*thyon* menstruation

mentiroso/a ⓜ/ⓕ men·tee·ro·so/a liar

menú ⓜ me·*noo* menu

menudo/a ⓜ/ⓕ me·*noo*·do/a little

a menudo a me·*noo*·do often

mercado ⓜ mer·*ka*·do market

mermelada ⓕ mer·me·*la*·da jam • marmalade

mes ⓜ mes month

mesa ⓕ *me*·sa table

meseta ⓕ me·se·ta plateau

metal ⓜ me·*tal* metal

meter (un gol) me·*ter* (oon gol) kick (a goal)

metro ⓜ *me*·tro metre

mezclar meth·*klar* mix

mezquita ⓕ meth·*kee*·ta mosque

mi mee my

microondas ⓜ mee·kro·*on*·das microwave

miel ⓕ myel honey

miembro ⓜ *myem*·bro member
migraña ⓕ mee·*gra*·nya migraine
milímetro ⓜ mee·*lee*·me·tro millimetre
millón ⓜ mee·*lyon* million
minusválido/a ⓜ/ⓕ mee·noos·*va*·lee·do/a disabled
minuto ⓜ mee·*noo*·to minute
mirador ⓜ mee·ra·*dor* lookout
mirar mee·*rar* look • watch
— los escaparates los es·ka·pa·*ra*·tes window-shopping
misa ⓕ *mee*·sa mass
mochila ⓕ mo·*chee*·la backpack
módem ⓜ *mo*·dem modem
(carne) molida (*kar*·ne) mo·*lee*·da mince (meat)
mojado/a ⓜ/ⓕ mo·*kha*·do/a wet
monasterio ⓜ mo·nas·*te*·ryo monastery
monedas ⓕ pl mo·*ne*·das coins
monja ⓕ *mon*·kha nun
monopatinaje ⓜ mo·no·pa·tee·*na*·khe skateboarding
montaña ⓕ mon·*ta*·nya mountain
montar mon·*tar* ride
— en bicicleta en bee·thee·*kle*·ta cycle
monumento ⓜ mo·noo·*men*·to monument
mordedura ⓕ mor·de·*doo*·ra bite (dog)
morir mo·*reer* die
mosquitera ⓕ mos·kee·*te*·ra mosquito net
mosquito ⓜ mos·*kee*·to mosquito
mostaza ⓕ mos·*ta*·tha mustard
mostrador ⓜ mos·tra·*dor* counter
mostrar mos·*trar* show
motocicleta ⓕ mo·to·thee·*kle*·ta motorcycle
motor ⓜ mo·*tor* engine
motora ⓕ mo·*to*·ra motorboat
muchas/os ⓜ/ⓕ pl *moo*·chas/os many

mudo/a ⓜ/ⓕ *moo*·do/a mute
muebles ⓜ pl *mwe*·bles furniture
muela ⓕ *mwe*·la tooth (back)
muelle ⓜ *mwe*·lye spring
muerto/a ⓜ/ⓕ *mwer*·to/a dead
muesli ⓜ *mwes*·lee muesli
mujer ⓕ moo·*kher* woman
multa ⓕ *mool*·ta fine
mundo ⓜ *moon*·do world
muñeca ⓕ moo·*nye*·ka doll • wrist
murallas ⓕ pl moo·*ra*·lyas city walls
músculo ⓜ *moos*·koo·lo muscle
museo ⓜ moo·*se*·o museum
— de arte de *ar*·te art gallery
música ⓕ *moo*·see·ka music
músico/a ⓜ/ⓕ *moo*·see·ko/a musician
— ambulante am·boo·*lan*·te busker
muslo ⓜ *moos*·lo drumstick (chicken)
musulmán(a) ⓜ/ⓕ moo·sool·*man*/ moo·sool·*ma*·na Muslim
muy mooy very

N

nacionalidad ⓕ na·thyo·na·lee·*da* nationality
nada *na*·da none • nothing
nadar na·*dar* swim
naranja ⓕ na·*ran*·kha orange
nariz ⓕ na·*reeth* nose
nata ⓕ **agria** *na*·ta *a*·grya sour cream
naturaleza ⓕ na·too·ra·*le*·tha nature
naturopatía ⓕ na·too·ro·pa·*tee*·a naturopathy
náusea ⓕ *now*·se·a nausea
náuseas ⓕ pl **del embarazo** *now*·se·as del em·ba·*ra*·tho morning sickness
navaja ⓕ na·*va*·kha penknife
Navidad ⓕ na·vee·*da* Christmas
necesario/a ⓜ/ⓕ ne·the·*sa*·ryo/a necessary
necesitar ne·the·see·*tar* need
negar ne·*gar* deny

O

negar ne·*gar* refuse

negocio Ⓜ ne·*go*·thyo business

— de artículos básicos de ar·*tee*·koo·los ba·*see*·kos convenience store

negro/a Ⓜ/Ⓕ *ne*·gro/a black

neumático Ⓜ ne·oo·*ma*·tee·ko tyre

nevera Ⓕ ne·*ve*·ra refrigerator

nieto/a Ⓜ/Ⓕ *nye*·to/a grandchild

nieve Ⓕ *nye*·ve snow

niño/a Ⓜ/Ⓕ *nee*·nyo/a child

no no no

— fumadores foo·ma·*do*·res non-smoking

— incluido een·kloo·ee·do excluded

noche Ⓕ *no*·che evening • night

Nochebuena Ⓕ no·che·*bwe*·na Christmas Eve

Nochevieja Ⓕ no·che·*vye*·kha New Year's Eve

nombre Ⓜ *nom*·bre name

— de pila de *pee*·la Christian name

norte Ⓜ *nor*·te north

nosotros/as Ⓜ/Ⓕ pl no·*so*·tros/ no·*so*·tras we

noticias Ⓕ pl no·*tee*·thyas news

— de actualidad de ak·twal·ee·*da* current affairs

novia Ⓕ *no*·vya girlfriend

novio Ⓜ *no*·vyo boyfriend

nube Ⓕ *noo*·be cloud

nublado noo·*bla*·do cloudy

nueces *nwe*·thes nuts

— crudas *kroo*·das raw nuts

— tostadas tos·*ta*·das roasted nuts

nuestro/a Ⓜ/Ⓕ *nwes*·tro/a our

Nueva Zelanda Ⓕ *nwe*·va the·*lan*·da New Zealand

nuevo/a Ⓜ/Ⓕ *nwe*·vo/a new

número Ⓜ *noo*·me·ro number

— de la habitación de la a·bee·ta·*thyon* room number

— de pasaporte de pa·sa·*por*·te passport number

nunca *noon*·ka never

O

o o or

obra Ⓕ *o*·bra play • building site

obrero/a Ⓜ/Ⓕ o·*bre*·ro/a factory worker • labourer

océano Ⓜ o·*the*·a·no ocean

ocupado/a Ⓜ/Ⓕ o·koo·*pa*·do/a busy

ocupar o·koo·*par* live (somewhere)

oeste Ⓜ o·*es*·te west

oficina Ⓕ o·fee·*thee*·na office

— de objetos perdidos de ob·*khe*·tos per·*dee*·dos lost property office

— de turismo de too·*rees*·mo tourist office

oír o·*eer* hear

ojo Ⓜ o·*kho* eye

ola Ⓕ *o*·la wave

olor Ⓜ o·*lor* smell

olvidar ol·vee·*dar* forget

ópera Ⓕ *o*·pe·ra opera

operación Ⓕ o·pe·ra·*thyon* operation

opinión Ⓕ o·pee·*nyon* opinion

oporto Ⓜ o·*por*·to port (wine)

oportunidad Ⓕ o·por·too·nee·*da* chance

oración Ⓕ o·ra·*thyon* prayer

orden Ⓜ *or*·den order (placement)

ordenador Ⓜ or·de·na·*dor* computer

— portátil por·ta·*teel* laptop

ordenar or·de·*nar* order

oreja Ⓕ o·*re*·kha ear

orgasmo Ⓜ or·*gas*·mo orgasm

original o·ree·khee·*nal* original

orquesta Ⓕ or·*kes*·ta orchestra

oscuro/a Ⓜ/Ⓕ os·*koo*·ro/a dark

ostra Ⓕ *os*·tra oyster

otoño Ⓜ o·*to*·nyo autumn

otra vez *o*·tra veth again

otro/a Ⓜ/Ⓕ *o*·tro/a other • another

oveja Ⓕ o·*ve*·kha sheep

oxígeno Ⓜ o·*ksee*·khe·no oxygen

P

padre Ⓜ *pa*·dre father

padres Ⓜ pl *pa*·dres parents

P

pagar pa·*gar* pay
página ① pa·*khee*·na page
pago ⓜ *pa*·go payment
país ⓜ pa·*ees* country
pájaro ⓜ *pa*·kha·ro bird
palabra ① pa·*la*·bra word
palacio ⓜ pa·*la*·thyo palace
palillo ⓜ pa·*lee*·lyo toothpick
pan ⓜ pan bread
— integral in·te·*gral* wholemeal bread
— moreno mo·*re*·no brown bread
panadería ① pa·na·de·*ree*·a bakery
pañal ⓜ pa·*nyal* diaper • nappy
pantalla ① pan·*ta*·lya screen
pantalones ⓜ pl pan·ta·*lo*·nes
pants • trousers
— cortos kor·*tos* shorts
pañuelos ⓜ pl **de papel** pa·*nywe*·los
de pa·*pel* tissues
papá ⓜ pa·*pa* dad
papel ⓜ pa·*pel* paper
— de fumar de foo·*mar* cigarette
papers
— higiénico ee·*khye*·nee·ko toilet
paper
paquete ⓜ pa·*ke*·te packet • package
para llevar pa·ra lye·*var* to take away
parabrisas ⓜ pa·ra·*bree*·sas
windscreen
paracaidismo ⓜ pa·ra·kai·*dees*·mo
skydiving
parada ① pa·*ra*·da stop
— de autobús de ow·to·*boos* bus stop
— de taxis de *ta*·ksees taxi stand
paraguas ⓜ pa·*ra*·gwas umbrella
parapléjico/a ⓜ/①
pa·ra·*ple*·khee·ko/a paraplegic
parar pa·*rar* stop
pared ① pa·*re* wall (inside)
pareja ① pa·*re*·kha pair (couple)
parlamento ⓜ par·la·*men*·to
parliament
paro ⓜ *pa*·ro dole
parque ⓜ *par*·ke park
— nacional na·thyo·*nal* national park

parte ① *par*·te part
partida ① **de nacimiento** par·*tee*·da
de na·thee·*myen*·to birth certificate
partido ⓜ par·*tee*·do match (sport) •
(political) party
pasado ⓜ pa·*sa*·do past
pasado mañana pa·*sa*·do ma·*nya*·na
day after tomorrow
pasado/a ⓜ/① pa·*sa*·do/a off (food)
pasajero ⓜ pa·sa·*khe*·ro passenger
pasaporte ⓜ pa·sa·*por*·te passport
Pascua ① *pas*·kwa Easter
pase ⓜ *pa*·se pass
paseo ⓜ pa·*se*·o street
paso ⓜ *pa*·so step
— de cebra de *the*·bra pedestrian
crossing
pasta ① *pas*·ta pasta
— dentífrica den·*tee*·free·ka
toothpaste
pastel ⓜ pas·*tel* cake • pie
— de cumpleaños de
koom·ple·a·*nyos* birthday cake
pastelería ① pas·te·le·*ree*·a cake
shop
pastilla ① pas·*tee*·lya pill
pastillas ⓜ pl **de menta** pas·*tee*·lyas
de *men*·ta mints
pastillas ⓜ pl **para dormir**
pas·*tee*·lyas pa·ra dor·*meer* sleeping
pills
patata ① pa·*ta*·ta potato
paté ⓜ pa·*te* pate (food)
patinar pa·tee·*nar* rollerblading • ice
skating
pato ⓜ *pa*·to duck
pavo ⓜ *pa*·vo turkey
paz ① path peace
peatón ⓜ&① pe·a·*ton* pedestrian
pecho ⓜ *pe*·cho chest
pechuga ① pe·*choo*·ga breast
(poultry)
pedal ⓜ pe·*dal* pedal
pedazo ⓜ pe·*da*·tho piece
pedir pe·*deer* ask (for something)

peine ⓜ *pey*·ne comb
pelea ⓕ pe·*le*·a fight
película ⓕ pe·*lee*·koo·la movie • film (camera)
— en color en ko·*lor* colour film
peligroso/a ⓜ/ⓕ pe·lee·*gro*·so/a dangerous
pelo ⓜ *pe*·lo hair
pelota ⓕ pe·*lo*·ta ball
— de golf de golf golf ball
peluquero/a ⓜ/ⓕ pe·loo·*ke*·ro/a hairdresser
pendientes ⓜ pl pen·*dyen*·tes earrings
pene ⓜ *pe*·ne penis
pensar pen·*sar* think
pensión ⓕ pen·*syon* boarding house
pensionista ⓜ&ⓕ pen·syo·*nees*·ta pensioner
pepino ⓜ pe·*pee*·no cucumber
pequeñito/a ⓜ/ⓕ pe·ke·*nyee*·to/a tiny
pequeño/a ⓜ/ⓕ pe·*ke*·nyo/a small
pera ⓕ *pe*·ra pear
perder per·*der* lose
perdido/a ⓜ/ⓕ per·*dee*·do/a lost
perdonar per·do·*nar* forgive
perejil ⓜ pe·re·*kheel* parsley
perfume ⓜ per·*foo*·me perfume
periódico ⓜ pe·*ryo*·dee·ko newspaper
periodista ⓜ&ⓕ pe·ryo·*dees*·ta journalist
permiso ⓜ per·*mee*·so permission • permit
— de trabajo de tra·*ba*·kho work permit
permitir per·mee·*teer* allow • permit
pero *pe*·ro but
perro/a ⓜ/ⓕ *pe*·ro/a dog
perro ⓜ **lazarillo** *pe*·ro la·tha·*ree*·lyo guide dog
persona ⓕ per·*so*·na person
pesado/a ⓜ/ⓕ pe·*sa*·do/a heavy
pesar pe·*sar* weigh

pesas ⓕ pl *pe*·sas weights
pesca ⓕ *pes*·ka fishing
pescadería ⓕ pes·ka·de·*ree*·a fish shop
pescado ⓜ pes·*ka*·do fish (as food)
peso ⓜ *pe*·so weight
petición ⓕ pe·tee·*thyon* petition
pez ⓜ peth fish
picadura ⓕ pee·ka·*doo*·ra bite (insect)
picazón ⓕ pee·ka·*thon* itch
pie ⓜ pye foot
piedra ⓕ *pye*·dra stone
piel ⓕ pyel skin
pierna ⓕ *pyer*·na leg
pila ⓕ *pee*·la battery (small)
píldora ⓕ *peel*·do·ra the Pill
pimienta ⓕ pee·*myen*·ta pepper
pimiento ⓜ pee·*myen*·to capsicum • bell pepper
— rojo *ro*·kho red capsicum
— verde *ver*·de green capsicum
piña ⓕ *pee*·nya pineapple
pinchar peen·*char* puncture
ping pong ⓜ peeng pong table tennis
pintar peen·*tar* paint
pintor(a) ⓜ/ⓕ peen·*tor*/peen·*to*·ra painter
pintura ⓕ peen·*too*·ra painting
pinzas ⓕ pl *peen*·thas tweezers
piojos ⓜ pl *pyo*·khos lice
piqueta ⓕ pee·*ke*·ta pickaxe
piquetas ⓕ pl pee·*ke*·tas tent pegs
piscina ⓕ pees·*thee*·na swimming pool
pista ⓕ *pees*·ta court (tennis)
— de tenis de *te*·nees tennis court
pistacho ⓜ pees·*ta*·cho pistachio
plancha ⓕ *plan*·cha iron
planeta ⓜ pla·*ne*·ta planet
planta ⓕ *plan*·ta plant
plástico ⓜ *plas*·tee·ko plastic
plata ⓕ *pla*·ta silver
plataforma ⓕ pla·ta·*for*·ma platform
plátano ⓜ *pla*·ta·no banana

plateado/a ⓜ/ⓕ pla·te·a·do/a silver

plato ⓜ pla·to plate

playa ⓕ pla·ya beach

plaza ⓕ pla·tha square

— de toros de to·ros bullring

pobre po·bre poor

pobreza ⓕ po·bre·tha poverty

pocos po·kos few

poder po·der can (be able)

poder ⓜ po·der power

poesía ⓕ po·e·see·a poetry

polen ⓜ po·len pollen

policía ⓕ po·lee·thee·a police

política ⓕ po·lee·tee·ka policy • politics

político ⓜ po·lee·tee·ko politician

póliza ⓕ po·lee·tha policy (insurance)

pollo ⓜ po·lyo chicken

pomelo ⓜ po·me·lo grapefruit

poner po·ner put

popular po·poo·lar popular

póquer ⓜ po·ker poker

por (dia) por (dee·a) per (day)

por ciento por thyen·to percent

por qué por ke why

por vía aérea por vee·a a·e·re·a air mail

por vía terrestre por vee·a te·res·tre surface mail

porque por·ke because

portero/a ⓜ/ⓕ por·te·ro/a goalkeeper

posible po·see·ble possible

postal ⓕ pos·tal postcard

póster ⓜ pos·ter poster

potro ⓜ po·tro foal

pozo ⓜ po·tho well

precio ⓜ pre·thyo price

— de entrada de en·tra·da admission price

— del cubierto del koo·byer·to cover charge

preferir pre·fe·reer prefer

pregunta ⓕ pre·goon·ta question

preguntar pre·goon·tar ask (a question)

preocupado/a ⓜ/ⓕ pre·o·koo·pa·do/a worried

preocuparse por pre·o·koo·par·se por care (about something)

preparar pre·pa·rar prepare

presidente/a ⓜ/ⓕ pre·see·den·te/a president

presión ⓕ pre·syon pressure

— arterial ar·te·ryal blood pressure

prevenir pre·ve·neer prevent

primavera ⓕ pree·ma·ve·ra spring (season)

primer ministro ⓜ pree·mer mee·nees·tro prime minister

primera ministra ⓕ pree·me·ra mee·nees·tra prime minister

primero/a ⓜ/ⓕ pree·me·ro/a first

principal preen·thee·pal main

prisa ⓕ pree·sa hurry

prisionero/a ⓜ/ⓕ pree·syon·ne·ro/a prisoner

privado/a ⓜ/ⓕ pree·va·do/a private

probar pro·bar try

producir pro·doo·theer produce

productos ⓜ pl congelados pro·dook·tos kon·khe·la·dos frozen foods

profesor(a) ⓜ/ⓕ pro·fe·sor/ pro·fe·so·ra lecturer • instructor • teacher

profundo/a ⓜ/ⓕ pro·foon·do/a deep

programa ⓜ pro·gra·ma programme

prolongación ⓕ pro·lon·ga·thyon extension (visa)

promesa ⓕ pro·me·sa promise

prometida ⓕ pro·me·tee·da fiancee

prometido ⓜ pro·me·tee·do fiance

pronto pron·to soon

propietaria ⓕ pro·pye·ta·rya landlady

propietario ⓜ pro·pye·ta·ryo landlord

propina ⓕ pro·pee·na tip

proteger pro·te·kher protect

protegido/a ⓜ/ⓕ pro·te·khee·do/a protected

protesta ⓕ pro·tes·ta protest

provisiones ⓕ pl pro·bee·syo·nes provisions

proyector ⓜ pro·yek·tor projector

prudente proo·den·te sensible

prueba ⓕ prwe·ba test

— del embarazo del em·ba·ra·tho pregnancy test kit

pruebas ⓕ pl **nucleares** prwe·bas noo·kle·a·res nuclear testing

pub ⓜ poob bar (with music) • pub

pueblo ⓜ pwe·blo village

puente ⓜ pwen·te bridge

puerro ⓜ pwe·ro leek

puerta ⓕ pwer·ta door

puerto ⓜ pwer·to port • harbour

puesta ⓕ **del sol** pwes·ta del sol sunset

pulga ⓕ pool·ga flea

pulmones ⓜ pl pool·mo·nes lungs

punto ⓜ poon·to point (tip/score)

puro ⓜ poo·ro cigar

puro/a ⓜ/ⓕ poo·ro/a pure

Q

(el mes) que viene (el mes) ke vye·ne next (month)

quedar ke·dar leave (behind)

quedarse ke·dar·se stay (remain)

quedarse sin ke·dar·se seen run out of

quejarse ke·khar·se complain

quemadura ⓕ ke·ma·doo·ra burn

— de sol de sol sunburn

querer ke·rer love • want

queso ⓜ ke·so cheese

— crema kre·ma cream cheese

— de cabra de ka·bra goat's cheese

quien kyen who

quincena ⓕ keen·the·na fortnight

quiosco ⓜ kyos·ko news stand • newsagency

quiste ⓜ **ovárico** kees·te o·va·ree·ko ovarian cyst

quizás kee·thas maybe

R

rábano ⓜ ra·ba·no radish

— picante pee·kan·te horseradish

rápido/a ⓜ/ⓕ ra·pee·do/a fast

raqueta ⓕ ra·ke·ta racquet

raro/a ⓜ/ⓕ ra·ro/a rare (item)

rastro ⓜ ras·tro track (footprints)

rata ⓕ ra·ta rat

ratón ⓜ ra·ton mouse

raza ⓕ ra·tha race (people)

razón ⓕ ra·thon reason

realista re·a·lees·ta realistic

recibir re·thee·beer receive

recibo ⓜ re·thee·bo receipt

reciclable re·thee·kla·ble recyclable

reciclar re·thee·klar recycle

recientemente re·thyen·te·men·te recently

recogida ⓕ **de equipajes** re·ko·khee·da de e·kee·pa·khes baggage claim

recolección ⓕ **de fruta** re·ko·lek·thyon de froo·ta fruit picking

recomendar re·ko·men·dar recommend

reconocer re·ko·no·ther recognise

recordar re·kor·dar remember

recorrido ⓜ **guiado** re·ko·ree·do gee·a·do guided tour

recto/a ⓜ/ⓕ rek·to/a straight

recuerdo ⓜ re·kwer·do souvenir

red ⓕ red net

redondo/a ⓜ/ⓕ re·don·do/a round

reembolsar re·em·bol·sar refund

reembolso ⓜ re·em·bol·so refund

referencias ⓕ pl re·fe·ren·thyas references

refresco ⓜ re·fres·ko soft drink

refugiado/a ⓜ/ⓕ re·foo·khya·do/a refugee

regalar re·ga·lar exchange (gifts)

regalo ⓜ re·ga·lo gift

— de bodas de bo·das wedding present

régimen ⓜ re·khee·men diet

reglas ⓕ pl re·glas rules

reina ⓕ rey·na queen

reírse re·eer·se laugh

relación ① re·la·*thyon* relationship
relajarse re·la·*khar*·se relax
religión ① re·lee·*khyon* religion
religioso/a ⓜ/① re·lee·*khyo*·so/a religious
reliquia ① re·*lee*·kya relic
reloj ⓜ re·*lokh* clock
— de pulsera de pool·*se*·ra watch
remo ⓜ *re*·mo rowing
remolacha ① re·mo·*la*·cha beetroot
remoto/a ⓜ/① re·*mo*·to/a remote
reparar re·pa·*rar* repair
repartir re·par·*teer* divide up (share)
repetir re·pe·*teer* repeat
república ① re·poo·*blee*·ka republic
requesón ⓜ re·ke·*son* cottage cheese
reserva ① re·*ser*·va reservation
reservar re·ser·*var* book (make a reservation)
resfriado ⓜ res·free·a·do cold
residencia ① **de estudiantes** re·see·*den*·thya de es·too·*dyan*·tes college
residuos ⓜ pl **tóxicos** re·see·dwos *to*·ksee·kos toxic waste
respirar res·pee·*rar* breathe
respuesta ① res·*pwes*·ta answer
restaurante ⓜ res·tow·*ran*·te restaurant
revisar re·vee·*sar* check
revisor(a) ⓜ/① re·vee·sor/ re·vee·so·ra ticket collector
revista ① re·*vees*·ta magazine
rey ⓜ rey king
rico/a ⓜ/① *ree*·ko/a rich
riesgo ⓜ *ryes*·go risk
río ⓜ *ree*·o river
ritmo ⓜ *reet*·mo rhythm
robar ro·*bar* rob • steal
roca ① *ro*·ka rock
rock ⓜ rok rock (music)
rodilla ① ro·*dee*·lya knee
rojo/a ⓜ/① *ro*·kho/a red
rollo ⓜ **repelente contra mosquitos** *ro*·lyo re·pe·*len*·te *kon*·tra mos·*kee*·tos mosquito coil

romántico/a ⓜ/① ro·*man*·tee·ko/a romantic
romper rom·*per* break
ron ⓜ ron rum
ropa ① *ro*·pa clothing
— de cama de *ka*·ma bedding
— interior een·te·*ryor* underwear
rosa *ro*·sa pink
roto/a ⓜ/① *ro*·to/a broken
rueda ① *rwe*·da wheel
rugby ⓜ *roog*·bee rugby
ruidoso/a ⓜ/① rwee·*do*·so/a loud
ruinas ① pl *rwee*·nas ruins
ruta ① *roo*·ta route

S

sábado ⓜ *sa*·ba·do Saturday
sábana ① *sa*·ba·na sheet (bed)
saber sa·*ber* know (something)
sabroso/a ⓜ/① sa·*bro*·so/a tasty
sacar sa·*kar* take out • take (photo)
sacerdote ⓜ sa·ther·*do*·te priest
saco ⓜ **de dormir** *sa*·ko de dor·*meer* sleeping bag
sal ① sal salt
sala ① **de espera** *sa*·la de es·*pe*·ra waiting room
sala ① **de tránsito** *sa*·la de *tran*·see·to transit lounge
salario ⓜ sa·*la*·ryo rate of pay • salary
salchicha ① sal·*chee*·cha sausage
saldo ⓜ *sal*·do balance (account)
salida ① sa·*lee*·da departure • exit
saliente ⓜ sa·*lyen*·te ledge
salir con sa·*leer* kon go out with
salir de sa·*leer* de depart
salmón ⓜ sal·*mon* salmon
salón de belleza ⓜ sa·*lon* de be·*lye*·tha beauty salon
salsa ① *sal*·sa sauce
— de guindilla de geen·*dee*·lya chilli sauce
— de soja de so·*kha* soy sauce
— de tomate de to·*ma*·te tomato sauce • ketchup

S

saltar sal·tar jump

salud ① sa·loo health

salvaeslips ⑩ pl sal·va·e·sleeps panty liners

salvar sal·var save

sandalias ① pl san·da·lyas sandals

sandía ① san·dee·a watermelon

sangrar san·grar bleed

sangre ① san·gre blood

santo/a ⑩/① san·to/a saint

sarampión ⑩ sa·ram·pyon measles

sartén ① sar·ten frying pan

sastre ⑩ sas·tre tailor

sauna ① sow·na sauna

secar se·kar dry

secretario/a ⑩/① se·kre·ta·ryo/a secretary

sed ① se thirst

seda ① se·da silk

seguir se·geer follow

segundo/a ⑩/① se·goon·do/a second

seguro ⑩ se·goo·ro insurance

seguro/a ⑩/① se·goo·ro/a safe

sello ⑩ se·lyo stamp

semáforos ⑩ pl se·ma·fo·ros traffic lights

Semana ① **Santa** se·ma·na san·ta Easter Week

sembrar sem·brar plant

semidirecto/a ⑩/① se·mee·dee·rek·to/a non-direct

señal ① se·nyal sign

sencillo/a ⑩/① sen·thee·lyo/a simple

(un billete) sencillo ⑩ (oon bee·lye·te) sen·thee·lyo one-way (ticket)

sendero ⑩ sen·de·ro mountain path • path

senos ⑩ pl se·nos breasts

sensibilidad ① sen·see·bee·lee·da sensitivity • film speed

sensual sen·swal sensual

sentarse sen·tar·se sit

sentimientos ⑩ pl sen·tee·myen·tos feelings

sentir sen·teer feel

separado/a ⑩/① se·pa·ra·do/a separate

separar se·pa·rar separate

ser ser be

serie ① se·rye series

serio/a ⑩/① se·ryo/a serious

seropositivo/a ⑩/① se·ro·po·see·tee·vo/a HIV positive

serpiente ① ser·pyen·te snake

servicio ⑩ ser·vee·thyo service charge

— militar mee·lee·tar military service

— telefónico automático te·le·fo·nee·ko ow·to·ma·tee·ko direct-dial

servicios ⑩ pl ser·vee·thyos toilets

servilleta ① ser·vee·lye·ta napkin

sexo ⑩ sek·so sex

— seguro se·goo·ro safe sex

sexy sek·see sexy

si see if

sí see yes

SIDA ⑩ see·da AIDS

sidra ① see·dra cider

siempre syem·pre always

silla ① see·lya chair

— de ruedas de rwe·das wheelchair

sillín ⑩ see·lyeen saddle

similar see·mee·lar similar

simpático/a ⑩/① seem·pa·tee·ko/a nice

sin seen without

— hogar o·gar homeless

— plomo plo·mo unleaded

sinagoga ① see·na·go·ga synagogue

Singapur ⑩ seen·ga·poor Singapore

sintético/a ⑩/① seen·te·tee·ko/a synthetic

soborno ⑩ so·bor·no bribe

sobre so·bre about • on top of

sobre ⑩ so·bre envelope

sobredosis ① so·bre·do·sees overdose

sobrevivir so·bre·vee·*veer* survive
socialista ⓜ&ⓕ so·thya·*lees*·ta socialist
sol ⓜ sol sun
soldado ⓜ sol·*da*·do soldier
sólo *so*·lo only
solo/a ⓜ/ⓕ *so*·lo/a alone
soltero/a ⓜ/ⓕ sol·*te*·ro/a single
sombra ⓕ *som*·bra shadow
sombrero ⓜ som·*bre*·ro hat
soñar so·*nyar* dream
sondeos ⓜ pl son·*de*·os polls
sonreír son·re·*eer* smile
sopa ⓕ *so*·pa soup
sordo/a ⓜ/ⓕ *sor*·do/a deaf
sorpresa ⓕ sor·*pre*·sa surprise
su soo her · his · their
subir soo·*beer* climb
submarinismo ⓜ soob·ma·ree·*nees*·mo diving
subtítulos ⓜ pl soob·*tee*·too·los subtitles
sucio/a ⓜ/ⓕ *soo*·thyo/a dirty
sucursal ⓕ soo·koor·*sal* branch office
sudar soo·*dar* perspire
suegra ⓕ *swe*·gra mother-in-law
suegro ⓜ *swe*·gro father-in-law
sueldo ⓜ *swel*·do wage
suelo ⓜ *swe*·lo floor
suerte ⓕ *swer*·te luck
suficiente soo·fee·*thyen*·te enough
sufrir soo·*freer* suffer
sujetador ⓜ soo·khe·ta·*dor* bra
supermercado ⓜ soo·per·mer·*ka*·do supermarket
superstición ⓕ soo·pers·tee·*thyon* superstition
sur ⓜ soor south
surf ⓜ **sobre la nieve** soorf *so*·bre la *nye*·ve snowboarding

T

tabaco ⓜ ta·*ba*·ko tobacco
tabla ⓕ **de surf** *ta*·bla de soorf surfboard

tablero ⓜ **de ajedrez** ta·*ble*·ro de a·khe·*dreth* chess board
tacaño/a ⓜ/ⓕ ta·ka·nyo/a stingy
talco ⓜ *tal*·ko baby powder
talla ⓕ *ta*·lya size (clothes)
taller ⓜ ta·*lyer* workshop
también tam·*byen* also
tampoco tam·*po*·ko neither
tampones ⓜ pl tam·*po*·nes tampons
tanga ⓕ *tan*·ga g-string
tapones ⓜ pl **para los oídos** ta·*po*·nes *pa*·ra los o·*ee*·dos earplugs
taquilla ⓕ ta·*kee*·lya ticket office
tarde *tar*·de late
tarjeta ⓕ tar·*khe*·ta card
— de crédito de *kre*·dee·to credit card
— de embarque de em·*bar*·ke boarding pass
— de teléfono de te·*le*·fo·no phone card
tarta ⓕ **nupcial** *tar*·ta noop·*thyal* wedding cake
tasa ⓕ **del aeropuerto** *ta*·sa del ay·ro·*pwer*·to airport tax
taxi ⓜ *ta*·ksee taxi
taza ⓕ *ta*·tha cup
té ⓜ te tea
teatro ⓜ te·*a*·tro theatre
teclado ⓜ te·*kla*·do keyboard
técnica ⓕ *tek*·ne·ka technique
tela ⓕ *te*·la fabric
tele ⓕ *te*·le TV
teleférico ⓜ te·le·*fe*·ree·ko cable car
teléfono ⓜ te·*le*·fo·no telephone
— móvil *mo*·veel mobile phone
— público *poo*·blee·ko public telephone
telegrama ⓜ te·le·*gra*·ma telegram
telenovela ⓕ te·le·no·*ve*·la soap opera
telescopio ⓜ te·les·*ko*·pyo telescope
televisión ⓕ te·le·vee·*syon* television
temperatura ⓕ tem·pe·ra·*too*·ra temperature (weather)
templado/a ⓜ/ⓕ tem·*pla*·do/a warm

T

templo m *tem*·plo temple

temporada f tem·po·*ra*·da season (in sport)

temprano tem·*pra*·no early

tenedor m te·ne·*dor* fork

tener te·*ner* have

— hambre *am*·bre to be hungry

— prisa *pree*·sa to be in a hurry

— sed seth to be thirsty

— sueño *swe*·nyo to be sleepy

tenis m *te*·nees tennis

tensión f **premenstrual** ten·*syon* pre·mens·*trwal* premenstrual tension

tentempié m ten·tem·*pye* snack

tercio m *ter*·thyo third

terminar ter·mee·*nar* finish

ternera f ter·*ne*·ra veal

ternero m ter·*ne*·ro calf

terremoto m te·re·*mo*·to earthquake

testarudo/a m/f tes·ta·roo·do/a stubborn

tía f *tee*·a aunt

tiempo m *tyem*·po time • weather

a— a *tyem*·po on time

a— completo/parcial a *tyem*·po kom·*ple*·to/par·*thyal* full-time/part-time

tienda f **(de campaña)** *tyen*·da (de kam·*pa*·nya) tent

tienda f *tyen*·da shop

— de comestibles de ko·mes·*tee*·bles grocery

— de fotografía de fo·to·gra·*fee*·a camera shop

— de eléctrodomésticos de e·*lek*·tro·do·mes·*tee*·kos electrical store

— de cámping de *kam*·peen camping store

— de recuerdos de re·*kwer*·dos souvenir shop

— de ropa de *ro*·pa clothing store

— deportiva de·por·*tee*·va sports store

Tierra f *tye*·ra Earth

tierra f *tye*·ra land

tiesto m *tyes*·to pot (plant)

tijeras f pl tee·*khe*·ras scissors

tímido/a m/f *tee*·mee·do/a shy

típico/a m/f *tee*·pee·ko/a typical

tipo m *tee*·po type

— de cambio de *kam*·byo exchange rate

tirar tee·*rar* pull

tiritas f pl tee·*ree*·tas band-aids

título m *tee*·too·lo degree

toalla f to·*a*·lya towel

toallita f to·a·*lyee*·ta face cloth

tobillo m to·*bee*·lyo ankle

tocar to·*kar* touch

— la guitarra la gee·*ta*·ra play guitar

tocino m to·*thee*·no bacon

todavía (no) to·da·*vee*·a (no) (not) yet

todo *to*·do all • everything

tofú m to·*foo* tofu

tomar to·*mar* take • drink

tomate m to·*ma*·te tomato

— secado al sol se·*ka*·do al sol sun-dried tomato

tono m *to*·no tone

torcedura f tor·the·*doo*·ra sprain

tormenta f tor·*men*·ta storm

toro m *to*·ro bull

torre f *to*·re tower

tos f tos cough

tostada f tos·*ta*·da toast

tostadora f tos·ta·*do*·ra toaster

trabajar tra·ba·*khar* work

trabajo m tra·*ba*·kho job • work

— administrativo ad·mee·nees·tra·*tee*·vo paperwork

— de camarero/a m/f de ka·ma·re·ro/a bar work

— de casa de *ka*·sa housework

— de limpieza de leem·*pye*·tha cleaning

— eventual e·ven·*twal* casual work

traducir tra·doo·*theer* translate

traer tra·*er* bring

traficante m&f **de drogas** tra·fee·*kan*·te de *dro*·gas drug dealer

tráfico m *tra*·fee·ko traffic

tramposo/a m/f tram·po·so/a cheat

tranquilo/a m/f tran·kee·lo/a quiet

tranvía m tran·*vee*·a tram

a través a tra·*ves* across

tren m tren train

— de cercanías de ther·ka·*nee*·as local train

trepar tre·*par* climb • scale

tres en raya tres en *ra*·ya noughts & crosses

triste *trees*·te sad

tú inf too you

tu too your

tubo m **de escape** *too*·bo de es·*ka*·pe exhaust

tumba f *toom*·ba grave

tumbarse toom·*bar*·se lie (not stand)

turista m&f too·*rees*·ta tourist

— operador(a) m/f o·pe·ra·*dor*/ o·pe·ra·*do*·ra tourist operator

uniforme m oo·nee·*for*·me uniform

universidad f oo·nee·ver·see·*da* university

universo m oo·nee·*ver*·so universe

urgente oor·*khen*·te urgent

Usted pol oos·*te* you

Ustedes pol pl oos·*te*·des you

útil *oo*·teel useful

uvas f pl *oo*·vas grapes

— pasas *pa*·sas raisins

vaca f *va*·ka cow

vacaciones f pl va·ka·*thyo*·nes holidays • vacation

vacante va·*kan*·te vacant

vacío/a m/f va·*thee*·o/a empty

vacuna f va·*koo*·na vaccination

vagina f va·*khee*·na vagina

vagón m **restaurante** va·*gon* res·tow·*ran*·te dining car

validar va·lee·*dar* validate

valiente va·*lyen*·te brave

valioso/a m/f va·*lyo*·so/a valuable

valle m *va*·lye valley

valor m va·*lor* value

vaqueros m pl va·*ke*·ros jeans

varios/as m/f pl *va*·ryos/as several

vaso m *va*·so (drinking) glass

vegetariano/a m/f ve·khe·ta·*rya*·no/a vegetarian

vela f *ve*·la candle

velocidad f ve·lo·thee·*da* speed

velocímetro m ve·lo·*thee*·me·tro speedometer

velódromo m ve·*lo*·dro·mo racetrack (bicycles)

vena f *ve*·na vein

vendaje m ven·*da*·khe bandage

vendedor(a) m/f **de flores** ven·de·*dor*/ven·de·*do*·ra de *flo*·res florist

vender ven·*der* sell

venenoso/a m/f ve·ne·*no*·so/a poisonous

venir ve·*neer* come

ventana f ven·*ta*·na window

ventilador m ven·tee·la·*dor* fan (machine)

ver ver see

verano m ve·*ra*·no summer

verde *ver*·de green

verdulería f ver·doo·le·*ree*·a greengrocery (shop)

verdulero/a m/f ver·doo·*le*·ro/a grocer (shopkeeper)

verduras f pl ver·*doo*·ras vegetables

vestíbulo m ves·*tee*·boo·lo foyer

vestido m ves·*tee*·do dress

vestuario m ves·*twa*·ryo wardrobe

vestuarios m pl ves·*twa*·ryos changing room

vez f veth once

viajar vya·*khar* travel

viaje m *vya*·khe trip

vid f veed vine

Y

vida ① *vee*·da life
vidrio ⓜ *vee*·dryo glass
viejo/a ⓜ/① *vye*·kho/a old
viento ⓜ *vyen*·to wind
vinagre ⓜ vee·*na*·gre vinegar
viñedo ⓜ vee·*nye*·do vineyard
vino ⓜ *vee*·no wine
violar vyo·*lar* rape
virus ⓜ *vee*·roos virus
visado ⓜ vee·*sa*·do visa
visitar vee·see·*tar* visit
vista ① *vees*·ta view
vitaminas ① pl vee·ta·*mee*·nas
vitamins
víveres ⓜ pl *vee*·ve·res food supplies
vivir vee·*veer* live (life)
vodka ① *vod*·ka vodka
volar vo·*lar* fly
volumen ⓜ vo·*loo*·men volume
volver vol·*ver* return
vosotros/as ⓜ/① pl inf
vo·*so*·tros/as you
votar vo·*tar* vote
voz ① voth voice
vuelo ⓜ **doméstico** *vwe*·lo
do·*mes*·tee·ko domestic flight

Y

y ee and
ya ya already
yip ⓜ yeep jeep
yo yo I
yoga ⓜ *yo*·ga yoga
yogur ⓜ yo·*goor* yogurt

Z

zanahoria ① tha·na·o·rya carrot
zapatería ① tha·pa·te·*ree*·a shoe
shop
zapatos ⓜ pl tha·*pa*·tos shoes
zodíaco ⓜ tho·*dee*·a·ko zodiac
zoológico ⓜ zo·o·*lo*·khee·ko zoo
zumo ⓜ *thoo*·mo juice
— de naranja de na·*ran*·kha orange
juice

Index

índice

For topics that are covered in several sections of this book, we've indicated the most relevant page number in bold.

10 Ways to Start a Sentence

When's (the next flight)?	¿Cuándo sale (el próximo vuelo)?	*kwan*·do *sa*·le (el *prok*·see·mo *vwe*·lo)
Where's (the station)?	¿Dónde está (la estación)?	*don*·de es·*ta* (la es·ta·*thyon*)
Where can I (buy a ticket)?	¿Dónde puedo (comprar un billete)?	*don*·de *pwe*·do (kom·*prar* oon bee·*lye*·te)
How much is (a room)?	¿Cuánto cuesta (una habitación)?	*kwan*·to *kwes*·ta (*oo*·na a·bee·ta·*thyon*)
Do you have (a map)?	¿Tiene (un mapa)?	*tye*·ne (oon *ma*·pa)
Is there (a toilet)?	¿Hay (servicios)?	ai (ser·*vee*·thyos)
I'd like (a coffee).	Quisiera (un café).	kee·*sye*·ra (oon ka·*fe*)
Can I (enter)?	¿Se puede (entrar)?	se *pwe*·de (en·*trar*)
Could you please (help me)?	¿Puede (ayudarme), por favor?	*pwe*·de (a·*yoo*·dar·me) por fa·*vor*
Do I have to (get a visa)?	¿Necesito (obtener un visado)?	ne·the·*see*·to (ob·te·*ner* oon vee·*sa*·do)